The Ecosystem of Group I

CW01394870

The unconscious dynamics that surface in groups when authority is exercised are of paramount importance in Group Relations Conferences; this volume addresses these considerations through research findings and speculation on the future of Group Relations both within conferences and outside of them.

This is the sixth instalment in a series of books based on Tavistock Group Relations Conferences and contains a collection of papers presented at the sixth Belgirate conference. Combining chapters on theory and practice, this volume delivers a meditation on the relationships between the physical spaces we inhabit or co-create, the psychic, inner or spiritual space, and the liminal space in-between. Group Relations provides a window of understanding into why inequity and intergroup hostilities pervade the modern world alongside a method that illuminates how people consciously and unconsciously contribute to these tensions, whether personally, in groups, or in organisations.

This will be an invaluable resource for practitioners, academics, and scholars of Group Relations, as well as managers and organisational members wanting to learn more about how Group Relations methods can contribute to their organisational success.

Coreene Archer is a Principal Consultant and Executive Coach at the Tavistock Institute. Coreene's interest lies in the study of leadership and identity. Her works have expanded Group Relations ideas to include work with emergent young leaders. Coreene teaches a number of programmes and her work has expanded Group Relations ideas to include work with young and emergent leaders.

Rachel Kelly is a Principal, Engagement/PR lead, and Group Relations Consultant at the Tavistock Institute of Human Relations. She explores relatedness between the unconscious and consciousness and journeys into the psychophysical by exploring concepts such as embodiment, sensation, and imagination.

Gordon Strauss is a Psychiatrist who has practiced and taught Group Relations for over 40 years. He is a Fellow and Board member of the A. K. Rice Institute for the Study of Social Systems.

Joseph Triest is a Training Psychoanalyst (IPS; IPA), Clinical Psychologist and Organisational Consultant. He is the head of the "Freud and Followers Root" at the Tel-Aviv University Psychotherapy Program and past President of the Israel Psychoanalytic Society.

'For some years now, Belgirate has been *the* place to gather for the most innovative thinking in the area of group relations. Based on a highly engaging conference at Belgirate, this volume brings together some of the foremost innovators and thinkers in the field. It makes for fascinating reading, and I whole-heartedly recommend it.'

Mark Stein, PhD, Emeritus Professor of Leadership and Management, University of Leicester and Associate Lecturer in Consultation and Organisation, Tavistock Clinic London, UK

'This book serves as a transitional space ship, for exploring new territories of Group Relations life, thinking and methodology. Various aspects of (the relationship between) outer physical and inner psychic worlds are being studied thoughtful and reflective. The crew skillfully guides you in crossing several boundaries, (re)visiting conceptual planets, shows comets of practice, bright stars of experience and also leaves enough black holes to grapple with yourself. Fasten your seatbelts for this inspiring flight.'

Martijn van der Spek, Senior Organisational Consultant and Program Leader Inside Dynamics in Organisations, Utrecht University, the Netherlands

The Group Relations Conferences Series

Group Relations conferences offer opportunities to learn about group, organisational, and social dynamics; the exercise of authority and power; the interplay between tradition, innovation, and change; and the relationship of organisations to their social, political, and economic environments. This series of books on the Tavistock Group Relations Conferences provides edited collections of papers presented at the Belgirate conferences, plus additional chapters which examine the respective conference as a whole.

Titles in the series:

Doing the Business of Group Relations Conferences
Exploring the Discourse: Volume V
Edited by Eliat Aram, Coreene Archer, Rachel Kelly, Gordon Strauss and Joseph Triest

Group Relations Work
Exploring the Impact and Relevance Within and Beyond its Network: Volume IV
Edited by Eliat Aram, Robert Baxter and Avi Nutkevitch

Group Relations Conferences
Tradition, Creativity, and Succession in the Global Group Relations Network: Volume III
Edited by Eliat Aram, Robert Baxter and Avi Nutkevitch

Adaptation and Innovation
Theory, Design and Role-Taking in Group Relations Conferences and their Applications: Volume II
Edited by Eliat Aram, Robert Baxter and Avi Nutkevitch

Group Relations Conferences
Reviewing and Exploring Theory, Design, Role-Taking and Application
Edited by Louisa Diana Brunner, Avi Nutkevitch and Mannie Sher

For further information about this series please visit: https://www.routledge.com/The-Group-Relations-Conferences-Series/book-series/KARNGRC

The Ecosystem of Group Relations

Culture, Gender and Identity in Groups and Organizations

Edited by
Coreene Archer, Rachel Kelly,
Gordon Strauss, and Joseph Triest

R Routledge
Taylor & Francis Group

LONDON AND NEW YORK

Designed cover image: pavlen | Getty Images.

First published 2023
by Routledge
4 Park Square, Milton Park, Abingdon, Oxon OX14 4RN

and by Routledge
605 Third Avenue, New York, NY 10158

Routledge is an imprint of the Taylor & Francis Group, an informa business

© 2023 selection and editorial matter, Coreene Archer, Rachel Kelly, Gordon Strauss, and Joseph Triest; individual chapters, the contributors

The right of Coreene Archer, Rachel Kelly, Gordon Strauss, and Joseph Triest to be identified as the authors of the editorial material, and of the authors for their individual chapters, has been asserted in accordance with sections 77 and 78 of the Copyright, Designs and Patents Act 1988.

All rights reserved. No part of this book may be reprinted or reproduced or utilised in any form or by any electronic, mechanical, or other means, now known or hereafter invented, including photocopying and recording, or in any information storage or retrieval system, without permission in writing from the publishers.

Trademark notice: Product or corporate names may be trademarks or registered trademarks, and are used only for identification and explanation without intent to infringe.

British Library Cataloguing-in-Publication Data
A catalogue record for this book is available from the British Library

ISBN: 978-1-032-19930-6 (hbk)
ISBN: 978-0-367-37072-5 (pbk)
ISBN: 978-1-003-26148-3 (ebk)

DOI: 10.4324/9781003261483

Typeset in Times New Roman
by KnowledgeWorks Global Ltd.

Contents

About the Editors and Contributors

Editors

Coreene Archer, MA, is a Principal Consultant and Executive Coach at the Tavistock Institute of Human Relations since 2007. She is Co-Director of the Coaching for Leadership and Co-Director of the Supervision for Coaches and Consultants Professional Development programmes. Also a keen learner, she is currently undertaking her Doctorate. She directs the Launching Young Leaders group relations conference and the Self Leadership workshops. Coreene's passion is in initiating new ways of working with and developing leadership for young people, informed by her belief that we are not defined by where we start but by how we finish.

Rachel Kelly, BA, mSTAT, is a Principal, Engagement and PR Lead, and GR & OD Consultant at The Tavistock Institute of Human Relations and a member of the Society of Teachers of the Alexander Technique. She explores relatedness between the unconscious and consciousness and journeys into the psychophysical by exploring embodiment, sensation, and imagination.

Gordon Strauss, MD, is a Professor Emeritus of Psychiatry at the University of Louisville School of Medicine. He is member, fellow, and currently Treasurer of the AK Rice Institute for the Study of Social Systems (AKRI). He is also former president and member of the Midwest Group Relations Center and a member of GREX, both affiliate centres of AKRI. He received advanced training in organisational consultation from the Cincinnati Psychoanalytic Institute.

Joseph Triest, PhD, is a Training Psychoanalyst (IPS; IPA) Clinical Psychologist and Organisational Consultant. He is the head of the "Freud and Followers Root" at the Tel-Aviv University Psychotherapy Program, and faculty at the Tel Aviv University Sackler Medical School Ph.D. program. Dr Triest was President of the Israel Psychoanalytic Society and (past) co-director of the Program for Organizational Consultation and Development (POCD). Since 2018, he is co-founder and co-director of the "Center for Research of the Psychoanalytic – Systemic Approach" (CROPSA). Member of OFEK. Beside his clinical work in "Triest-Sarig Clinic" (Founded at 1985) he took up a variety of roles in GR conferences, including the director's role in some of them. Triest is the author of several papers in the field of Psychoanalysis and Group Relations.

Contributors

Daphna Bahat is a clinical psychologist and consultant to organisations. She teaches psychotherapy and the Psychoanalytic-Systemic Approach for groups and organisations in various institutions, including 'Touch OFEK,' which she also co-directs. She leads workshops for women's empowerment using Oriental Dance and is past Chairwoman, OFEK.

Diane Forbes Berthoud, PhD, is Vice President and Chief Diversity Officer at the University of Maryland Baltimore; Affiliate Faculty at the George Washington University; and Faculty emeritus of the RISE San Diego Urban Leadership Fellows Program. She is a member and past executive committee member of the Washington-Baltimore Center and has served as lead consultant to organisations such as the American Psychological Association, the UN High Commissioner for Refugees (UNHCR), and the US Capitol.

Giada Boldetti, MD, is a freelance psychiatrist working in public health until 2016. Since 2000 she has been responsible for psychiatric residential rehabilitation in TCs. From 2014 to 2016, she was deputy director of the Mental Health Service Psichiatria I in Padua. She has been part of many GRCs as a member and as a consultant. She is a member of Il Nodo Group.

Fabio D'Apice is the Director of Centro Coaching (UK and Gibraltar) and the Executive Director of the International Society for the Psychoanalytic Study of Organisations (ISPSO). He trained within the Tavistock tradition and is working with private and public sector organisations with the application of Systemic and Psychoanalytic thinking.

John Diamond is the Director of the Mulberry Bush UK. He is an international expert in Mental Health Communities for children and adolescents and is the author of several papers and books in this area. He is an associate of OPUS and a member of the *International Journal of Therapeutic Communities*. He has a passion for painting.

Shmuel Erlich, PhD, is Sigmund Freud Professor of Psychoanalysis (Emeritus) at The Hebrew University of Jerusalem. He is a psychoanalyst in private practice, a consultant to organisations, and a Founding Member, OFEK, PCCA.

Giovanni Foresti, MD, is a psychiatrist and training and supervising analyst of the Italian Psychoanalytic Society (SPI) and the IPA, associate member of OPUS, London, and a member of the scientific committee of IL NODO group, Turin. He teaches at the School of Psychiatry of Milano-Bicocca University and at the Department of Psychology of the Catholic University. He works as a supervisor and organisational consultant in several institutions.

Zachary Green, PhD, Founding Circle, Group Relations International and Professor of Practice, University of San Diego, California. Zachary devoted a year's leave from the university to discern the direction and focus of his life's journey. Through reading, writing, and working with one local and one global organisation, he is sharpening his focus on a collective call to consciousness that embraces our common humanity.

Jaume Benavent i Guàrdia, MA, is a project manager and organisational consultant at the Innova Institute for organisational and social innovation in Barcelona. He specialises in development of family business programs.

Yermi Harel, MD, a senior psychiatrist at Lewenstein Rehabilitation Hospital in Raanana, Israel. He is a lecturer in the Sackler Faculty of Medicine, Tel-Aviv University, Israel. He is a member and former board member of OFEK, the Israeli Association for the study of Group and Organizational Process. He works in a private practice as psychiatrist and psychotherapist in Bet-Halevi, Israel.

Seth B. Harkins, EdD, Harkins Educational Consulting and Advocacy; Adjunct Professor, National Louis University, Chicago; chairperson, board of directors, Illinois Community and Residential Services Authority; executive director and board member, Serenity Academy Chicago; board member; Chicago Virtual Charter School; Associate, AK Rice Institute; past president and member, Chicago Center for the Study of Groups and Organizations; vice president, Midwest Group Relations Center.

Patricia Kummel, JD, PhD, has a private practice for psychotherapy and organisational consultation in New York City and is a consultant for CHE Behavioral Health Services. Prior to becoming a psychologist, Patricia practiced law as a prosecutor in Washington, DC, at a law firm in New York City, and as a Director in the Enforcement Division of the New York Stock Exchange. She is a former chair of the A. K. Rice Institute for the Study of Social Systems (AKRI) Training and Certification Committee; chair, 2021 AKRI Dialogues Planning Committee; AKRI Fellow; member, New York Center for the Study of Groups, Organizations, and Social Systems; former President, Philadelphia Center for Organizational Dynamics; co-creator, Group Relations International; member, Organisation for

Promoting Understanding of Society (OPUS); and member, American Psychological Association (APA). She is a member of California, New York, and Washington DC Bars.

David Sierra Lozano, MA, is partner and organisational consultant of the Innova Institute for organisational and social innovation in Barcelona. He specialises in Soft Systems Methodology, Viable Systems, and Systemic Contributions Methodology for organisations.

John Lundgren, MD, is a training and supervising analyst at the Psychoanalytic Center of California and a member of GREX and the A. K. Rice Institute. He served as co-director of the Group Relations Leadership training program at the UCLA Department of Psychiatry.

Jack Marmorstein, EdS, was President of the A. K. Rice Institute from 2018 to 2020. He is currently Chief Learning Officer at a multinational education technology company.

Simona Masnata is a health educator, social manager, coach, consultant, member of GRC ALI staff (2012–2015), member of LFA Staff (2013–2018), member of Il Nodo Group, and member of the scientific committee of CSS – Redancia Group.

Luca Mingarelli is a psychologist, social entrepreneur, founder, and director of therapeutic communities for adolescents. He is president of the charity "Rosa dei Venti Foundation" and past president of the Il Nodo Group, Italy. He is an OPUS member, a staff member of GRC ALI since 2006, and in other international GRCs, and from 2010 he was director of LFA and ECW. He is a Michelangelo Pistoletto Third Paradise's Ambassador, a journalist, and a previous basketball coach. His last book, with R. D. Hinshelwood, was *Learning from Action: Working with the Non-Verbal* (Phoenix Publishing House, 2022).

Gilad Ovadia is a senior clinical psychologist and senior educational psychologist, as well as therapist, organisational consultant, and entrepreneur. She is a member of the Tel Aviv Institute for Contemporary Psychoanalysis, a friend of Ofek, and is taking part in the LFA since 2013.

Sandra Carrau Pascual, MA, is a partner and organisational consultant of the Innova Institute for organisational and social innovation in Barcelona. She specialises in the research and development of creative collaboration dynamics in teams.

Sivanie Shiran, PhD, is Faculty Head of leadership area in the MBA programs at the Interdisciplinary Center (IDC) Herzliya. She also serves as a senior organisational consultant and executive coach at IMD Business School (Switzerland) and at the Wexner Foundation (Israel). She is a clinical psychologist, Jungian psychoanalyst, and a member of OFEK.

Ellen L. Short, PhD, is Chairperson and Associate Professor in the Department of Counseling and School Psychology, Long Island University, Brooklyn. She is a consultant, member, New York Center, AKRI Member, Fellow and former board member.

Lili Valko is a clinical psychologist, psychotherapist, and part of the therapeutic community in Thalassa Ház in Budapest, Hungary, for more than nine years in different roles and is currently deputy manager.

Joan Roma I Vergés, MA, is president and organisational consultant of the Innova Institute for organisational and social innovation in Barcelona. He specialises in applied research from the integrative "Organisational Transnovation" approach.

Rosemary Viswanath, PGDM, consults on organisational strategy, leadership, and change processes primarily with social development, social justice, and human and environmental rights organisations and people's movements. Passionately involved in Group Relations work in India and internationally since 1987, she is the Founder–Managing Trustee of Group Relations India.

Janice K. Wagner, LICSW, is a psychotherapist in private practice in Boston, MA. She is a Fellow at A. K. Rice Institute, past president Center for the Study of Groups and Social Systems, and co-creator at Group Relations International.

John Wilkes is a freelance coach and consultant who is grateful for the learning he has derived from over 20 years of Group Relations experiences and for the opportunity to explore the complex and multi-faceted issues that encompass difference and diversity, working with Barbara Williams and Fabio D'Apice.

Barbara Williams, EdD, MSW, MSc, is Director of Bureau Kensington Consulting in Toronto; member, ISPSO, AKRI & Center for the Study of Groups and Social Systems; Guest Toronto Psychoanalytic Society & Institute; Associate Editor for *Journal Organizational and Social Dynamics*.

Katherine M. Zwick, MA, LPCC, CGP, C-DBT, is Associate Director of Clinical Services, Queer Asterisk, Denver, CO (Telecommute); Principal, Consultant & Therapist, Ride The Wave Recovery, Santa Cruz, CA (Telehealth); Co-Creator, Group Relations International; Associate, AK Rice Institute; member, GREX West Coast Affiliate; clinical member, American Group Psychotherapy Association; member, GAYLESTA; Member, WPATH; past Secretary, Chicago Center for the Study of Groups and Organizations.

Belgirate Conference: A Memory

In Belgirate it is autumn.
A warmth that softly resonates with the past heat of summer, wraps
around me.
I climb from the taxi, remembering the winding roads that the driver
seemed carelessly, even recklessly to traverse.
I leave my luggage at the hotel and begin walking.
Baskets of flowers hang from balconies over narrow streets and I smell
sweet scents;
Sometimes the delicious smell of bread newly baked.
Turning back, the splendid vista of Lake Maggiore spreads before me
and I sigh with contentment at my safe arrival.
Next.
The excitement starts.
Colleagues are hugged, cheeks kissed, new faces spied.
The anticipation of things to come hangs in the air.
Will this be a place of new discoveries?
Or simply a place where we reassure each other in our beliefs and
practices?
We listen to and make our own and our collective judgments of
papers, generally with appreciation and sometimes with questioning.
We attend experiential events,
Challenge each other.
And ourselves.
Have discussions over coffee.
It's as if we have found a box full of layers of fascinating foods,
Many recognised although newly presented.
The basic comfort food we all need.
Others exotic and new so we have to accustom ourselves to their taste.

Susan Long

Foreword

The Place Where We Live: The Space for Group Relations – a book developed from a conference in 2018.

The task of the conference on which this book is based: *To explore the ecosystem called Group Relations Conferences and reflect upon our lived experience of that ecosystem in relation to our different spaces and contexts.*

A foreword written in early 2021 to a book about 'the ecosystem called Group Relations conferences' is not so much an introduction (that is done excellently in each of the section introductions) as it is a place to raise associations and connections. So, I take that as my purpose here.

One thing about ecosystems is that although everything is interconnected in co-dependent dynamics, each separate part, in its own skin, has a unique niche: comprising that part and its environment; i.e. its habitat, interactions, activity patterns, and resources: each of these being in connection with other niches. A niche is metaphorically equivalent to the spaces and contexts named in the conference task. In the discipline of Ecology, the law of competitive exclusion argues that different species of approximately the same habits cannot inhabit the same resource niche. One of the two (or more) will have better adaptation and survive. The others become extinct or evolve in new ways. Is this the case with different theories or practices within Group Relations? Those that survive through their use and those that evolve into quite different ideas and practices are yet to be discovered. And, despite the principle of competitive exclusion, the 'competition-colonisation trade-off principle' amongst other dynamics allows co-existence. 'Species that are better competitors will be specialists, whereas species that are better colonisers are more likely to be generalists' (Wikipedia). That is, within the same ecological niche. This is an interesting idea when we think about relations within the Group Relations community; itself having a hierarchy of specialists and generalists. That is the specialist roles in conferences and the more generalist roles of applying conference learning to a broader setting.

Ecological niches sit alongside one another, sometimes even inside one another. And, a creature in one niche may be oblivious to other different niches, registering only a niche competitor. So it is, in many ways, with the phenomenon called the human mind (and I see mind as a collective phenomenon): out of sight of our own special niches, we may be oblivious to those of the other. Rosemary Viswanath's chapter, amongst others in this book, illustrates this. And, as object relations practitioners and Group Relations experiences indicate, one human mind may inhabit another through projection, introjection, and projective identifications. The group mind does this also when groups psychologically inhabit each other – sometimes destructively.

But there are limits to the metaphorical leap of a concept from one discipline to another. Bion utilised ecological concepts in many ways including his understanding of relations between humans as commensal, parasitic, and symbiotic (Bion 1970). Natural ecological systems have all of these relations between and sometimes within species, where some such relations are life giving and others disastrous to individuals.

An ecological system maintains its own balance, irrespective of the individual. But as potentially ethical beings, beyond our basic biology, we seek both to maintain system balance and preserve individuals in all of their complex dimensions. Our ecology stretches beyond the biological to political, identity, emotional, otherness, and spiritual dimensions – all discussed in this book.

Contexts

The world of COVID-19 is a world of being 'lost in familiar places' to use a term coined by Shapiro and Carr (1991). In the many lockdowns that have taken place throughout 2020 and into 2021, people have lost their normal everyday lives and have faced being in their homes in new ways. Some have been stranded in places other than their own (both physically and mentally) and forced into quarantine, sometimes lonely. The anxieties washed in with covid have colonised the mind just as the virus has colonised the body. I wrote about this in a blog (Long 2020) where I examined how we are caught between BA(Me) and BA(Oneness). Bahat's chapter explores 'Nothingness' as occupying a space here – a frightening vista of the future were we to fall into such an assumption. A more positive place is co-operation and collaboration.

Climate change and species extinction are perhaps even more serious than COVID-19. Perhaps because in the COVID context, humans are interested in maintaining their health and lives in the face of an immediate threat, hence collaboration across nations has occurred (well at least to some extent) and vast amounts of resources have been poured into creating vaccines. Meanwhile, interests are solidly different with respect to ways of reducing carbon emissions and maintaining habitats for endangered species. The recent glacial fall causing dams to collapse in India, with many lives lost (Reliefweb, 2021), and the Australian bush fires are but two examples of devastation from climate change to human communities. Meanwhile, species are being lost at a frighteningly rapid rate, including, for example, many mammals, frogs, birds, and plants (Scientific American, 2021).

Our political world seems increasingly split as demonstrated in many elections and uprisings around the globe – the US and Hong Kong being but two examples. One issue in the split is the nature of authority – a concern traditionally approached by Group Relations. Linked to this is a question that I have heard raised during lockdowns about whether or not the various populations have become too simply compliant with the regulations. I'm not referring to those who object to wearing masks on the grounds that this is an attack on personal liberties or those deniers or followers of the multitude of conspiracy theories now circulating. I refer to liberal thinkers and colleagues. Compliance, co-operation, and identification are ranged along a dimension of responses to influence. My own thinking is that where populations have had leadership that has listened to the science, moved decisively and made it possible for communities to collaborate together, the virus has had less of a grip – again both physically and mentally.

And splits between those who have, and those who have not, grow. The 'Black Lives Matter' and 'MeToo' movements have brought these 'unthought knowns' into some prominence, as has the political situation in places like Myanmar and many other such places that continue to suffer from oppression of minorities.

These contexts are not isolated but interconnected:

> While the COVID-19 pandemic's most immediate impacts have been on public health and economic performance, the longer-term legacy of the current crisis is more likely to be political and social upheaval. The pandemic is already showing signs of amplifying ongoing crises around the world, whether it's racial inequality in the United States, government spending on social programs in South America, unsustainable debt in Europe, or the ongoing geopolitical stand-off between the United States and China. In addition to the wave of challenges governments and companies have faced amidst the immediate COVID-19 crisis, the long-term repercussions on political and social stability will generate more uncertainty for years to come.
>
> (West, 2020).

What Is the Place Now of Group Relations in These Contexts?

Inequities, intergroup hostilities, and cruelty continue as does trauma as a result. Group Relations both provide a window of understanding into why this is, and a method for showing people how they contribute, personally and in groups and organisations. Can we bring Group Relations thinking and practice to board rooms? See, for instance, Brissett et al (2019) and the work of Lionel Stapley at OPUS. Or to government policy where broad changes can occur? See, for example, Boccara (2016). While in this tradition, we have written about climate change denial, its psychology and its consequences (Long, 2015; Hoggett, 2019), there is now talk of species extinction denial and an unwillingness to look at the way factory farming and what we eat is destructive to the planet as well as embodying cruelty (Oppenlander 2012; Ricard 2016). Can Group Relations face whole world systems? And importantly, can Group Relations inform our daily lives for ongoing transformations in challenging contexts?

This book brings together different approaches to theory and practice in Group Relations, including innovations into new places and contexts, showing the place that Group Relations thinking and practice can bring to different communities and workplaces; to the issues of otherness and differing languages – even at home, wherever that is. This raises questions about core identity. Whenever Group Relations practitioners come together issues of task, territory, time, and boundaries are raised along with well-established theories such as basic assumptions and social defences. Here, the various authors not only illustrate such fundamentals but also question and propose new ideas. If Group Relations thinking and practice is to have an influential place in today's contexts, we must all maintain healthy scepticism alongside an imaginative curiosity while building strongly on the work of the past. Importantly we must find ways to make a difference – an enterprise at the core of Group Relations.

Susan Long

References

Bion, W. R. (1970) *Attention and Interpretation*. Routledge.

Boccara, B. (2016) *Socioanalytic Dialogue: Incorporating Psychosocial Dynamics into Public Policies*. Lexington Books.

Brissett. L. B., Sher, M. and Smith, T. L. (eds) (2019) *Dynamics at Boardroom Level: A Tavistock Primer for Leaders, Coaches and Consultants*. Routledge.

Hoggett, P. (ed) (2019) *Climate Psychology: On Indifference to Disaster*. Palgrave McMillan.

Long, S. D. (2015) 'Turning a blind eye to climate change: integrating psychological, philosophical and cultural perspectives.' *Organisational and Social Dynamics* 15:2, 248–262, 346.

Long, S. D. (2020) https://www.nioda.org.au/we-are-all-in-this-together/

Oppenlander, R. (2012) *Comfortably Unaware: What We Choose to Eat Is Killing Us and Our Planet*. Beaufort Books.

Reliefweb (2021) https://reliefweb.int/report/world/glacier-collapse-india-worrying-sign-what-s-come

Ricard, M. (2016) *A Plea for the Animals: The Moral, Philosophical and Evolutionary Imperative to Treat All Beings with Compassion*. Shambhala Publications, Inc.

Scientific American (recovered 12 Jan 2021) https://www.scientificamerican.com/article/what-weve-lost-the-species-declared-extinct-in-2020/

Shapiro, E. and Carr, W. (1991) *Lost in Familiar Places: Creating Connections between the Individual and Society*. Yale University Press.

West, B. (September 2020) https://www.securityinfowatch.com/security-executives/article/21152093/how-political-and-social-unrest-affect-global-security-in-the-age-of-covid19

Introduction

This book, like all the others in the series, is based on the Belgirate meetings that take place every three years for anyone who has taken up a staff role in a group relations conference. The meetings have been held in Belgirate, Lago Maggiore in Italy since 2003.

The theme of the meeting in 2018 was *The Place Where We Live: The Space for Group Relations* in terms of the conscious and unconscious assumptions, phantasies, forces, and perceptions that shape and influence the Group Relations Conference space. Its task was to explore the ecosystem called Group Relations Conferences and reflect upon our lived experience of that ecosystem in relation to our different spaces and contexts.

The phrase: 'the place in which we live' is taken from Donald Winnicott's paper on the location of cultural experience. It refers to a third place, a liminal, potential zone, which is located 'neither outside nor inside [of us] – and yet outside and inside – at the same time'. If you want to imagine this dialectic definition, you can think about our oxygenic surrounding. It is outside (the oxygen in the atmosphere), and at the same time, it is inhaled – so it is also inside; the process of inhalation transforms the oxygen inside and is then exhaled (as it turns into CO_2), thus changing the outside environment. Then it is inhaled again … and so it goes on and on. Our action – breathing in this case – changes 'the place in which we live' inside and outside simultaneously. And more than that: it is an ongoing process which is constantly and dynamically evolving – while keeping its characteristic features and boundaries. This allows us to define it in specific moments, either as a 'life giving' place, or as a 'deadening' place, etc.

The focus was on context, i.e. on the relationship between our physical place we inhabit or co-create, and the psychic, inner or spiritual space we are part of.

The three keynote lectures and three rounds of parallel presentations were the raw material from which this book has emerged. In addition, we have once again included several personal reflective pieces from the participants at the meeting.

DOI: 10.4324/9781003261483-1

Table 0.1 Previous GRC roles taken by Belgirate VI participants

Role	Total
Administrator	1
Associate Director, Consultant	8
Associate Director, Consultant, Administrator	5
Consultant	17
Consultant, Administrator	21
Consultant, Translator	1
Director	1
Director, Associate Director, Consultant	13
Director, Associate Director, Consultant, Administrator	21
Director, Associate Director, Consultant, Administrator, Associate Administrator	1
Director, Consultant	2
Director, Consultant, Administrator	1
MAT	5
Total	**97**

Belgirate VI was the largest meeting since the series was founded. Ninety-seven people attended from eighteen countries. The average age was 58, and the gender distribution was 59% women and 41% men. We asked participants to indicate which roles they had held in Group Relations Conferences. As Table 0.1 shows, 21 participants had held four roles, 19 had held three roles, and another 32 held two roles. Nineteen participants had only experienced one role in a GRC, while one participant had held five roles.

The definition we use for the discourse has been consistent across the meetings. We mean the language we use, our terms, our ethical values (explicit or implicit), the nature of the concepts we use in our theoretical writings; our metaphors and their hidden meanings, the tools and methods we use in our practice, the nature of our work – in short, our professional culture (doing the business of group relations to use a phrase from the Belgirate V meeting).

As mentioned before[1] – the discourse we create may not only represent the way we understand reality – but it may actually create the reality we understand – and at the same time, leave outside of our consciousness all that we don't understand and, perhaps, don't want to understand. That may be true not only for our profession, but it actually may be relevant to all scientific disciplines. For example – when Stephen Hawking talks about 'Baby Universes'[2] it is not just a metaphor; it is a metaphor which shapes our physical concepts and the way we understand our universe. This time we are considering place and space.

Space, place, or territory has always been one of the three key T boundaries for the design of a Group Relations Conference (alongside Task and Time). Many of our conferences are known for the place in which they happen, most notably Leicester and Belgirate. We also remember by their place, rather than by their theme, the series of group relations conferences which came together around a particular theme, for example: the Nazareth conferences, the Cyprus conferences, the Robbin Island conferences, the Boston conferences, the NOLA conferences, the Peruvian Amazon conferences, amongst others.

The book is divided into four sections. The first focuses on the place of psychoanalysis in group relations. The second section explores the place of social, political, and spiritual issues. The third section looks at the place of practice and methodology. The book concludes with the final section which contains reflections from participants who were at the meeting.

As with the previous volumes in this series, chapters in this book are largely based on presentations made at the Belgirate VI meeting. Some of the authors updated their presentations and others (notably Green) refocused the chapter (and added a co-author). Hence, even if the reader attended the Belgirate VI meeting, we believe the chapters in this volume offer new and additional opportunities for learning. This is in addition to the chapters offering reflection on the meeting experience.

Coreene, Gordon, Rachel, and Yossi

January 2021

Notes

1 Doing the business of group relations introduction.
2 Hawking, S. (1993) 'Black Holes and Baby Universes'. Bantam Books.

Section I

The Psychoanalytic – Systemic Approach

Introduction

This section explores the "Place in which we live" from a psychoanalytic-systemic perspective. Each of the three chapters of this part sheds new light on different corners of our Group Relations (GR) world.

Shmuel Erlich's chapter *Unbounded Worlds – A Challenge for Group Relations?*, based on his keynote lecture, starts with a short historical review of the theory and practice of GR and introduces a new type of GR conference where the focus is not so much about exploring authority, leadership, and organizational dynamics, but on "collective trauma, the threat of changing identity, and the fear of betraying one's social network". In retrospect, Erlich offers a hypothesis that the focus on "organizational life" may have served unconsciously also as a defense against dealing with the unbearable pain and repressed horror of the collective trauma following WWII. Erlich hints that perhaps now it is ready to be explored and worked through. The chapter offers a new design implemented by a new organization: Partners in Confronting Collective Atrocities (PCCA) which brought together Germans and Israelis to allow each group to do "its own work in the actual presence of the other". Theoretical as well as practical conclusions close this fascinating and thoughtful chapter.

Daphna Bahat's chapter is a provocative analysis of what she defines as the "Seventh Basic Assumption": Nothingness. The chapter *Nothingness – A Group Phenomenon or a Seventh Basic Assumption. Does It Really Matter? Does Anything Matter at All?* describes a phenomenon where the group actually adopts the view that "there is no sunrise so beautiful that it is worth waking me up to see it" (Mindy Kaling: Molidzon, 2017). Bahat's discussion touches several crucial points. Some of them she defines as meta-theoretical, for example: should there be more than Bion's original three Basic Assumptions ("are we allowed?" she asks). Is "Nothingness" actually a Basic Assumption, reflecting primitive, unconscious aspects of the inner world – or is it a group culture, more than mentality? The chapter extends the discussion to include current social and cultural characteristics.

DOI: 10.4324/9781003261483-2

This section ends with a powerful report about a GR-oriented organizational intervention in a psychoanalytic society which had become totally paralyzed. It is an honest and respectful description of the difficulties psychoanalysts face when exposed and analyzed as a group. John Lundgren's chapter *The Place Where Psychoanalysts Live: Introducing Group Relations to Psychoanalytic Institutes* describes this very thoughtful and systematic intervention. The theoretical background suggests that the work was based on Winnicott's "model of the social and cultural process that engage both external reality and internal reality with the creation of a third or intermediate zone where play, creativity, and group life may emerge". Lundgren proposes that "we live together with a paradox, that of being both joined together and separate from each other. Our social engagement recurrently evokes, at our infantile core, the experience of our movement from dependency to autonomy". The sensitive way the author deals with this situation and the outcomes close this chapter.

Chapter 1

Unbounded Worlds

A Challenge for Group Relations?[1]

Shmuel Erlich

I would like to begin my contribution by referring to the theme of this volume, which is *the relationship between physical place we inhabit or co-create, and the psychic, inner or spiritual space we are part of.* It is from the vantage point of this relationship that we aim to reflect upon our lived experience of the Group Relations (GR) ecosystem in our different spaces and contexts. In what follows, I wish to address the relationship between our physical place and the psychic, inner, or spiritual space that we are part of, and to examine its implications to the present state of GR and the future directions it may take.

I must confess: The argument that persuaded or seduced me to accept the invitation to write this chapter was that the theme under discussion plays on Winnicott's well-known title, *Home Is Where We Come from* (1986). This, I thought, somewhat naively, should make it easy for me, based on my affinity with some of Winnicott's ideas and writings. I had a fresh look at the chapters of this book and discovered that in a book about "Home", there was a heading, *Reflections on Society*, under which was a chapter titled, *Some Thoughts on the Meaning of the Word Democracy.* Interestingly, it was published on June 1, 1950, not in a psychoanalytic journal but in *Human Relations.* It is noteworthy that this article preceded by several years the inception of GR (1957) and was probably as close as Winnicott came to it. So, in addressing "Home" as where we come from and the place we live in, Winnicott extended the scope of "home" to reflect on the nature of the social and even the political. Winnicott's perspective and intention in this book and chapter define GR quite well: GR represents the combined look at what is closest to home, in the most intimate sense of one's personal experience, and what in this experience belongs to the social order in its widest and most systemic sense.

I find the thoughts in this chapter both timely and provocative. Winnicott, being a psychoanalyst, distinguishes between how conscious and unconscious thoughts and feelings affect democracy. The secret ballot, for instance, enables and ensures that the vote will "express deep feelings *apart from conscious thoughts.* If there is doubt about the secrecy of the ballot, the

DOI: 10.4324/9781003261483-3

individual, however healthy, can only express by his vote his *reactions*" [my emphasis] and compliance. Thus, even in the conscious act of casting our vote, we are expressing deep unconscious aspects of ourselves. Furthermore, he claims that democracy is only possible "if there is sufficient maturity in the emotional development of a sufficient proportion of the individuals" comprising the society at that moment in time (we may want to relate this to present developments). *Freedom* is made possible through the willingness of individuals to tolerate being outvoted and not getting their own way if they cannot get the support of the majority. This, he observes, is a remarkable human achievement since it involves tolerating much strain and pain, which interestingly "can only be possible if the gratification is allowed of a period-ical illogical riddance of the leader".

"A periodical illogical riddance of the leader"? Do we detect a connection to the incipient theme of GR conferences of "Authority and Leadership" a few short years hence? Winnicott's idea of a sufficient proportion of "healthy" and mature individuals seems problematic, if not inflammatory, in our times when political correctness is a supreme value. Yet it echoes longstanding debates and attempted solutions at the socio-political level, such as the debate in the early stages of American democracy about who should be qualified and can be entrusted with the newly created democ-racy. Among those not to be entrusted were people who did not own land or enough financial means and, of course, women who were barred from the vote. This historical debate led eventually to the structural solution of differently elected Two Houses, and nearly 150 years later, to enfranchise women. But it is pertinent to our subject today if we wish to focus on the place and space in which GR conferences came into being, how they have evolved, and where they may be heading.

GR came into being and evolved against the background of the world as constituted in the 1950s and in the aftermath of WWII. Its universe was not only clearly bounded – it was super-bounded. Good and evil were sharply separated and demarcated through the opposition between Democracy and its nemeses: Fascism, Communism, and Totalitarianism. The opposing forces vying for world domination were soon to be physically set apart by the virtual iron curtain, the concrete barrier of the Berlin Wall, and the barbed wire borders all over Europe.

The emergence of GR at that time and era stemmed from the serendipi-tous confluence of two currents: An enlarged perspective of social science, expounded by Kurt Lewin's field theory (1951) and Bertalanffy's Open Systems Theory (1950) on the one hand, and the group-as-a-whole trans-ference and mentality, coupled with psychoanalytic defensive activity, as formulated by Bion (1961) on the other hand. Trauma played a significant behind the scenes role as well: the emergence of GR in England took place against the background of a severely injured and declining empire and the residual traumata of war, to wit also Bion's work with traumatized soldiers and his own traumatic experience in WWI. Thus, advances and new discoveries were intertwined with the breakup of the old order, together with the comfort and safety it provided, of knowing all too well one's place in the world.

Psychoanalysis was a major input that informed and saturated the newly created GR theory, methodology, and practice, along with Systems Theory. In the history of psychoanalysis as well, this was a period marked by the interplay of trauma and a struggle between rigidification and innovation. WWII brought about the temporary decline of European psychoanalysis: many analysts perished by Nazi persecution, and many others sought refuge in North and South America and the UK. The psychoanalytic center of gravity shifted to the US, where for a variety of reasons and factors it became popular, academically respectable, and financially successful, but at the same time increasingly stiff and removed from experiential immediacy. The psychoanalytic movement, represented by the International Psychoanalytic Association (IPA), avoided a traumatic split by granting the Americans exceptional autonomy. This resulted eventually in what may be a paraphrase on what Churchill aptly described, albeit in a different context, as two psychoanalytic entities separated by a common language. When GR was imported in 1966 to the US by Kenneth Rice and Pierre Turquet, which is when I first encountered it, it felt like being colonized by the British once again – by a language, a mode of articulation, and a set of concepts that were at one and the same time immensely appealing and strange. "Authority and Leadership" were indeed the order of the day and what it felt to be all about.

I must explain why I took you on this historical journey through facts that must be familiar to most of the readers. GR teaches us to investigate the roots of processes, the "how", the "what", and the "why" of its coming into being. It is therefore only appropriate that we explore what went into the creation and evolution of GR. My main point in this regard is this: Implicit in the major innovations represented by GR are the residues and impingements of traumas, of national and international struggles, of losses, and decline, but also of hopes for a new world and a better social order. It is much beyond my abilities to explore the unfolding of these trends in European and world history over the following decades of the 20th century and the beginning of the 21st. But I think it is pertinent to a perspective of where GR is in the present world and in its own developmental track. Surely such a perspective on areas pertinent to GR must take account of the changes that have occurred and those that we are still embroiled in.

This brings us to today's world, and again, any attempt to reduce it to a few sentences or paragraphs must be terribly oversimplified. Nonetheless, and with this apology, I would like to describe several aspects of our present social environment that I alluded to in my title, namely, the unbounded worlds we live in and how this must affect GR practice.

If we look at the evolution of the titles of GR conferences, we may note a tendency toward a shift, sometimes subtle and sometimes deliberate: Authority and Leadership seem to have relinquished their first line prominence, which in the beginning phase, they occupied for decades. They have either been dropped, moved to a less prominent subtitle, or were otherwise modified. At the same time, various other components of GR methodology, as well as other terms, have acquired greater prominence and titular visibility. To name a few recent examples: "Discovering Leadership: Authenticity, Action and Responsibility – a group relations conference"; "Identity, culture, and class in group and organisational life: a group relations conference"; "Working in organisations – the unconscious at work – a group relations conference"; "Role, mask, and person in groups and organisations"; and so on. In our own history of OFEK[2] conferences, it is remarkable that for the first two conferences, "authority" was dropped in favor of Task and Organization. The reason given was that in post-Holocaust Israel, the word "authority" carried offensive negative associations, and no one would come. After the first two conferences, "authority" was restored to the title, later to be dropped again, and more recently, "authority and leadership" have experienced at least a partial revival. The upcoming OFEK international conference, for example, bears the title: "Leadership, Identity and Role: Fantasy and Reality". In a similar vein, this year's Leicester brochure bears the title: "Task, Authority, Organization", bracketing Authority with the notions of Task and Organization.

Multitude factors are involved in this shift, and I wish to single out only two of them. First, the wish/need for innovation, for distinguishing and differentiating oneself from previous work, as if a mere terminological change of emphasis connotes novelty, freshness, and progress; and second, the pressures of competing in a crowded marketplace, where "task" and "organization" possess greater immediate familiarity and appeal. This is not a criticism; it is an attempt to draw attention to certain evolutionary changes. But it does raise the question: are authority and leadership no longer the issues they represented at the beginning of GR? They certainly were "the" issues in the 50s, 60s, and even the 70s and 80s. And I believe that they are just as relevant today. Yet something has changed in the social world we live in and therefore also in the focus of GR work.

It seems to me that the early phases of GR have unconsciously avoided the traumas that affected and burdened the world in which they were conceived. Rather than deal with trauma and painful feelings, the focus was on structure and system, on institutional functioning, on the nature of boundaries, the clarity of task, and the exercise of authority. In all this, the individual was not exactly irrelevant but treated substantially as a signifier of the social structure he was embedded in – the group, the nationality, the nature of the organization he represented. In a sense, this may even be construed as an unconsciously totalitarian, meta-individual approach, whether it is regarded through the systemic lens or the group-as-a-whole transference and basic assumption mentality.

Has the world indeed changed since then? Admittedly, this is a silly question since the answer seems rather commonsensical and obvious. Indeed, the changes we have all experienced and lived through in the last decades are not only momentous and multiple, but the rate and speed of change are rising exponentially. Yet we know that the answer to this question depends on the focus and tools that are employed for studying and gauging change. To add a bit of information from a different area: questions and doubts are currently being raised about the capacity of our evolutionary molded brain to keep up with the explosion of information it is required to deal with. Very recent studies (Fiebelkorn et al, 2018) have demonstrated that our brain becomes *unfocused* about four times every second [!], or 240 times a minute, implying that our consciousness is absent during these lapses and we are *unconsciously* attuned to potential dangers and inputs in our surroundings. Such findings are in line with psychoanalytic notions about the limited place and nature of consciousness and especially in agreement with Freudian ideas. Moreover, the psychoanalytic understanding of human nature – the place and impact of drive, desire, conflict, and early experience – all suggest that at the heart of the rapid changes created and perfected by mankind stands a human being whose internal world and experience are seriously, and quite often dangerously, out of sync with these external, fast-paced developments. In a recent session, for instance, analyst and analysand found themselves in agreement over the sweeping generalization that, faced with the seemingly unlimited proliferation of sexual and gender identities and object choices, in addition to blurred identities and role definitions, people are increasingly experiencing confusion, anxiety, and loss, associated with the limitless freedom of choice.

The question I want to pose is therefore: Given that the place we live in is poignantly marked by and struggling with this duality – increasingly rapid external change that is out of step with our basically unchanging (or slow changing) internal psychic makeup – a duality that characterizes our current lives and the social dynamics that stem from it – given all that, what is the place and role of GR? Are we to be part of the forward propulsion of change, adapting ourselves to the shifting and constantly renewing styles and fashions? Or should we rather be the keepers and guardians of unyielding constancy and stability in the midst of change, with the risk of becoming anachronistic and out of step? If the objective of a GR conference is learning and granted the well-known fact that each participant has his/her own conference and learning, what is to be the focus of this learning? Should it still be on latent institutional dynamics governed by the impact of authority and the role of leadership? Have these issues become obsolete in the face of trends toward horizontal authority and shared leadership?

It may be rightly objected that these questions are irrelevant since we have already moved beyond them, given some of the innovations that have been introduced into the classical GR format. Nevertheless, I maintain that GR as a *theory,* a practiced *methodology,* and a *movement* is faced with these issues and embroiled in the process of coping with them, and hence it is only appropriate to surface and focus on them. If these are the prominent trends in the place we live in, and if we are part of this place and space, these issues are with us, and we are part of them.

Obviously, the dichotomous choices I have described are quite polarized and the answer cannot be simply lie in one extreme or the other. But it may help us to frame what we are struggling with.

As a tentative contribution toward the exploration of the options we face, I would like to share our experience in a series of conferences that began in 1994 and have since evolved to their present form and shape. I am referring to the "Germans and Israelis, the Past in the Present" conferences, known in Germany as "the Nazareth Conferences". I hope that the story and approach represented by them will contribute to the theme I am trying to develop.

These conferences grew out of the felt need and recognition that the residual effects and aftermath of the Holocaust were an underlying, only partially and unsatisfactorily addressed dynamic in both German and Israeli-Jewish mental health professionals, hampering their capacity to work fully and well with these residues in themselves and in their patients. Recognizing both the pain and agony, as well as the real difficulty in addressing this poignantly sensitive and painful area, the idea of applying the GR methodology promised a fresh and potentially meaningful approach. We were aware of other approaches, of a quite different nature, that aimed at reconciliation, expiation, and forgiveness. We eschewed this goal and thought we needed to aim for the kind of learning that would expand the capacities of participants, to which the GR method seemed uniquely appropriate. Yet obviously, the traditional GR methodology could not accommodate a structure in which two *a priori* identified nationality groups constituted the membership. A special design and adaptation were created by Eric Miller together with the German and Israeli initiators of the project. This original design consisted of mixed-nationality SSGs, single-nationality RAGs, an Institutional Event (IE) that began in simultaneous separate openings for the two nationality groups, and several Plenaries throughout the conference.

You may have noticed the absence in this design of an event commonly present in GRCs (except the earliest ones), namely the LG. It bears testimony to the tremendous anxiety felt by all of us. The LG was deemed potentially too explosive and dangerous for the encounter between perpetrators and victims. That this fantasy projection was not altogether mad was confirmed by the following encounter in the opening plenary of the first Nazareth Conference. A German woman said she was so disappointed because there were so few Israelis present. An immediate response came from an elderly Israeli woman: "If you hadn't killed so many of us, there would have been more". Notwithstanding and perhaps owing to this dramatic opening, the conference evolved and became institutionalized in mind, with people expecting it and planning for their joining and participation. But the initial level of anxiety took several years to diminish. In the first three conferences, Eric Miller as director steadfastly refused to include an LG.

What was this anxiety? Obviously, the immediate fear was of the aggression that would be liberated and insufficiently contained, the rageful attack and revenge of the victims, and the guilty submission of the perpetrators to punishment, perhaps in turn mobilizing their counter-aggression. The anxiety of staff had to do with doubts about the resilience and strength of the structure to contain such aggression. But the source of anxiety was still deeper. In our book that describes the first three conferences (Erlich et al, 2009), we note that the main sources of anxiety and resistance were the *threat to identity*, coupled with the feeling of *betrayal*. Let me elaborate.

Taking a broad perspective, it is a daring and courageous act to engage with the residues of historical and collective trauma. It must involve the restoration of pain as well as the unleashing of enmity, aggression, and destruction in the worst and most poignant manner. And yet, and this is my central point, it is desperately needed in the unbounded world we live in, more so than focusing on organizational structure and dynamics. The latter still have their place, which I shall address presently, but they can be employed in the service of different needs and goals.

The structure and design of these conferences provide opportunities for encountering the other, as well as oneself and one's own group. A possible outcome of this encounter is the changed image of the other, which brings about a shift in the perception of oneself. The other is an invaluable determinant of one's own identity, and as the image of the other undergoes change, the personal and collective group identities change with it. This change is experienced as a serious threat on all levels: it destabilizes one's sense of the world as an organized, coherent, meaningful place. It undermines the clear delineation of good from bad objects, upsetting habitual patterns of projection. It challenges the primitive schizo-paranoid order without immediately moving to a depressive integration. Worst of all, it undermines one's ties and roots in psychic and social reality. The changed perception of the other works against the world view that is part of the emotional ties with one's parents and family.

Such threats to identity emerged because Germans and Israelis came in actual close contact. Because the conference had shaken deeply established identity patterns by changing one's view of oneself and the other, it produced disarray, tension, and upset. It is difficult to give up familiar roles, such as the role of perpetrator for the Germans and that of victim for the Israelis. But the overriding danger that may block change is the fear of *betrayal* – of parents, relatives, and culture – and the associated shame and guilt.

Beyond these dangers and difficulties, the emergent lesson of these conferences and this design was the fundamental need and value for each group *to do its own work in the actual presence of the other.* This lesson was carried forth in the next series of conferences which took place in Cyprus, gradually extended their scope to include diaspora Jews, affected others, and Palestinians. We founded a new organization that took charge and responsibility for this work – *Partners in Confronting Collective Atrocities* (PCCA). The mission of this organization is to take forward the understanding and methodological approach we have gained in this work and to apply it in areas and with memberships suffering from residual traumas due to violence and atrocities, whether national or international, ethnic or religious, political or historical. The focus of the work has shifted somewhat with time, although the shadow of the Holocaust is still very much a leitmotiv affecting our understanding of what we meet.

You may well ask: Where is authority and leadership in these conferences? What makes them GR conferences? The question was indeed raised by staff members who joined this work. Some new staff were troubled by the seeming absence of clear reference to authority and authorization. In my view, this is a pseudo issue. Authority and leadership are always present explicitly as well as implicitly, as in all institutions and organizations. The conference is structured along the familiar roles of management – a director, associate director, and administrator. Staff are clearly allocated, deployed, and authorized in their dual role as consultants and collective management. Boundaries – of task, role, times, language, and territories – are carefully and mindfully monitored, as are the points on the continuum of authorization for members in the IE (our version of the Organizational Event [OE]). The conference comprises the usual events – Small Study Group (SSG), Large Study Group (LSG), Review and Application Group (RAG), IE, and Plenaries, in addition to such recent additions as a Social Dreaming Matrix.

Thus, the structure, events, and role definitions are the familiar GR ones. Yet the focus in these conferences is not learning about authority and leadership. The focus has shifted in accordance with the precariously unbounded worlds we live in to harness the unique lens developed by GR to enable us to attend to collective trauma, the threat of changing identity, and the fear of betraying one's social network.

So, wherein lies the difference? The answer is: in the Primary Task. The Primary Task of these conferences does not aim at learning about institutional unconscious dynamics as these unfold, but rather at *using* these, in whatever way the GR frame enables, to manage and to interpret, in line with the overall theme of the conference, feelings, and fantasies about Germanness and Israeliness/Jewishness; Victims and Perpetrators; Identities and Cultures in Violent Conflict; Exclusion, Resentment, and the

Return of the Repressed; and so on. Put differently, the focus has shifted. The dynamics of authority and leadership, of role and task, etc., are important and omnipresent. It is the GR methodology that allows us to perceive, identify, and work with them – with the staff, with the membership, and with the conference institution-as-a-whole. Yet all of these are in the service of a different dynamic understanding and learning, which hopefully also creates the change that comes with the experience of new insight. In this sense, it is a figure and ground exercise.

Before I come to some tentative conclusions or suggestions, let me share an instance from one of our conferences in Poland, which I hope will illustrate what I have been saying.

The conference membership was dominated by Germans and Israelis as the two major groups, though of unequal numbers, and an assortment of others from various European countries. There were two or three Polish members, as well as two members whose mother tongue was Polish but who lived in different countries. In the IE the membership formed various groups which, for the most part, bore titles that were somewhat compliant and perhaps placating to the management, as if to gain recognition for the good work being done. As often happens, the groups were moderately active, meeting and negotiating on their issues. The emergent map of these groups seemed to reflect striving for a measure of cooperation and peaceful coexistence, perhaps invoking the image of the European Union. Slowly and belatedly, however, it emerged that while these intergroup activities and interactions with management went on, a clandestine and unreported meeting of the Poles and the two Polish-speaking members was taking place, without anyone mentioning it or being explicit about it, and certainly outside the awareness of management. These meetings took place within or at the outskirts of the territorial boundaries and within the time boundaries, and management learned of it rather late in the event. It was as if there was an additional unrecognized group within the event. In the final plenary of the IE this finally emerged, and the explanation given by these members was that they met to speak Polish, their native or mother tongue.

Clearly, this bit of enactment could be understood and interpreted in many ways. For one, it underscores the tremendous and insufficiently recognized significance of language – as a boundary but also as a container, a matrix of identity, roots, and early life experience. Significantly, a somewhat similar event took place in one of our Cyprus conferences, when the Palestinian members closed themselves off in a room and refused to emerge from it and to interact with staff or other groups because they wanted to speak their own language, Arabic.

Now this could be interpreted in terms of the need to violate the boundaries set by management, and hence as a rebellious protest against authority and perhaps even a bid for alternate leadership. However, I chose to interpret it along different lines: I thought it was an *in vivo* demonstration that to assert and maintain one's identity as a national minority in this compliant and complacent European world could only be done by avoiding contact with both the authorities and the dominant majority, risking or even creating a break with the law of the land. If national identity is threatened, felt to be outlawed, and forbidden, it can only be maintained clandestinely and in defiance of authority. In such a cultural context, language becomes a refuge for identity. At the same time, its clandestine character poses a serious threat to democracy, for which transparency and participation are guiding values and norms. We may wish to reflect on the pertinence of this observation to current socio-political trends. For me this was the most telling event of the conference.

Hopefully, these developments and illustrations help us to focus the challenges GR faces under conditions of a rapidly changing sociocultural milieu and the unchanged elements of human constitution, mind, and soul. I would like to share my own conclusions and tentative suggestions.

As I have tried to demonstrate, GR came into being through the amalgamation of psychoanalytic and systemic insights. These two different components represent essentially opposed emphases on the internal *vs.* the external world. While their fusion in the GR practice has been no less than brilliant and hence immensely powerful, there has always been a certain strain between them. I remember the comment of the SSG convener the first time I served as an SSG consultant in Leicester. When I shared the experience and contents of my group with the team, she remarked, "Clearly a psychoanalyst's group!" It took me a long time to understand what she meant and what was right about it. I have often witnessed this tension as it manifests in the different approaches and backgrounds we bring to the work. More importantly, it appears that if this tension remains unrecognized and unattended it may become problematic.

In GR we are currently trying to hold together two very distinct aspects of our human existence, namely the duality of our nature, which Bion (1961) described as the tragic dimension of human existence: the conflict between two inherent and fundamental aspects of the human being: that of being a herd animal which can fully exist only within a matrix with others, and that of possessing an individual subjectivity that only knows itself and seeks to follow its own individual course. It corresponds to what I described earlier as the dilemma of emphasizing the group, the institution, and the organization as against the experience of trauma and pain. Recent GR conferences have developed awareness of this dilemma and have attempted to somehow accommodate both these aspects by including events and experiences that may address the internal world and inner space. The question is: has this resolved the issue or merely obscured it? Or: is there a price for holding both ends of the stick?

Let me clarify to avoid misunderstanding: In no way am I advocating turning GR in a more therapeutic direction aimed at healing individual pain and suffering. To the contrary, I am suggesting that perhaps what we need, faced with the challenge of a turbulent, violent, and unbounded world, is to proceed simultaneously in two parallel, equally valid, and important tracks. One track would preserve the initial aims of GR, i.e., providing opportunities for learning about unconscious dynamics in groups and organizations that will contribute to participants' functioning in roles in their organizations. Prominently, this would entail the unabashed clear emphasis on authority and leadership, as well as other familiar aspects, such as boundaries, tasks, and roles.

The other track that I envision is GRCs in which the learning and experience gained in the first track are brought to bear on a variety of current and/or historical issues, where individual issues are contingent upon group identity, historical struggles, and aspirations. The trauma, pain, and suffering are at one and the same time, the individual's and the group's, and the individual is affected *because of his "groupiness"*, as Bion put it, and therefore it is best to be dealt with at the group level. Jews and Armenians, Serbs and Chechens, Vietnamese, and Americans were all persecuted and murdered not for any individual issue but because they belonged to a specific group and identity. There are naturally less gruesome examples to be found, such as workers, people of color, or Mexican immigrants, each with its oppressors and counterparts. Examples are endless. The point is that GR can contribute significantly toward providing a way of working with them *as a group,* employing a method gained through its experience with the exploration of unconscious institutional dynamics.

In closing, let me simply reiterate what we have learned from GR: If we can re-focus and be clear about our Primary Task, there is every reason to believe that we will meet these challenges.

Notes

1 Keynote address for Belgirate VI Conference, "The Place Where We Live: The Space for Group Relations", 1–4 November 2018.
2 I am a Founding Member of OFEK (Organization, Person, Group), the Israel Association for the Study of Group and Organizational Processes. It was founded in 1983 with the assistance and guidance of the Tavistock Institute of Human Relations with the mission of introducing and fostering GR conferences in Israel.

References

Bion, W. R. (1961) *Experiences in Groups*. New York: Basic Books.

Erlich, H. S., Erlich-Ginor, M. & Beland, H. (2009) *Fed with Tears – Poisoned with Milk. The "Nazareth" Group-Relations-Conferences: Germans and Israelis: The Past in the Present*. Psychosozial Verlag: Gießen.

Fiebelkorn, I. C., Pinsk, M. A. & Kastner, S. (2018) A dynamic interplay within the frontoparietal network underlies rhythmic spatial attention. *Neuron*, 99:842–853.

Lewin, K. (1951) *Field Theory in Social Science: Selected Theoretical Papers* (Edited by Dorwin Cartwright). Oxford, England: Harpers.

von Bertalanffy, L. (1950) An outline of general systems theory. *British J. Philosophy & Science*, 1:134–165.

Winnicott, D. W. (1986) *Home Is Where We Start from.* London & New York: Norton.

Chapter 2

The Place Where Psychoanalysts Live

Introducing Group Relations to Psychoanalytic Institutes

John Lundgren

Introduction

The title of this Belgirate VI meeting, "The place where we live, the space for Group Relations," draws from Donald Winnicott's last book *Playing and Reality* published the year of his death in 1971. He sets out a model of the social and cultural process that draws both from external reality and internal reality with the creation of a third or intermediate zone where play, creativity, and group life may emerge. We live together with a paradox, that of being both joined together and separate from each other. Our social engagement recurrently evokes, at our infantile core, the experience of our movement from dependency to autonomy. Thus, we separate in our development from infancy, yet we are never separate and thus are compelled to co-create potential spaces where we can develop trust that the symbols we deploy for external world phenomena will safely (as he puts it, "in a relaxed state") generate play, creativity, and the experience ourselves as human beings. This was and is always rooted in the earliest experience of annihilation anxiety. "It is a joy to be hidden, but a disaster not to be found" (Winnicott 1965, p 186).

My aim in this chapter is twofold: to explore the world where psychoanalysts live and the approaches we have developed to both studying this world and create interventions to modify it by bringing the culture or world into contact with the group relations approach to study of groups. I will first describe the seminal opportunity where I encountered my institute in crisis and looked to my group relations and organizational consulting background for assistance. I will follow this by setting out the development of an experiment to combine an experiential group relations workshop with a traditional psychoanalytic symposium with the working hypothesis that this combined experience would enhance the safety and reliability of the containing sponsoring institution and lead to greater depth of participation of the individual analysts in their work groups. This would be accompanied by less destructive schism formation, less inhibition, and reduced emergence of at-home political roles and narcissistic displays. We believed that this approach would both enhance and deepen the cultural experience

DOI: 10.4324/9781003261483-4

of the psychoanalyst (Winnicott, 1971). I will conclude by a very selective discussion of this "case material" from a group-as-a-whole perspective and plans for future development of these experimental conversations.

Caveat

I, the author, have been a member of a psychoanalytic institute for nearly four decades. Over about the same period, I have served as consultant and director to Tavistock group relations conferences as well as to organizations and family businesses (Benson, Lundgren, West, 1988). I have long sought opportunities to bring the two psychoanalytic traditions into a functional dialogue, in an effort to preserve and anchor the psychoanalytic roots of group relations and draw from this tradition to, in turn, enrich the organizational experience of psychoanalytic institutes. The two case vignettes below arise through serendipity, where both opportunity and requisite authority emerge to productively bring these two traditions into dialogue. A full description of the rationale and methodology of the first case, an institute consultation, was recently published (Lundgren, 2019).

Historical Background

Psychoanalysis has been beset with conflicts, schisms, and dysfunctional group dynamics since its founding as a movement and organization. Freud expressed his ambivalence about leadership and anxiety about succession in several modes. In "Totem and Taboo" he posited the image of the primal horde of sons consuming the father (Freud, 1913). The creation of the IPA saw him withdraw from public leadership and the creation of the "secret" committee of loyal followers who were unquestioning of his authority. Rank, Jung, and Adler were split off and later Ferenczi joined in the "un-anointed" over manifestly doctrinal issues (Roustang, 1986).

As psychoanalysis grew both geographically and generationally, the schismatic group dynamics were passed down. Europe, North America, and Latin American, the three regions of the International Psychoanalytic Association, all have painful histories of schisms and splits after the founding of institutes. Raw power struggles coupled with contentious transfer of authority are amply documented (Fine, 1979). The impact of schisms and dysfunction is well documented along with the emergence of "independent" institutes, recognized directly by the IPA, bypassing the authority of the American Psychoanalytic Association (Eisold, 1994; Kernberg, 2009). These authors chronicle not only the formal splitting off of new institutes, but also the pervasive culture of factional wars and intellectual intimidation. Lest these social and historical dilemmas appear unique to Freudian psychoanalysis, Jungian institutes also experience similar group dynamics (Eisold, 2003, Kirsch and Spradlin, 2006).

The paradox of mature, well-meaning, and presumably well, if not fully analyzed members of institutes behaving individually and collectively in very irrational and "unscientific" ways has been richly documented in the literature. This is often to the dismay of "helpless" colleagues as institutes sink into disarray, fragmentation, and stasis. It is also particularly distressful to candidates in training as they are impacted by the destructiveness and are pressured both to internally idealize their training and supervising analysts and to externally adopt unquestioned loyalty to factions in their institutes.

Primitive group fantasies and anxieties driven by envy, competition, and aggression are acted out, with narcissistic individuals emerging to represent factions and spar in meetings, significantly impacting the culture of inquiry, innovation, and governance.

The effect of this is to create an unsafe environment for expression and integration of thought and emotion resulting in silent withdrawal from participation and fueling demoralization more generally in the field.

The place where analysts live has a particularly distinct culture, notably influenced by Freud and his attitudes and practices with groups and sustained across successive generations of analysts. Freud wrote of working in "splendid isolation" during his early formative years. This attitude toward the world appears to have been passed on to his earlier followers and persists today. This dynamic in the genesis of psychoanalytic culture was augmented by the formation of the secret Committee, the "band of brothers" (Grosskurth, 1986) that effectively held power in the international movement for the next 20 years. There are many factors which contribute to the "closed" culture of psychoanalysis, richly explored by Ken Eisold. He notes that given the attitude of "privileged apartness," superiority and arrogance toward the rational, transparent processes of the business and administrative worlds, institutes tend to become "overbounded," a term introduced by Alderfer (Eisold, 1994). Eisold goes on to describe how institutes by "centrifugal forces" devolve into systems that have "excessively impermeable boundaries, rigid hierarchies and inflexible role and task assignments" (Eisold, 2018). The two vignettes to be presented will illustrate engagement of this culture both in an institute and in a private group of analysts who choose to meet outside any official psychoanalytic authority structure. It will be shown that even under conditions of a purely volunteer self-authorized temporary learning setting, analysts carry into this temporary institution their "organizations in their minds" (Armstrong, 2005).

Case Studies

Introduction: The cases represent a serendipitous "moment," each opening an unexpected opportunity to actively engage group relations with psychoanalytic institutional and scientific meeting cultural life. Each emerged as a potential space, where the two fields could approach a collaboration or synergy. In Bion's terms, the tension between our narcissism and our socialism could be creatively held in a space with the prospect of growth and development. There was opening to develop binocular vision and reflective depth perception in the groups, so that individuals are encouraged to hold both their individual view and that of the group-as-a-whole at the same time.

Case Study #1 – Action Research Intervention at a Psychoanalytic Institute

The Presenting Situation: A psychoanalytic institute reached crisis in leadership manifested by the following:

- Not one faculty member would run for either of two key offices: President of the organization or Dean of the training program. This threatened the two core elements of the primary task of the organization, the maintenance of the professional organization for the members and the recruitment and training of candidates.
- Several of the founding members had recently died and others were withdrawing their active participation. These members had large imprints on the identity of the institute. The next generation hesitated to step up to assume leadership.
- Members and training candidates expressed apathy and emotional withdrawal. There was a fear of speaking up ascribed to a hostile and unsafe atmosphere. Fewer members were volunteering for participation on committees and attending meetings related to governance of the Institute and training programs.
- The Institute experienced the active presence of cliques and factions with intimidating, covert, and demoralizing power struggles.
- The Society was formally "leaderless," as was the Institute training program.

Local Historical Context of the Intervention

The Institute was founded in a region where there had been previous splits with new institutes formed. More recently, a schism grew out of protest against the arrival of British Object Relations by the then dominant American Ego Psychology orthodoxy. In reaction with another schism, the Institute was created with a curriculum including year-long courses on Freud, on Klein and her followers, on Bion and his followers, and on the British independents. Bion's work with groups was limited to one class without experiential group relation experience.

Further Context: Organizational Structure of the Institute

A Board of elected members governs the Institute. Authority is delegated to an Institute training committee, to administer the programs in psychoanalysis and psychoanalytic psychotherapy. At the founding of the Institute, a third governing body was created, the Faculty Senate (FS). The FS is delegated authority to monitor the training programs, to approve all curriculum changes and to appoint the Dean and his/her training committee. The FS has functioned to assure checks and balances, as "third leg," seeking to stabilize the Institute development and engage the balancing of power and authority between two historically contentious factions in institutes. The FS meetings are open to all members and candidates.

Establishing the Institute Consultation

In the face of the above crisis of leadership, the FS authorized an organizational "self-study." A self-study committee (SSC), comprised of faculty and candidates, was formed under the leadership of the author. While titled a "self-study," the SSC took as its mandate the creation of an intervention that had the potential to deeply engage the existing culture of the Institute. At issue was the challenge to secure requisite authorization of the SSC to create optimal conditions to implement organizational change and analyze the organizational dysfunction. In clarifying the primary task of this consultancy, we sought to establish our credibility and trust. Furthermore, by mounting the consultation from *within,* we endeavored to mitigate the organizational paranoia that emerges with an outside organizational consultant. As we learned later, we were applying the insights set out by Erlich, in his discussion of the challenges facing an individual external consultant to an institute (Erlich, 2013).

The SSC also set out to clarify the roles within our consultancy group and the boundaries associated with the task. All committee members were simultaneously members or candidates. The observance of these dual roles and the monitoring of the role boundaries was a central issue. The SSC had to evolve a separate group identity and then work in our roles to conduct the intervention. Having a separate group identity provided an internal as well as external boundary to observe, monitor, and utilize the countertransference to the projections from the community at large. Several committee members had experience with the Tavistock group relations model and drew upon concepts of "action research," an interventional approach developed at the Tavistock Institute (Trist and Murray, 1990). Thus, the intervention was framed to support a psychoanalytic situation with the Institute, such that access to covert and unconscious anxieties and fantasies could emerge and be studied. The work of the SSC was strictly confidential in terms of the community at large. This boundary maintenance allowed us to move back and forth between our member and candidate roles in the Institute, and our psycho-social research and consultant roles in our committee work, thus facilitating the unconscious flow of transference and countertransference.

Conceptual Framing of Consultation

Given the crisis situation of substantial withdrawal from participation in the institute, and with the prospect of a leaderless society and training program, the SSC faced the challenge to create an intervention that would reach deeply into and influence the existing social process or culture. We had to account for the centrality and power of pairs in the institute, particularly the training and supervising analyst/candidate pairs, and for the covert power this pair culture exercised (Eisold, 1994). Concerned with competing and being confused with this pair culture, we chose not to develop consulting relationships with individuals in the institute. Thus in contrast to the customary consultant/client relationship, the SSC chose to work as a group and engage with the client group as a whole. No one-to-one interviews or consulting relationships were developed throughout this intervention. By framing the intervention in this manner, we sought not to be drawn into the strong culture and existing roles of the pairs, particularly the "secret" training analyst/candidate pair (Rustin, 1985). We sought to facilitate all members and candidates to speak freely, extensively, and confidentially about what they were carrying: their explicit concerns, their anxieties, and their fantasies, as well as their hopes and visions for the future. Akin to the psychoanalytic situation, we sought to create a safe and trusted container and boundary across which the individual members and candidates could externalize and locate with us, for our preliminary "group analysis," their deeper worries and aspirations for the Institute.

To that end, our first step was the development and administration of a comprehensive survey, administered by the SSC as a group and not in pairs. This survey endeavored to elicit the underlying issues and anxieties of the organization while also serving as a container to foster safety in reflection. Almost all questions were invited and elicited text responses with no restrictions on length. Each respondent was invited to be unconstrained and to free associate.

Self-Study Survey

The survey consisted of two modes and fifteen questions. It was administered online by Survey Monkey, where each respondent was provided with a private site to access as many times as needed until they completed the survey. Thus, all respondents were guaranteed absolute confidentiality. The first mode of inquiry included direct questions with space for unlimited text responses. The four core questions followed the SWOC format: "what are the Institute's *strengths, weaknesses, opportunities* and finally, *challenges?*" The second mode was a series of questions with responses noted on 9-point Likert scales. These questions explored dimensions of cohesion and alienation, core clinical identity, the experience of individual and institutional affiliation, transparency, issues of respectful communication, assessment of the educational programs, and the experience of institute governance. Of note, each of the Likert questions also provided space for unlimited text comments and reflections.

Survey Data Analysis

At the close of the survey, there was a 70% response rate for both members and candidates. There were a total of 600 text responses. The SSC organized the data analysis by endeavoring to minimize our biases, both as a group bounded by confidentiality from the rest of the community and by our individual bias since we were also member of community as well as respondents to the survey ourselves.

We developed a system first to identify and consensually agree on major themes in each question's up to seventy responses, then establish a coding system to identify all themes in each response and finally determine the weighting of each theme across all responses to a question. What emerged was a reliable identification of themes in each question's responses and then a weighting for that theme for each set.

SSC Countertransference

Following an action research model of organizational intervention, the management of the SSC's countertransference became a key element in the work of the SSC. As noted above, as both subjects of the survey as well as responsible for the data analysis and reporting to the community, we were challenged to manage our countertransference in our SSC roles. Thus we were participants/observers in our roles, both internally as well as across the boundary to our "client." This was at times very tedious and frustrating with "relapses" into a "we-they" conflict within subgroups of the SSC and with factions within the institute. As expected, we enacted and mirrored the splits within the Institute, particularly between senior and more junior members and members and candidates.

We were guided by a goal to establish an intervention that was experienced as credible and trusted by the community. In psychoanalytic parlance, we received their "free associations" and both respectively contained their anxieties and generated "group as a whole" data that could be digested and used toward a collectively negotiated interpretation of our troubled functioning. We also colluded with an instance of organizational denial and the powerful scapegoating when we did not pursue a suggestion that we interview individuals who had resigned from the Institute, either as members or candidates. While there was scattered and anecdotal gossip, we found there was no policy of follow-up. We acted out this denial, with the defense that we were already "overworked" as unpaid volunteers.

Findings of Survey – Steps to an Interpretation to the Institute

The final report to the community was 25 single-spaced pages (38 with appendices). It schematically reviewed the organizational crisis and authorization of the intervention. It gave a detailed accounting of the survey methodology and the findings. The text responses to all questions of the categories for each text answer contained quotes as illustrative of the emerging themes giving flesh and emotional substance to what was carried in the Institute.

The essential *strengths* of the Institute were its focus on primitive mental states and strong embrace of British object relations, particularly Kleinian and Bionian approaches.

Perhaps the most complicated and important survey question was the inquiry into the *weaknesses* of the Institute (Question #2). The responses were the most challenging to analyze as they contain the rich and deep essence of the dysfunction. Between a quarter and a half of all respondents, both members and candidates alike, extensively noted and discussed the following institute weaknesses:

- Presence of factions and cliques.
- Rigid adherence to a party line.
- Massive cronyism.
- Clique-like atmosphere bordering on a cult along with dogmatic adherence to a "party line" with arrogant dismissal of different points of view, that created an inhibited and stifled climate, discouraging freedom of thought.
- Significantly impaired volunteerism and withdrawal.
- "Organizational Oedipus complex" – a fear of founding generation authorizing succeeding generations. "We don't bring along our young," "the old guard is holding on to power."
- Impaired organizational processes – arrogance, rigidity, mistrust, and lack of safety. "The Board treats the membership as disenfranchised. Fear of retribution of one is 'disloyal' to one's clique."
- The lack of transparency in organizational processes was noted.

The questions about the *opportunities* and *challenges* for the institute generated a rich array of issues that dealt with both internal issues of governance and functioning and with the external relations of the institute to the outside world and issues of adaptation and survival. There was significant concern expressed for addressing or challenging the hierarchy of power and culture of secrecy and lack of transparency within the governing bodies of the Institute. This was coupled with concerns that the elitist, arrogant stance was maladaptive to the institute surviving in the community.

Action Phase – Making the Interpretation to the Institute

Soon after publication of report, a meeting has held of all members and candidates where the SSC gave a detailed presentation of findings, followed by discussion and clarification. No interpretations were given by SSC. The group was asked to begin to collectively formulate interpretations. We asked them to own *their* data The SSC sought to generate a "reflective space" (Krantz, 2010) space for discovery, actively resisting the regressive pull of quick closure, certainty, and existing group dynamics that would avoid taking responsibility for their survey findings. The FS encouraged a "negotiated interpretation" (Shapiro, Carr, 1991). Finally, two actions were consensually authorized. First, the SSC was discontinued; its work was completed. A new FS ad hoc committee was authorized with the task of implementing action items that emerged at this meeting. Second, an all-day retreat was scheduled for all members and candidates. Formatted to take up the four SWOC questions described above, the goal of the retreat was to invite all stakeholders to personally cross a boundary into the group-as-a-whole to find a voice and explore alignments and creation of a new shared vision of the Institute. The retreat was structured with an opening plenary, followed by small breakout groups to address the SWOC questions. Membership in the groups was randomly assigned to inhibit the natural gathering of the cliques and factions. Each group had a co-facilitator pair of one member and one candidate, again to further minimize the existing power dynamics. The retreat culminated with an extended plenary session where the seating was arranged in concentric circles, thus non-hierarchical. After brief reports back from each small discussion group, the task was to collectively discuss and integrate the emergent findings, inviting both members and candidates to find their voice in the collective endeavor. A key finding of the survey, the desire for greater transparency, was now enacted. Several members and candidates with group relations experience offered group-as-a-whole interpretations. Following this, a full report of the retreat was distributed to the community, specifying the action items raised in the plenary.

There followed a series of meetings of the new FS ad hoc committee where the proposed action items from the survey and initial meetings were followed out. The existing chairs of Institute committees attended to reframe the task systems and their leadership necessary to accomplish these revised tasks.

Long-Term Follow-Up

The self-study intervention has now been underway for seven years. The Institute elected a new President and Dean not long after the intervention was undertaken. In the spirit and practice of transparency, what was before covert and behind the scenes, has become increasingly overt and accountable. Appropriate boundaries to protect privacy and confidentiality have been clarified. FS meetings were held every 2–3 months. More recently, through the repeated process of confidential surveys, reports, and community retreats, a significant rebalancing of the curriculum has occurred, bringing the several "schools" of British object relations into contemporary focus and dialogue. This has had the effect of adding depth to the identity of the Institute, as the covert and rigidified power of the several factions has waned and subordinated to the task of organizational survival.

About 25 members and candidates have attended public three-day group relations conferences with follow-up application groups for psychoanalyst conference members. Planning is underway to add an experiential group relations training track to the core curriculum of the psychoanalytic training program.

CASE STUDY #2 – Psychoanalysts in an Experiential Learning Community

In response to the death of James Grotstein, MD, a founding member of the Institute and a Wilfred Bion scholar who dreamed of an academy or symposium of psychoanalysts where the struggle for political dominance could be set aside, the Regional Bion Symposium (RBS) was created. The goal was to create a safe and collegial setting where controversial discussions could unfold while minimizing the acrimony and sectarian emotional violence, along with the emergence of narcissistic "leaders." The RBS was conceived to maximize intellectual dialogue and emergent depth of presented clinical work while minimizing the regressive group tensions traditionally and chronically enveloping scientific meetings and symposia within psychoanalytic institutes and larger assemblies of analysts. Invitations went out to five centers of Bion study and seventy graduate analysts from ten institutes in the US and Europe attended the first RBS.

RBS1 – 2016 – Launching a Model of a Symposium

The first year of the RBS celebrated the publication of the collected works of Wilfred Bion and featured Chris Mawson, the editor. RBS1 was formatted with several papers, discussants, panels, all occurring in only large group discussions. As with Case Vignette #1 above, Survey Monkey was deployed for confidential post-symposium feedback, yielding three key responses: We observed that a regressive large group including an underlying pervasive anxiety about being heard and recognized and a splitting into camps ("early Bion" and "late Bion"), with several participants attempting to commandeer the discussion. This experience of dislocation in the plenary meeting also yielded a wish to explore Bion's clinical work and also work in small groups at the symposium. They had read Bion's *Experiences in Groups* but had no experiential exposure. There was also expressed a wish to study Bion in relation to Winnicott. One co-founder dropped out of leadership and I joined the leadership team as RBS co-director.

RBS2 – 2017 – Innovations – The Introduction of Group Relations

Responding to the survey feedback from the first year, RBS2 had several goals:

- Introduce a comparison between the approaches of Bion and Winnicott to treatment of primitive mental disorders and difficult to treat patients.
- Create further opportunities for working in small discussion groups.
- Introduce the heir to Bion's work at the Tavistock Institute, the group relations model.

To accomplish the comparison of the two British theorists, two leading analysts from the UK were invited: Bob Hinshelwood, "representing" the British Kleinian/Bionian school and Leslie Cauldwell, "representing" Winnicott and the British Independent School. As well, Leslie Cauldwell was co-editor of the just published collected works of Winnicott. In addition to their compare and contrast presentations with discussants, two further innovations were mounted.

All participants were assigned to a small discussion group, meeting twice, once each for the two presentations. Each group had a facilitator. Their work as a group was reported back to a plenary session designed to create a dialogue between what had emerged in each group and the two British guests.

The second innovation was the addition of an optional one-day Tavistock group relations introductory workshop that was held the day preceding the symposium. We believed that this additional experience would address the curiosity about Bion and groups, and that it would also create a boundary across which awareness of the institutional group dynamics imported to the symposium could be engaged and the learning might be subsequently applied during the symposium to reduce the regressive anxieties and deepen the exploration of Bion and Winnicott.

Group Relations Workshop – RBS2

A one-day, "mini" group relations conference with experienced, trained Tavistock consultants was held the day preceding the RBS. It became nicknamed the "taster." It was co-sponsored by RBS and Grex, West coast affiliate of AK Rice Institute. The task was to study leadership and authority in groups. Membership was optional for RBS attendees with almost a half (30) of the total RBS members (70) attending. For most, it was their first group relations experience. The events were tightly packed into a daylong schedule in the following order: Opening plenary – small group – large group – lunch – large group – small group – role application group and closing plenary.

At the opening of RBS the next day, the full RBS group was invited to explore the influence of the intergroup created by those who attended the workshop and those who did not. This followed the RBS2 conference theme of deepening group work, both in small discussion groups and the large plenary presentations. A follow-up, online confidential survey of all RBS participants with a separate section for members of the workshop was conducted. A detailed survey report was sent to all participants. See Aguayo and Lundgren (2018), for a richer description of this experiment.

Findings of the survey:

- Strong endorsement of experience of the group relations workshop
- Experience of "leaving" their institutes behind with freedom to explore roles that usually emerge at psychoanalytic meetings
- Greater experience of safety in groups with deeper access to internal experience when their clinical vignettes were presented in the symposium

RBS3 – 2018 – Further Innovations

Based on the above feedback, a decision was made to create a shift toward greater clinical immersion for the next year. Two different British analysts, one from the Klein group and one from the Independent group, each to present detailed clinical material of their own analytic work with difficult patients to the RBS. This was to be taken up by small discussion groups offered again with experienced facilitators who would hold a focus on safety during the immersion into reactions to the presented case material.

There was also a Tavistock group relations workshop offered again the day preceding the RBS, again with Grex consultants. The workshop brochure highlighted the dialectic between the narcissistic or personal self-explored in dyadic personal analysis and the "group self" analyzed from the group-as-a-whole vertex in the group relations event. Thus, the continuity between the two psychoanalytic situations, that of the dyad and that of the group was explicitly set out. In addition to a change in the order of events (Opening Plenary – LG – SG – Lunch – LG – SG – RAG – Closing Plenary), an Application group was added the next morning. Sixty percent of the RBS enrollees attended the GR workshop.

The survey again strongly endorsed the workshop as facilitating a group experience of safety and depth in the subsequent exploration of clinical material presented in the RBS and now more deeply exploring experientially a comparison of the approaches of Klein/Bion and Winnicott. The

Application group was experienced as very valuable in the exploration of the challenges of taking up roles in psychoanalytic institutes as well as effects of pathological leadership/followership regressions. Two readings were assigned for the Application group.

Workshop Outcome

The survey examining the outcome of RBS3 is reflected in the following comments:

> "I would say the conscious abandonment of institute affiliation and/or roles facilitated a high degree of safety and inclusivity often missing in institute-sponsored meetings and conferences."
>
> "RBS is very different from any other psychoanalytic conference. The idea of a 'temporary community' is palpable" "There was hardly any 'posturing' throughout the weekend."
>
> "I could not be more enthusiastic about something that was so awkward! Bion was devoted to letting something new emerge instead of the repetition of over-familiar forms. I think the group relations aspect was completely consonant with this purpose."
>
> "I feel free to listen to myself as I listen to others, and I let something new emerge rather than just repeat old stuff."

The experiencing of the "group self" was strongly endorsed as an inventive, creative experience. The outcome of the newly added application group is noted next.

Outcome of RBS3 Application Group

The invitation to this event presented an opportunity to reflect on the implications of the workshop learning experience for their at-home institutions, particularly their institutes. Two papers were suggested, "The Intolerance to Diversity in Psychoanalytic Institutes" by Ken Eisold (1994) and "Intervention into an Institute at Crossroads: A Methodology and Rationale" by the author (Lundgren, 2019). There was a rich recounting of the perils and loneliness of taking on leadership roles in their institutes. The leadership role strain was experienced as personal and left to the leader to metabolize, perhaps evidence of personal pathology left to be analyzed. Another major theme intensely engaged was that of ethical and boundary violations, particularly of senior members of an institute. The insidious corruption of very senior leaders of institutes holding on to power was explored in the context of the generational transfer of authority. There was a critique made that the focus on what was "outside," in the institute, deflected us from what lived inside of us that led to roles being taken (the issues of personal valency).

Discussion

The two projects or case studies reported above represent opportunities to bring the perspective and practices of the group relations model into engagement with the culture of created by psychoanalysts, one in an existing psychoanalytic institute and one in a volunteer, temporary institution of comprised of analysts from institutes across the US. Both projects created venues for a dialogue about the following dialectics:

- The tension between our narcissism and socialism or groupishness, in struggle to attain "bi-nocular" vision or depth perception, in Bion's phrase.
- The boundaries between person and role, the private self and group self.
- The valency to unconsciously assume roles in psychoanalytic groups.
- Holding a group-as-a-whole perspective in the face of the narcissistic vulnerability of joining a group, particularly where intimate clinical material is explored.
- The pressure to idealize leaders and the hatred of groups and splitting into factions and cliques ostensibly based on doctrinal and theoretical differences.
- The tension between the secret pair culture and group-as-a-whole institute.
- The dual focus on what was being discussed and how it was being discussed.
- Illuminate distinction between person and role and the institute factions as social system defenses (Jaques, 1955).

Questions raised:

- What is meant by a "pair heavy" culture of psychoanalytic institutes?
- As a social defense, what is projected by and into the pair culture that undermines organizational functioning of an institute?
- With the RBS experiment, the question of how the addition of the GR workshop facilitated the "de-centering" to sustain two simultaneous vertices of observation: of what was being discussed and how it was being discussed.

Challenges Facing the Institute Studied and the Psychoanalytic Community

- Sustain momentum and coherency of organizational development.
- Encouraging attendance at GR conferences.
- Establishing a group relations training track within the core psychoanalytic training program (now underway at the Institute).
- Is this the 4th leg of training? (Bolognini, IPA Institutional Issues Task Force, 2016).

Challenges Facing the RBS

- Deploying the RBS one-day experiential workshop model inviting analysts from multiple institutes as a "taster" introduction sponsored by another psychoanalytic institute.
- As of writing this chapter, RBS4 has occurred, accruing a four-year experience with this experimental symposium.
- Is the RBS evolving from a "temporary" learning experiment into a more permanent institution? If so, what are the implications and challenges?
- Influence of RBS on local institutes, a collaborator or competitor? Intergroup phenomenon.

Broader Impact of Self Study and RBS on the Psychoanalytic Culture

About 30 analysts and candidates in training from several local institutes have attended several three-day non-residential conferences.

A three-day non-residential conference is in the planning stages for psychoanalysts not only from potentially eight institutes on the west coast of the US, but open to any IPA analyst.

Summary and Conclusions

The culture of psychoanalytic institutes and group meetings, "the place where psychoanalysts live," historically manifests distinctive dynamics of dysfunction leading to chronic "self inflicted" damage to these groups and to individual members and training candidates Two case studies of organizational intervention were described that provided an opportunity to engage and explore the place where psychoanalysts live through the introduction and impact of Tavistock group relations methods. An institute in crisis responded productively to an in-house consultation adapted from the action research approach developed at the Tavistock Institute. This engagement led to the steady introduction of a system, group-as-a-whole working perspective into the culture of that institute. The second case study is of a symposium mounted outside of any formal psychoanalytic institutional authority that joined with an experiential group relations workshop directly engaging and modifying the traditional culture of that scientific meeting. The social dynamics of these two engagements are discussed, drawing from the Tavistock group relations literature. Recommendations for further development of this cultural dialogue are made.

Bibliography

Aguayo, J, Lundgren, J (2018). Introduction to a comparative assessment of W.R. Bion and D.W. Winnicott's clinical theories. *British Journal of Psychotherapy*, 34(2):194–197 and Concluding Remarks, *ibid, 248–254.*

Armstrong, D (2005). *Organization in the Mind: Psychoanalysis, Group Relations and Organizational Consultancy*. Karnac Books.

Benson, MC, Lundgren, JT, West, K (1988). Psychiatric residency training in the dynamics of groups and organizations. *Journal of Psychiatric Education*, 12(2):102–110.

Bion, W (1961). *Experiences in Groups*. Basic Books, p 131.

Bion, W (1991). *Cogitations*. Karnac, p 106.

Bolognini, S (2016). www.psihoanalitiki-ipa.si/files/Bolognini-Towards.pdf

Eisold, K (1994). The intolerance of diversity in psychoanalytic institutes. *International Journal of Psychoanalysis*, 75:785–800.

Eisold, K (2003). The profession of psychoanalysis: past failures and future possibilities. *Contemporary Psychoanalysis*, 39:557–582.

Eisold, K. (2018). *The Organizational Life of Psychoanalysis: Conflicts, Dilemmas and the Future of the Profession*. Routledge.

Erlich, S. (2013). 'Psychoanalytic Societies on the Couch' in *The Couch in the Marketplace: Psychoanalysis and Social Reality*. Karnac, pp 145–175.

Fine, R (1979). *The History of Psychoanalysis*. Columbia University Press.

Freud, S (1913). *Totem and Taboo*. Routledge Classics.

Gittleson, FH (1983). 'Identity Crisis: Splits or Compromises – Adapative or Maladaptive' in *The Identity of the Psychoanalyst*. Eds: E. Joseph, D. Widlocher. International University Press, pp 157–180.

Grosskurth, P. (1986). *Melanie Klein: Her World and Her Work*. A. Knopf.

Hinshelwood, R (2008). Systems, culture and experience: understanding the divide between the individual and the organization. *Organizational and Social Dynamics*, 8:63–77.

IPA Institutional Issues Task Force – Working Note (2016). http://ipa.informz.net/IPA/data/images/Institutional%20Issues%20Task%20Force_Working%20Note_English.pdf

Jaques, E (1955). 'Social Systems as a Defense against Persecutory and Depressive Anxiety' in *New Directions in Psychoanalysis*. Eds: M. Klein, P. Heimann, E. Money-Kyrle. Basic Books, pp 478–498.

Kernberg, O (1986). Institutional problems of psychoanalytic education. *Journal of the American Psychoanalytic Association*, 34:799–834.

Kernberg, O (1996). Thirty methods to destroy the creativity of psychoanalytic candidates. *International Journal of Psychoanalysis*, 77:1031–1040.

Kernberg, O (2010). A new organization of psychoanalytic education. *The Psychoanalytic Review*, 97:997–1020.

King, P, Steiner, R (eds) (1992). *The Freud-Klein Controversies 1941–45*. Routledge.

Kirsch, J, Spradlin S (2006). Group process in Jungian analytic training and Institute Life. *Journal of Analytic Psychology*, 51:357–380.

Kirsner, D (2009). 'Fear and Loathing in Los Angeles' in *Unfree Associations: Inside Psychoanalytic Institutions: A Dilemma of a Profession*. Jason Aronson Inc, pp 139–231.

Krantz, J. (2010). Social defences and twenty-first century organizations. *British Journal of Psychotherapy*, 26:192–201.

Long, S (ed) (2013). *Socioanalytic Methods: Discovering the Hidden in Organizations and Social Systems*. Karnac.

Lundgren, J (2019). Intervention into an institute at a crossroads: a methodology and rationale. *International Journal of Psychoanalysis*, 100(4):674–692.

Roustang, F (1986). *Dire Mastery: Discipleship from Freud to Lacan.* American Psychiatric Press.

Rustin, M (1985). The social organization of secrets: towards sociology of psychoanalysis. *International Review of Psychoanalysis,* 12:143–160.

Shapiro, E, Carr, W (1991). *Lost in Familiar Places: Creating New Connections between the Individual and Society.* Yale University Press, pp 140–141.

Trist, E, Murray, H (1990). *The Social Engagement of Social Science.* University of Pennsylvania Press, p 171.

Turquet, P (1975). 'Threats to Identity in the Large Group' in *The Large Group: Dynamics and Therapy.* Ed: Kreeger, L. Routledge, pp 87–144.

Winnicott, D (1960). The theory of the parent-infant relationship. *International Journal of Psychoanalysis,* 41:585–595.

Winnicott, D.W (1965). 'Communicating and Not Communicating Leading to a Study of Certain Opposites (1963)' in *The Maturational Processes and the Facilitating Environment: Studies in the Theory of Emotional Development,* 64, pp 179–192.

Winnicott, D. (1971) 'The Location of Cultural Experience' in *Playing and Reality.* Tavistock Publications, pp 95–103.

Chapter 3

Nothingness a Group Phenomenon or a Seventh Basic Assumption

Does It Really Matter? Does Anything Matter at All?[1]

Daphna Bahat

The first parts of this chapter will describe a phenomenon that occurs in groups and the last will address some meta-theoretical aspects of Basic Assumptions.

About 25 years ago, in my university days, I was a sorcerer's apprentice for a short while. The sorcerer – a friend of mine – thought it would be a good idea to run birthday parties for children together (it wasn't). I joined him for a six-year-old child's birthday party. Mostly, he did his tricks – some of which were really marvellous and not trivial at all. But with each trick, the children would react with a snobbish-trying-to-look-bored-devaluing look: "Ah ... I know this trick, I've seen it already!" It was quite frustrating. Yet, we had a saviour – the grandmother – a 70-year-old woman of Iraqi descent. Coming out of the kitchen once in a while, she would gape at the sorcerer in action. My friend claimed that only five years ago, things were very different. Children were more likely to joyfully "surrender" to his shows. These six-year-old boys must be in their thirties today – belonging to the so-called Y Generation.

Twenty-five years later, on a Friday evening in Tel-Aviv, I am half-listening to one of my favourite radio shows while preparing for Shabbat – good music with the radio show host's commentary in between: "Ever since I was a child, sleeping always seemed to me like a waste of time. On weekends (Shabbat), I used to set an alarm clock to get up early." He relates it to his fears of death and adds that nowadays, he likes sleeping more. Then he quotes Mindy Kaling[2]: "There is no sunrise so beautiful that it is worth waking me up to see it" (Molidzon, 2017). As I listened, I thought, "I disagree. There are sunrises worth getting up early for." And then I thought, "This is Nothingness."

A Groupish Phenomenon

Nothingness is a group phenomenon that I have identified, and which I see quite often in Group Relations conferences, group therapy and society as a whole. I had seen it appear so many times in such contexts that I began to question whether I see it everywhere simply because I am in love with it. Nothingness is a state of devaluing what can be gained from a group;

DOI: 10.4324/9781003261483-5

the assumption that nothing can come out of the group and from its work (or from the Work Group). In Bion's words, if the "group approximates too closely, in the minds of the individuals composing it, to very primitive phantasies about the contents of the mother's body" (Bion 1961, p162), then the mother's breast is empty; there is no milk, or at least no good milk. Of course, the group also cooperates in emptying the group of its potential content, outcomes, or work. In this sense, Nothingness corresponds to Smith and Berg's (1987) idea of paradoxes in groups. The group members can complain about the worthlessness of the group. But the group can only be worthwhile if the members make an effort to make it so. If they sit and wait for the value to appear – it won't. It requires taking a risk.

Some examples of Nothingness in Group Relations conferences I have encountered are Training group members devaluing the group work; claiming there is nothing to get from it; that there is no difference between the T group and other groups; failing, as consultants in training, to prepare for the group (i.e. not setting up the chairs). In some of these cases, it could be discussed later and members would see their defences against high ambitions, envy, competition, and fear of differentiation in capacities and success: "If everything is not worthwhile, we are OK, nobody gets more than anybody else." Interestingly enough, I have found that sometimes those who had the valency and held Nothingness for the group – claiming there is nothing to learn, that our work is all one big lie, etc. – are those who declared their wish to learn a lot from the group work, but were, so it seems, threatened by their wishes. So as a defence, these groups not only devalued the content, but also made it shallow.

Other ways of shallowing the work can be seen in a group style of raising good questions, touching upon clues and evidence of what happens in the group without really exploring them, without articulating any feelings, emotions, or phantasies as to what happens in order to make meaning. Some groups tend to touch upon and name social issues such as societal gaps, race, competition, and envy, in order, so it seems, to bury them deep in the dungeons of the un-thought or unspoken known. For example, if race is mentioned, the group will immediately attempt to scrutinise all forms of exclusion in history – Jews, Palestinians, homosexuals, etc. in a way that leaves no room for … Nothing.

Some groups fail to articulate feelings and integrate thoughts and emotions. A rather extreme form of this is of split between members who are too theoretical and those who mainly feel without saying anything about it – "I have a headache." In Bion's words (1961, pp128, 159) – "there is none of the painful bringing together of initiated and uninitiated, primitive and sophisticated, that is the essence of the developmental conflict."

Nothingness is also apparent in therapeutic groups, particularly noticeable with adolescents: in weekly adolescent groups, exactly a week after there was meaningful, touching, moving, or appreciated work – strong needs arise to claim that there is nothing in the group, question its purpose, propose discontinuing it, etc. I am not referring here to mere devaluation but rather the actual aim to deplete, empty, and impoverish the group of its content and potential. The devaluation is not always noticeable, but in fact the group is emptied of its meaning and group efforts continue in a way that is unfruitful. This off-course can operate simultaneously with vectors that operate towards realisation of the Work Group's tasks and aims. Sometimes the devaluation itself is conscious and spelled out, but its motives and the anxiety underneath it are unconscious.

Nothingness as a Societal Phenomenon

On the broader, societal level, I suggest that, in many ways, we are now in an era of Nothingness. This can mainly be felt within the so-called "Y Generation" (those who were born between 1980 and 1995). The Israeli Sociologist, Oz Almog, together with Tamar Almog (2016), describes the Israeli Y generation in the context of the worldwide Y Generation: the Ys are the inheritors of the X generation, who moved the world into globalisation, softening the collective authority, and from the Patriot to the Yuppie. The Ys were the first generation born into these changes. This generation is, among other things, described as passively rebelling against the ambition and diligence of their parents by refusing to enslave themselves to making a living, less wishing to lead and initiate, and moving from a culture of work to a culture of leisure. They are late in growing up and perceive maturity as a prison, best delayed. They fear responsibility.

The phenomenon of being childish began in the previous generation and is commonly represented in American television shows from the 80s and 90s – mainly in series about groups of young people, and best exemplified by "Seinfeld."[3] In a book called "Seinfeld and Philosophy (a Book about Everything and Nothing)," different writers attach doing nothing to Plato, the Tao, and other philosophies – claiming that Nothing is a basic power in the world (Irwin, 2000). One of the contributors, George A. Garcia, claims that the secret of Seinfeld humour lies in emphasising the importance of the unimportant things.

Nothingness prevails even in the fashion of this generation; and is looked down upon by fashion experts, who refer to a trend they consider cheap, tasteless with the worst combinations, and childish: "Toddlercore" (toddler+hardcore) (quoted in Almog & Almog 2016, p48). I personally see the way youngsters in Tel Aviv dress today, so as to make the statement: "I don't care, I threw on whatever I found in my grandmother's wardrobe or 'boidem',[4] if possible her worst outfits." I believe that this is partly to display effortlessness (which is sometimes very effortful) and to send the message that the world is their home, as if to say: "I just went down to my home-ish coffee shop after sponging my flat or doing Nothing."

In a fashion critique of the series "Girls" – a series about the Ys and a mirror of "Sex and the City" of the Xs – Karen Schwartz writes about what she calls the show's "sartorial crimes": "You watched Sarah Jessica Parker et al and thought, I wish I had those shoes. You watch Lena Dunham and crew and think, There, with the grace of God, I wenteth." She also cites Ms Rogien, the show's costume designer: "In fact, sometimes we tailor the clothes to fit her even worse"[5] (Schwartz, 2013).

The Almogs describe the well-known paralysis of the Y generation due to the overabundance of possibilities. They do everything simultaneously and therefore they actually do nothing (also considering the attention deficit hyperactivity disorder (ADHD) that prevails, with all the parallel stimulations in the environment). This may be partly explained by the promises this generation received from its parents: that they are special and can do anything they want. This is also because competition is global and not limited to "the neighbourhood," so apparently, they can, through the Internet, see what is happening everywhere. On Facebook, it seems that everyone is doing well. A large part of my clinic consists of Ys, and some of them don't even know why they come to therapy. Something is wrong – but they can't express what it is. Many are characterised by avoidance as a defence against taking risks and fear of failing (and not being perfect as they were told they are); it reaches a level of having difficulty even defining their wishes in any area. I really see it as a malaise of our time.

In this context, the Almogs refer to the characters in Girls as "a generation that went to learn an occupation, knowing it will not provide for them in the long run, if at all. They compromise on wages that are not enough for their living and on mediocre partners, because they have already learnt from the media and from their own experience that romance is mainly a frustration. They are Youngsters who grew up in a culture of Selfishness and Cynicism (MeNess, db) and became futile and cold emotionally. They don't really suffer conscience pains neither towards the other nor towards themselves. Life passes by for them in a tired yawn with some sections of laughter and crying. They live on the verge, exhausting the moment, as a person on the verge of doom" (Almog & Almog, 2016, p76). Of course, we can say all this is the natural criticism of a previous generation towards its successors, but there still may be truth in it. I believe the Ys carry the transition from post-modernism, which, in a way, taken to its end, may empty all meanings, into yet unknown post–post-modernism. It is a post-ideology generation – the "death of" all "isms" has taken over this generation's perception of reality.

According to the Almog and Almog (2016, p373), the Y generation is "a frightened and depressed generation, since it is exposed to 'radiation' of negative information. To protect themselves, the Ys had to blunt their senses and wrap themselves with a protective layer of indifference. They are focused on the present because their future has become blurred and intimidating." They continue: "Above all, the Y generation is an outcome of a democratic freedom of a new order. The unlimited permission to criticise and denounce is part of this democracy, but it also gives birth to cynicism and nihilism" (p374). We could say this "unlimited permission" is related to the downfall of authority.

The canonic American author David Foster Wallace best describes the cynicism and irony that characterise this generation (and in a way the X generation) in an interview: "One of the big reasons why irony – you know it's been the kind of mode of discourse in the culture for the last thirty years – has really ceased to be palliative or helpful, is that **irony is this marvellous carapace that I can use to shield myself from seeming to you to be naive or sentimental, or to buy the lush banalities that television gives, right**? If I show you that I believe that we're both bastards and that **there's no point to anything** and that I was last naive at about age six, then I protect myself from your judgment of the worst possible flaw in me, sentimentality and naivete ...."[6] Kaling (2013), in her previously mentioned quote: "No sunrise so beautiful that it is worth waking me up to see it" embodies the same generation – sounding ironic rather than sentimental and naïve.

Sophisticated Manoeuvres of Nothingness

The phenomenon of Nothingness may be dressed up in an even more sophisticated look. I will describe one such example that seemed to come about when there was interplay between basic assumptions since the use of a certain basic assumption induces anxieties that make room for the use of another one (Bion, 1961, p163).

As we know, Bion sees the Work Group as the group being rationalist thinking, looking for some kind of truth using what he calls "a scientific attitude." The BA Group, the group in its unconscious dimension, follows the force that works against intellect, rationalism, and thinking. In other words, the group is in the position or mode that expresses the "hatred of learning by experience" (Bion, 1961, p86). One way to look at it is to ask: what part of reality is skewed, in each Basic Assumption? Principally, the primary task, or the purpose of the Work Group, is somehow skewed anyway if we say the group behaves as if it gathers in order to have one person above the others in order to take care of them all, or to fight an enemy and so forth. But I think there is another aspect of reality that is either denied, skewed, or doesn't meet reality as it is, in each BA.[7] We can look at each BA this way, but in order to explain the example, I will move on to Oneness and MeNess.

In Oneness, the group denies differentiation and individuality, the fact that people are different, that it is not possible for everybody to get the same, and for all of us to feel the same. We are not one sticky mass. The group is oblivious to the fact that the illusion of unitedness doesn't save it but distances it from thinking of reality. If we take MeNess, the group denies that there is interdependency among group members; it denies the fact that group members are not just a number of individuals with no connection among them. The denial of interdependency enables the rise of narcissism and greed. Mobilising Nothingness may solve the inherent conflict between Oneness and MeNess, and the anxiety accompanying it.

An OFEK GR conference, about a year after the "tent protest" in 2011 – where hundreds of thousands of mainly young people protested against the social-economical system in Israel; the air was filled with contagious optimism that swept the older generations as well. At the conference Institutional Event, to encourage social leadership and explore contem-porary processes, we notified the members that they could negotiate the planning and running of the event's closing plenary. Indeed, leadership was established among the members, and delegates came to negotiate. They were impressive and had two suggestions: the first, which was easy to accept, was to hold an exhibition of the learning. However, we were less keen on the second: to hold a discussion in round tables, each table with members of different groups (that would continue discussions within each round table). Very tempting, very "Zeitgeist," very in the spirit of the protest – representation for each and everyone, a discussion of "the people." To refuse made me as director feel old and part of the corrupted establishment.

"But wasn't that what we had just done?" I thought. "Hadn't we sat until now around metaphoric round tables – each group in its own territory? What would be the benefit of continuing the discussion around round tables, so that each person from each group could state opinions to people from other groups? Yes, there would be a chance for each person to voice their thoughts in the plenary; the groups would be mixed and, supposedly, all ideas would be heard – but it wouldn't converge anywhere. It would remain in the round tables. It has meaning and value, but it ain't no plenary. It does not collect nor continue any learning.[8] A plenary is an "Agora," a marketplace in which one discusses in front of "the whole nation." Indeed, in an hour-long plenary with 80 people – not everybody has the courage or the opportunity to talk. So – what is the problem and what is the solution?"

We have said that in MeNess, the group denies the interdependence of the group's members, such that each takes care of him or herself and greed prevails. In this sense, the wish to have round tables gives everybody an opportunity to deliver, to say what they have to say, for themselves and by themselves; not by proxy, not by representation. "I will say what I think." The discourse that is enabled is again and again a discourse of individuals, of Me's. As we have said, in Oneness, the denial is of differentiation and individualisation between people. Not everybody will necessarily get the same. How do round tables correspond with this? We will feel all together, there will be no leaders, there will be no representation, there won't be those who are more or less seen, heard, or noticeable; there won't be envy. There will be one mass, almost no structure, and no vertical hierarchy. But the integrative reality is that we do have connectedness, albeit that we are separate individuals. We are different and with different interests – but we are interrelated and interdependent.

It seems that in the round tables, in the conference as well as in the protest, there was an attempt to join the two poles of the pendulum. In other words – "I will be there, and everybody will be like me; no one will be heard more than me – even if it means that not much will be said. No one will get more than me – even if it means that no one will get anything." The outcome is that there is no progress, we supposedly gain the two sides, a win-win, but actually we gain neither. Politically – the power of protest in what is common to thousands (the disgust with corruption, social gaps, the hard work without any economic prospect, etc.) is of no use in making another move forward, a political move, that will have meaning; that will influence decision-making. There is no negotiation with the government (or the conference management), in which, granted, not everybody will be heard and we will not be identical, but we may be getting somewhere. In many ways, the protest did not have a larger influence despite it being the largest in the history of Israel because no decision could be made in favour of any interest or goal. We lost the potential to talk, to address some of the needs. Indeed, it is hard to decide whose needs will be met. It is hard to agree on common ground, because this would leave some less happy than others. In this conference, as well as in the marvellous protest, there was such a great effort to give everybody what they wanted – that eventually no one got anything. So actually, we can see here a blurring and conflating of everything in such a way that what we finally have is – nothing. As if there is an unconscious drive to get nothing. And it becomes part of the group's culture – with its structure and mechanisms (i.e. round tables).

I think we all move on this pendulum between Oneness and MeNess, and Israeli society certainly does: moving from Kibbutz and from a united Oneness connected to Fight-Flight and being in survival mode, towards modern capitalistic-narcissism, where everything is privatised out of the aspiration to be a nation like all nations. I would like to suggest that when a society moves on this pendulum between Oneness and MeNess, as there is a human need for both, one solution or compromise that may be made is sterilising both. Allegedly – we will solve the problem of competition, greed, and MeNess by me feeling that I get my share through the fact that nobody gets more than me, and we also address the Oneness by giving an answer to the unity. How? We all equally get … nothing. We can hang out together in this Nothingness swamp, we can grumble, complain, and be united in our Nothingness. If we can flatten the experience and devalue the wishes as well as the resources we have, we may succeed in being in that place.

Some Meta-Theoretical Considerations

I will now move into a more meta-theoretical discussion, beginning with two meta-theoretical comments:

1 The first comment: It may be claimed, that the assumptions following Bion's first three – including what I am talking about – are not in fact BAs, such that Oneness, Me-ness, and Nothingness should be regarded as something else, perhaps the group culture, as opposed to the group mentality (i.e. basic assumptions).

   This comment is somewhat "religious" in the sense that it relates to Bion's writings in a narrow way, as an untouchable and unchangeable "bible."

2 The second comment (less religious in that sense): I think there is room to be less religious regarding Bion's theory and draw on it to look at groups through the lens of the gap between the visible and the invisible; between their conscious declarations and their unconscious aspects. In this sense, there are so many unconscious stories in groups that taking up only 3, 5, or 7 Basic assumptions would be a reductionist waste.

Armstrong (2005, pp12–13) poetically describes his encounter with Bion when he participated in a group that Bion took up: "Bion never gave the slightest impression of being the author of 'Experiences in Groups'. Some of us had read this beforehand ... We were primed to spot 'basic assumptions' at work ... we were to be sadly disappointed and then intrigued. Nothing Bion said seemed to connect to this bit of conceptual apparatus; whereas in the inter-group events run by Ken Rice, Isabel Menzies, Bob Gosling, Pearl King and, I think, Pierre Turquet over two weekends, dependence, pairing and fight-flight were everywhere, and I think genuinely to be found. Bion's preoccupation was elsewhere." It thus seems that Bion was not so religious himself.

Armstrong goes on to describe Bion's exploration of the limitation put on enquiry by using names as restriction. He writes: "A limit is set; the unknown is robbed of its power to disturb. The revenge of the unknown is that one can be left feeling curiously empty, unable to make contact with the group, or even with oneself in any way that has the ring of something authentic" (p13). In this sense, we may see a vicious cycle of robbing and "nothingnessing."[9]

Toress (2003) writes about Trotter's tremendous and somehow unrecognised influence on Bion. He shows that "Bion's conception of a triad of basic dispositions is parallel to Trotter's triad of basic instincts: self-preservation (BaF), sex (BaP), nutrition (BaD)" (pp96–97). On one hand, one might ask if there is room for any other BAs. On the other – if we go with Trotter's instincts – could Oneness be the parallel to the herd instinct, which Trotter also designates (and which Bion opposed)? And then – what is Me-ness? Is it a failed Oneness? Is it a counter Oneness? Is it a failed or a counter Dependency?

Another explanation of why there are only three dispositions is the relatedness or the influence of Melanie Klein on Bion. Robert Gosling (1994) claims that there is a difference in the level of "tone and primitiveness" that is felt between Dependency and Fight-Flight as opposed to Pairing, which is also somehow less intuitive. Gosling suggests that BaD and BaF "derive from the infant's first struggle for survival, in which its experience is split so that its goodness is separated and protected from its badness" (p8). In this sense, BaD goes with the goodness, the "good breast," and BaF goes with the badness, "the bad breast." Towards integration, and the constitution of a relationship between two actual people, there also come phantasies of the primal scene and of the third in the Oedipus complex – hence the Pairing Ba. In other words, BaD and BaF derive from the schizo-paranoid position, and BaP derives from the depressive position. It is worth mentioning that at one point, Bion himself wrote that the three basic assumptions groups "seem each in turn to be aggregates of individuals sharing out between them the characteristics of one character in the oedipal situation, which are depending on whichever basic assumption is active" (Bion, 1961, p161). Does this mean we are only allowed to use three BAs? Would saying that to ourselves be an expression of Dependency? Relating to the "bible" without any change and development? Personally, I would like to find a more structural immanent reasoning for the "only 3" claim.

I suppose it depends on the basic unit one defines as motives for human behaviour, or in other words – the level of reduction. Is the need for love, recognition, or being accepted a basic one? Or is it merely a vicissitude of the sex instinct? This, I think, is determined mainly by our belief systems, which become theories.

I think that regarding the basic unit question, my proposal of Nothingness as a basic assumption is on solid ground here, because even if we stay with only widely agreed upon basic instincts, we may say that Nothingness corresponds to the death instinct, Thanatos, aspiring to an un-organic state of cessation and nirvana.

And yet, what is the theoretical status of BAs? Are they mostly like instincts? Are they phantasies? Bion viewed them as connected to impulses and defending against anxiety: "Approached from the angle of sophisticated work-group activity, the basic assumptions appear to be the source of emotional drives to aims far different either from the overt task of the group or even from the tasks that would appear to be appropriate to Freud's view of the group as based on the family group. But approached from the angle of psychotic anxiety associated with phantasies of primitive part-object relationships, described by Melanie Klein and her co-workers, the basic-assumption phenomena appear far more to have the characteristics of defensive reactions to psychotic anxiety ... In fact I consider the latter to contain the ultimate sources of all group behaviour" (Bion, 1961, p189).

In that case, there are a few building blocks (denial, projection, reaction formation, etc.), as designated by Anna Freud (1937), but the possibilities of stories each group can create with them are as infinite as the stories people as individuals can create in their defensive phantasies. We may reduce everything to the Oedipal complex, Oral fixation – which we all have, or to other theoretical structures, such as mirroring, twin-ship, or grandiose self-object needs. But this would be, in my view, too boring. And we know that anything can be a defence against anything, so whatever structure we create cannot be too stable. Whatever we name the phenomena we see, whatever theoretical status we give them; it is worth widening our vocabulary and shedding light on the prism through which we look at the world and at groups in particular.

Another claim that stems from the instinctual framework and tends to differentiate Bion's three basic assumptions from the rest of the basic assumptions that were suggested over the years, relates to the existence of phenomena over time.

Bion differentiates between the group mentality – the BAs – and the group culture: "Group culture is a function of the conflict between the individual's desires and the group mentality. It will follow that the group culture will always show evidence of the underlying basic assumptions" (Bion, 1961, p66). He includes in culture: "the structure which the group achieves at any given moment, the occupations it pursues, and the organisation it adopts" (Bion, 1961, p55).

Bergstein (2014) claims that BAs correspond to universal, unchangeable basic human drives and culture refer to the different temporal group stories that can be seen across different groups and at different times. If so, we are not in a better state meta-theoretically. For example, if we look at Tao philosophy, we can see evidence for Nothingness ideas, and it also goes back to Ecclesiastes "Vanity of vanities ... all is vanity."[10] Many phenomena come and go like fashion trends and can be seen from time immemorial, as, too, was said by Ecclesiastes – "that which has been, is that which shall be; and that which has been done is that which shall be done: and there is nothing new under the sun."[11] Does the aforementioned evidence for Nothingness in different eras, different places around the globe and different human cultures, support Nothingness being a temporal phenomenon, or quite the opposite? I think it shows that Nothingness is indeed connected to basic emotions and shared by all humankind, as it is connected to the death instinct. Hence it could be considered as a basic assumption.

In this chapter I suggested a basic assumption that I call Nothingness, I offered examples from clinical groups, Group Relations conferences and wider society. I also developed the idea at the meta-theoretical level. I hope my efforts have fallen on curious ears. As Aristotle is reputed to have said: "There is only one way to avoid criticism: do nothing, say nothing, and be nothing."

Notes

1 A very early version of this chapter was given in "The Dreaming Consultant," a conference held by OFEK in Israel, 2014, in memory of Gordon Lawrence.
2 Mindy Kaling – an American actor, writer, producer, and director.
3 To see representative vignettes watch: https://www.youtube.com/watch?v= EQnaRtNMGMI and its outcomes at: https://www.youtube.com/watch?v= ofOSlsNz5I8
4 "Boidem" is a term originating in Yiddish referring to a storage space above the ceiling.
5 For example, the main character, Hannah, wears a cardigan festooned with tomatoes to her first paid job at a law office.
6 My emphasis.
7 For example, if we take BaD, we can say that in believing there is one person who can take care of everybody – a person who is god-like, who is the only one with wisdom and competency – the group denies the strength of the rest of the members, their capabilities to think and to work.
8 It is actually a kind of creating another Institutional Event.
9 When I began to wonder about the meta-theoretical status of these phenomena, I naturally found that others had written about it. And here, I thank David Armstrong and Moshe Bergstein for helping me find part of the bibliography.
10 Eccl. 1:2 American Standard Version.
11 Eccl. 1:9.

Bibliography

Almog, T. & Almog, O. (2016) *As If There Is No Tomorrow, How Generation Y Is Changing the Face of Israel.* Modan Publishing House (Hebrew).
Armstrong, D. (2005) *Organisation in the Mind.* Karnac. pp 12–13.
Bergstein, M. (2014) The BAs as a basis for a psychosomatic model, and the place of me-ness in this model, lecture notes, *The Dreaming Consultant,* an OFEK conference, delivered 12 December 2014.
Bion, W.R. (1961) *Experiences in Groups and Other Papers.* Tavistock Publications.
Freud, A. (1937) *The Ego and the Mechanisms of Defence.* Hogarth Press and Institute of Psychoanalysis.
Gosling, R.H. (1994) 'The everyday work group'. In: B. Sievers and D. Armstrong (Eds), *Discovering Social Meaning: A Festschrift for W. Gordon Lawrence on the Occasion of his 60th Birthday.* Unpublished.
Irwin, W. (Ed.) (2000) *Seinfeld and Philosophy (A Book about Everything and Nothing).* Open Court.
Kaling, M. (2011) *Is Everyone Hanging Out Without Me? (And Other Concerns).* Random House. p 5.
Molidzon, T. (Host). (2017, September 1) *Kan, Sham Uvechol Makom (Here, There and Everywhere)* [Radio Program – KAN – Israeli Public Broadcasting].
Schwartz, K. (2 January 2013) The Clothes Make the 'Girls', in: *Fashion & Style, New York Times.*

Smith, K.K. & Berg, D.N. (1987) A Paradoxical Conception of Group Dynamics, *Human Relations* 40:10, pp 633–658.

Toress, N. (2003) 'Gregariousness and the Mind, Wilfred Trotter and Wilfred Bion'. In: R.M. Lipgar, and M. Pines (Eds), *Building on Bion: Roots Origins and Context of Bion's Contributions to Theory and Practice*. Jessica Kingsley.

Wallace, D.F. [Adsp_ace]. (27 March 2011). *Endnotes. David Foster Wallace. BBC Documentary*. https://www.youtube.com/watch?v=DIjS4K2mQKY.

Section 2

Social, Political and Spiritual Issues in Group Relations

Introduction

This section begins with Rosemary Viswanath's chapter, "Unbounded Worlds – A Challenge for Group Relations?," based on her keynote lecture. She explores three themes: activism, group relations (GR), and engaging spiritual traditions, in this case, Buddhism. She describes her journey to Buddhism by way of Catholicism (her family of origin) and Hinduism (by marriage). She explores how a GR framework speaks to "place." She asserts her belief that GR work is "designed to be political." She also explores her belief that "we are hesitant to recognise spirituality infuses the depth and richness of GR."

The chapter by Zachary Green and Rene Molenkamp, "A Call to Consciousness on the Unknown Known of Dominance," based on Green's keynote lecture, begins by discussing the importance of recognising "the perpetuation of a dominance discourse in GR," and that "our method may actively be an enactment of dominance." They introduce two new basic assumptions: BA Authority and BA Identity. Much of the chapter then shifts to a description of three themes from Collective Consciousness Conversations sponsored by Group Relations International: connection, collective consciousness, and constructive action.

Coreene Archer's chapter, "A Nomadic State of Mind: In Search of a Place to Live," reflects a personal and professional journey of growth and discovery using a GR program for young people. She explores using established "space" in a new way. She discusses the first few conferences for 18–30-year-olds and how the design and title changed. She also explores how and whether "race and privilege can comfortably co-exist in an individual."

Joan Roma et al, in "Co-constructing a Society that Promotes Life," considers how the relationship between terrorism, immigrant identity, and the processes of exclusion and difference affect the state of mind of new members of a community by asking them to consider whether this the "place they live" is a space they are welcome, can belong or consider home. Roma et al further reflect on the impact on the whole community when the answer is negative.

DOI: 10.4324/9781003261483-6

The chapter by Ellen Short and Janice Wagner, "In the Shadow of Envy: Shame in Group Relations Conferences," is an exploration of shame both in general and in Group Relation Conferences. They also describe "the shame of learning in public in a counselling and group dynamics graduate course." They relate this to similar shame experiences in GRCs.

Chapter 4

Unbounded Worlds

A Challenge for Group Relations

Rosemary Viswanath

This chapter[1] brings together three aspects of my life on the same page – activism, GR, and the beginnings of an engagement with a spiritual tradition, which in my case is Buddhism.

I was drawn to activism first – to the idea of changing the world and quit a corporate career quite early to jump, somewhat naively into the arena of social justice and development. My choice of spaces to engage with helped me articulate my politics: feminist, socialist, environmentalist, but the way I articulated it was in terms of what I was against:– patriarchy, caste, racism, colonisation, neoliberal economics, and corporate impunity. Admittedly, a long list to fight against!

An engagement with GR came soon after. Learning how to learn, the way unconscious processes jostled with the more conscious ones, recognising that there was no, absolutely no situation, where I could run away from my personal authority. It was in the littlest things, in the mundane, in the granularity of the everyday that its beauty shone, and my reliance on this lens grew.

My fellow activists in their commitment to political struggles, defined and challenged the enemy outside. I admired their courage, their resilience, and their lifelong dedication to the causes they believed in, but I could also see that we were often not getting the results or changes we so desperately wanted, and the consequent cynicism and burnout worried me. GR taught me that living systems cannot isolate one part from another. If we want to change the big problems that we face, we need to begin to see the system as a whole and craft systemic interventions. A part of the system, howsoever "right-thinking," could not make progress by affixing blame for the mess on the other parts. This position did not make me popular with my fellow activists though!

My engagement with trying to find my own relationship with spirituality was more subtle and grew on me without my even realising it. Underlying the feisty exterior, were many questions that troubled me: What really gives meaning, what was I really trying to achieve, and were my methods helpful?

DOI: 10.4324/9781003261483-7

In the face of unpredictability in life, and the certainty of death, what are worthwhile pursuits? Nothing is ever by chance, and when these questions began to grow louder, and I was willing to acknowledge them, opportunities to engage with the frameworks of Buddhism emerged.

I had spent many years rejecting the oppressive structures that religions built or condoned – both in the religion I was born into – the Catholic faith – and the religion I had a close brush with by way of marriage – Hinduism. The baby that got thrown out with the "religion bath water" was spirituality. By spirituality, I mean consciousness of the world around us, shown through wonder, compassion, and love towards everything and everyone in it. Meeting extraordinary Buddhist masters led me to think that if I really very seriously worked at this, I could also someday in a future life perhaps, hope to be like them – consistently good human beings, with compassion that shone and with a clarity that was startling.

This brief personal narrative is about how these three strands of activism, GR, and spirituality, came to be woven into my own life, even if the pattern of the weave is just beginning to emerge!

Engaging with the Theme

The Primary Task of Belgirate VI was: *To explore the ecosystem called Group Relations Conferences and reflect upon our lived experience of that ecosystem in relation to our different spaces and contexts.*

I decided to approach this task from the other end, viz. to explore the reality and lived experiences of place – our spaces and contexts – and reflect on the extent to which GR frameworks are able to articulate place.

There are two aspects in the title of my paper that are linked to this lived experience of place:

> First: **Transforming the World**: I believe GR work is ***designed*** to be political work. It becomes potent when it recognises issues of place. I believe we are hesitant to use this political activist–subversive aspect, or at least possibility, of GR work.
> Second: **Transforming Ourselves**; I also believe we are hesitant to recognise that spirituality infuses depth and richness to GR work. When we don't recognise spirituality, or are embarrassed or diffident about it, we end up reducing GR' potential.

When I first used the term transformation in a title of a Group Relations Conference (GRC) "Transforming Systems," an activist colleague and friend[2] said – "Transform? hmm, that's kind of ambitious is it not?" That helped me to think about what I really meant when I used the term. What is transformation? Changed behaviour? No, it is a willingness to radically change our frameworks – change the shape of things in our minds to start with!

Transforming the World, Transforming Ourselves; is about transforming the world, actual bits of it, **through** transforming ourselves. I am often not able to draw a neat boundary between a political process and a spiritual process – because when transformation is genuinely sought, then the lines between them get blurred. The interconnections between the focus on change outside (activism) and the focus on change inside (spirituality) are very strong. Can one really bring about a change outside without change inside?

Drawing mainly on my experience in and with GR India, I offer three propositions, two related to the political and one related to the spiritual:

Proposition 1: The "inconvenience" of the political in group relations

The more we believe in group relations' capacity to be political, the more work we can do in conferences on the dynamics of places we live in.

I use "place" in multiple ways – I use it to signify geographies, to signify culture, to signify hierarchies of place such as the global north and global south, first world to third-world, etc. I also use place as the experience being in a fixed location as in being put in one's place/shown one's place.

The conference you get is the one in the mind of the Director, I have heard. In stating the more **we** believe in GR capacity to be political, I am referring to the sponsors and Directors initially and also to the conference staff. The conference **we offer** depends on all of **us,** including the members, as they can push boundaries even more than what we are prepared to offer!

Those of us who engage directly in activist roles in our everyday life and work, also offered conferences that spoke more directly to the politics of our contexts. For me, this came from a sense of despair that our political, economic, religious, and even educational systems are not providing freshness and nourishment to encourage much transformational thinking. Can GR assert its relevance by speaking to the issues of our times, exploring fault lines in our institutions and societies, help redesign futures? Can GR take a position on corporate greed, narcissistic cultures, omnipotent and authoritarian trends, hierarchies, and environmental destruction? Should it?

The activist in me felt responsible for furthering this enquiry. Without this attempt, I felt GR would have little relevance to the people I admired deeply – those engaged in everyday struggles for justice and a better world. I thought GRCs should be able to put up the subversive/disruptive signage of the Occupy Movement[3] "Sorry about the inconvenience, we are trying to change the world."

With its focus on leadership, authority, structures, and role, and its inherent focus on dynamics, both conscious and unconscious, GR, I believe has the potential to understand and explore the politics of a space; how power is obtained; how it is used or deployed; by whom and to what ends. It can explore how systems can be transformed to be less exploitative and more generative. The opening up of space to confer and explore though formulating hypothesis, offers the possibility of curiosity and reflection without being too anxious or too defended. Very often, this helps people holding different, even opposing ideologies and beliefs to recognise each other, acknowledge their place in the system, and the possibility of dialogue.

My own experimentation on a political agenda[4] for GRC's began with my taking on a Director role in Indian GRC's – A 2003 conference focussed on the dynamics of caste, in 2007 and 2008 we explored leadership in a gendered world, in 2009 and 2011 we offered a conference on exploring and working with difference. Each of these focussed on systems that are built on structural violence. We followed this in 2016 with a shorter workshop with a bolder invitation – the Brahmin in the Mind, which invited an exploration of the pervasive need to construct of hierarchies[5] as a way of coping with the complexities and challenges of building meaningful relationships.

Through a series of conferences from 2012 to 2017, we focussed on unpacking the idea of what leadership was. In contrast to the prevailing macho models of leadership, we suggested that vulnerability and compassion, intention and risk, knowing and not knowing, were important dimensions in reconstructing leadership itself. Through the title phrase the "Courage to Lead" the opportunity was to explore courage, ethics, vulnerability, and its links to leadership. For me, this series of conferences on leadership was very personal and very daring as I intended to challenge models and assumptions of leadership that were preferred in systems that I was part of, including the world of GR. In 2017, we also spoke more directly to socio-political realities in force, such as the strangulation of space for dissent in India. In June 2018, "Meeting the Other/Meeting Oneself" was an invitation to work on an issue that is tearing the fabric of our nation apart: the intractable nature of the other, and the cruelty and pervasiveness of the process of othering.

As we kept pushing the boundaries of the political, I felt that I was relying more and more on the GRCs to be a space where we could get some glimpse, explore in some way how we could deal with these large and pressing issues, which impacted us on an everyday basis, and from which we could not distance ourselves in our citizen and community roles. Thus, choosing the title itself became a very important process. A meditative process of immersion and discernment of societal dynamics; of listening deeply to what we needed to find the courage to work on. Courage for me is the first sign of spirituality at work, because spirituality leads to the reduction of fear. Courage and compassion then follow as two sides of a coin.

A whole section in our brochures describes the context and why the theme we choose has relevance to the way we experience context. We tend to have long brochures, with our initial thoughts about context and the relevance for the theme clearly laid out. Placing them in a brochure we believe is our way of bringing "place" to the centre of GR, and to place more publicly what our politics and our ideology is. We also believe this is a way to signal an invitation to slow down, reflect, hypothesise, and explore.

This was not without risk. Brochures of GRCs the world over are compact and pithy, offering participants the possibility of greater effectiveness in globalised, fast-moving organisations. Would our approach scare away members? I must confess this has crossed our minds – when recruitment has been painfully difficult, and our lack of commercial pragmatism stared in our face. But we persisted. Over the last few years, we have had more and more instances of members wanting to join because a particular issue reflected in the title drew them into the conference.

In the initial years of these more political and unusual titles, some of my colleagues felt that the title was just a way to make the conference sound interesting. That irrespective of the title, one did work of a certain kind in any case in a GRC (on organisation, leadership, authority, and managing of oneself in the role). The other debate among staff in India has been why the title did not appear conspicuously in the statement of the Primary Task. I believe both these views (or were they defences?) led to a situation where very often members were able to work more intensely and directly than staff on engaging with the theme.

My position as Director has been that the title was an invitation to work on that issue via the methodology of GR – but it was only an invitation, as we did not want to decide on how, in what ways, on what aspects of the issue the members would work, if at all. Theme provided a context to the task – in the sense of a "first circle of context" in which the temporary institution of the GRC was situated.

With this becoming clearer to me, and articulated more clearly in the brochures, recent editions of the conferences have seen both staff and members risk more explorations around the theme. In the 2018 conference which focussed on the process of the "Other," the dynamics of class was brought to the fore in a delicate yet direct way, and members of staff had to work with their own feelings of what their class privileges or positions meant to them.

Apart from signalling its intention via the title, Group Relations India has invested significantly to create a microcosm of society through the invitation to the membership and our work on recruitment. This is perhaps a very important reason why we can work on these broader issues – as the essential feature of exploration is experiential and not just intellectual.

Membership of the Group Relations India conferences is so diverse that it is probably one of the few spaces in our country where people of different caste, class, religion, sexual preferences, occupations, sectors, political ideologies, regional identities, language groups, and nationalities engage in the "same" role and common task as members, to which they bring in their particular histories of privilege, dis-privilege, and other life experiences. The resultant work that is possible can be very moving and a description of what is termed the human condition. Interestingly, in all this diversity, the most difficult issues to work with have been class, caste, patriarchy, religious bigotry, and disability – perhaps in that order– as these have very deep roots in prejudice and structural injustice in our society.

This diversity (in membership and to a lesser extent in the staff) has also been possible because of our politics. Our conferences are economically accessible without any external or grant-based support. This is possible because many of us offer many months of work on a voluntary basis to make a conference happen, and to run Group Relations India as an institution. We also offer a huge number and range of bursaries to members. In terms of number of people and proportion of income we forgo, this is significant – nearly a third of our income is "given away" as bursary. Given the slim margins of conferences and given that our published fee is itself really low – this is foolish economics, but very deliberate politics. This requires a very active engagement as Director that I have had with potential members over the years, having conversations with so many of them about why this conference, how much they could afford, and seeing how we could make arrangements on bursary and instalments to help them participate. We believe this is not charity or generosity but a political position we take about the importance, rather necessity, for such diversity as an essential component of the work that needs to be done. Our politics also comes into the picture when members particularly from marginalised groups and positions join the conference because they trust the politics that some of us on the staff represent as seen via our professional and personal choices over the years. An important aspect of truly political work is when people are representations, and yet not objects.

Do GRCs really transform? I believe they don't! In themselves, they are not the primary transformative tools – but they provide a rare space where we can pause and think about the frameworks we have attached ourselves to – so quickly and so firmly. We begin to recognise that the process of arriving at these frameworks has a huge unconscious component to it. We can try, hopefully without too much fear or anxiety, to revisit our frameworks and explore other frameworks. Once we are able to do that, or at least have an experience that beginning to do that is not too frightening, there is hope to try and work in the world on some form of transformation.

I believe that the primary architecture of a GRC is to create spaces for exploration. Through that experience, we gain the faith that spaces can be created anywhere – if we can work with intention, an ability to contain, courage, skilful means, and an approach of never giving up on people. Easy answers may be found in this process, and often we leave a conference a little more troubled, some assumptions shaken, even if not dislodged. In this sense, the work can also be seen as spiritual; by spiritual, here I mean the ability to be less attached to a view. If one is attentive to the actual dynamic at play, one may well recognise that this attachment is almost always evidence of one's attachment to ego identity, one's sense of "I."

Colleagues from the US, Bernie Gertler and Charla Hayden in their thoughtful analysis of place "Uneasy on the boundary" (Gertler B, 2019) speak poignantly of the shifts in GR focus in the US. They voice concern that some of the fundamental contributions of GR are being lost, such as – an organisational and societal focus, a focus on experience, and a describing and exploring stance. They also make an interesting observation of the focus of conferences increasingly shifting from role-system to person-role.

Extending this thought, whilst a GRC may be a temporary institution, it is also critical to see the work of building GR institutions as political and spiritual work. The sponsoring institution's vision, role, and intention is a key aspect of the conferences we offer, as this impacts the culture of our conferences in important ways. To invest as institutions, in the development of staff colleagues, and a wider community of people associated with GR – who see it as a worthwhile way to learn and become better human beings, not just skilled human beings. This development comes when they not only experience GR as a methodology of integrity, rigour, and beauty, but also as a useful framework for meeting challenges/dilemmas of contemporary societies and in everyday life. Building of the long-term Group Relations Institutions I believe must be done in a spirit of generosity and love, even if it is tough love, through the purposeful creating of spaces[6] for engagement, development, and belonging, with the spirit of GR evident in the institutional spaces and relationships. I think the care we put into the temporary institutions, viz. our conferences, needs to be replicated in the building of our more "permanent" institutions, the sponsoring organisations.

Proposition 2: The politics of global group relations

"An aspect of the politics of group relations – is that it has not adequately addressed issues of place as in language or culture or dominance."

GR origins are in the west, and subsequently much of GR work has grown in places and cultures that are western. It has been a point of interest to me as to why colonisation has never troubled western countries enough to wish to offer a GRC with it prominently in the theme or title. Conferences have been offered on the theme of race, I think largely in the US, and on the holocaust in Europe, and South Africa has worked on diversity dynamics. Colonisation – a particularly virulent and destructive form of hierarchy has been a predominantly (though not exclusively) western phenomenon – and at a point in history about 80% of the world was under the subjugation of one western coloniser or the other.

The politics of place influences in significant ways what is seen, what is appreciated and what is remembered! I am reminded of my first instance of GR work in the UK, when over a dinner conversation a well-intentioned British colleague told me that I seemed to be biased about British rule in India, and that the British had contributed many good things, including railroads and education! I wondered then where the shame around collective acts of exploitation greed and violence had been tucked away.

GR work has not been embraced by former colonies with the same commitment to tradition as the western countries have. Some of this may be undoubtedly an issue of language, culture, and mismatch of political and social structures and conceptual frameworks. It may also signify a deep-seated resentment and frustration at the longstanding euro-centrism of the world, of having to valorise all things western, as if our societies have not produced deep knowledge and established practise of how community functions, how the mind works, and how to be wiser.

There are examples of this that have some relevance to the practise of GR. I pick this up for instance in the "difficulty" in understanding why work on mind-body-spirit connection established partly through yoga has a place in GR. A colleague from the west may say – sure, but I know nothing about yoga, and I will accede that that may well be true, but I would ask them to think about why that is so. Why is it so easy to affix the label of esoteric or abstruse for something from the east, while something western is more quickly assumed to be mainstream or familiar?

Psychoanalytic frameworks are less popular and perhaps less relevant[7] in South Asia and East Asia where the relationship between individual and community and the understanding of spirituality is more nuanced, and these serve as containers for healing.

Whilst we may privilege the mind and thinking in our work in GR, western psychology is only beginning to get a handle on some process of the so-called mind – mind consciousness or mental processes, via neuro-psychology and neurosciences. Eastern societies have studied the mind for millennia, as they understood that genuine happiness can come only from the mind, and does not, or hardly depends on, external circumstances. A wealth of work for instance has been accomplished by Buddhist[8] masters through 2500 years of lived practise and conceptualisation based on experience.

As a part of its colonising process, the west has often cherry picked what has suited it, what fits in with the west's frameworks, rather than engage with the paradigm as it is. Thus, for instance, Buddhism has been almost equated with meditation, and in turn meditation has been reduced to mindfulness, which has then found a place in the healing professions in the west. Traditionally, the practice of meditation is placed between the practice of its foundation of ethics and its culmination in insight[9] into the way things actually are. The price meditation has paid to become seriously considered by modern western psychology has been separation from these core elements of its context and logic.[10]

I refer here to a certain covert dynamic of power and hierarchy – the process of privileging one kind of source over another. Consider this; overtly romanticising or secretly, perhaps unconsciously, denigrating non-western cultures comes easier than the hard work on the legacy of colonisation and what it means individually and collectively to us – west and east.

This work may also be avoided as a defence against facing and taking a position on the current newer forms of colonisation[11] – neoliberal economic frameworks, unregulated corporate power (as against other forms of organisation such as cooperatives, collectives or peoples' movements), and the power that the global north wields and arrogates to decide the fate of the world. The West builds its "better life," even today, based on lower labour costs, unfair trade practices, military attacks, and arbitrary withdrawals from global treaties to keep wealth and advantage in their favour.

This may be seen as a particularly scathing attack on the west, and I must say that neo colonisation and oppression, are equally of concern in non-western societies. GR work in India may have made beginnings in challenging caste, class and forms of othering, but are we ready to face our own colonisation of many parts of the country that fight for their autonomy and self-determination, branding them as separatists? It is perhaps still too hot to handle, and as an activist and GR colleague[12] pointed out, we don't yet have the courage. We may in our work in GR prefer to duck the wider politics by assuming these are givens; that this is how the world is, and is going to be.

Proposition 3: Skirting the spiritual

Group Relation's uneasy relationship with spirituality may be because of our need to preserve a certain notion of individualism and autonomy. But with this, tags along (unintentional but inevitable?) self-centeredness and narcissism.

It may be time to think deeper about why we offer GR conferences; do we offer them because we want more effectiveness and more progress in a material sense, or because we are interested in contributing to a world that is more humane, more wholesome, more sustainable, has less suffering, greater inner happiness?

In the latter half of the 19th century, western philosophy and psychology distanced themselves from spirituality. Spirituality was conflated with religion, conflated with mysticism and seen as incompatible with modernity and a scientific temper, both modernity and science being seen as inherently superior. One of the reasons why GR may be a bit wary about naming the spiritual as being of interest may be its legacy of the unease of psychoanalysis with religion and the tendency to conflate religion and spirituality, as if they are identical.

Psychoanalysis tried to fill the void left by religion but was not yet filled by science. Freud's antipathy towards religion was that it took people away from the task of facing life's realities – the hardships, the unfairness of it, by offering what he saw as the illusory comfort[13] of salvation or the threat of damnation. In a lot of writing in the west about psychoanalysis and spirituality,[14] there is the tendency to refer directly or obliquely to a Judeo-Christian religious framework, without references to other frameworks, or to use the terms religion, mysticism and spirituality interchangeably.

My colleague Gouranga Chattopadhyay hypothesised that religion was a defence against spirituality (1999). I believe that science, the way it is often understood, is also a defence against spirituality. Science, with its reliance on a third person-based evidence, can never hope to find an answer to what is essentially a first-person project of spiritual transformation. They work to different aims and employ different frameworks and hence are not adequate substitutes for each other, although they can co-exist. When cognitive science which is at best 135 years old engages with contemplatives who have inherited living traditions (often in an unbroken experiential lineage of thousands of years), the scientists ask them what can we learn *from* you? It doesn't strike the scientist to approach this with what can we learn *about* you? The first has a framework that is fixed and what is learnt is what can fit the framework. The second approach, which is what experiential traditions are about, is an open approach where the framework itself is assembled or modified.

GR, while relying on the psychoanalytic pillar, has other legacies too – many of them lending themselves to the idea of spirituality quite naturally. Interdependence, community, and interrelationship are natural characteristics of systems, and inherent aspects of spirituality. The idea of not knowing, working with the here and now, learning from one's direct experience, developing personal authority, are aspects of GR that also develop spiritual capacity.

Without memory and desire, is the mind that allows us to enter each moment, relationship and encounter free of history and bias, with openness and wonder, seeing with new eyes, with fresh eyes. Our images judgements and assumptions protect us from "not knowing" – an experience we see as fearful. It then becomes difficult to revisit our reactions, judgements opinions and conclusions as we end up investing absolute truth in them. The view of the system that GR encourages is a spiritual view – going out of myself, not reifying "me,"[15] and seeing the interconnectedness of all things, which makes me not small/insignificant, but neither makes me the centre of things. It simply makes me a "part" – I am unique – just like everyone else!

When Lawrence, Bain and Gould postulated "basic assumption me" BaM (Lawrence G 1996), they linked this to a defence against the culture of increasingly industrialised societies, which expressed itself as the need to always seek "what's in it for me," rather than "how does this serve the system and its task?" What the authors chose to call industrialised, can perhaps be described today as neoliberalism, where making choices which keep others' interests at heart would be considered foolish and naive. This is by no means a uniquely western phenomena. In contemporary non-western cultures, we struggle equally with an increasing draw towards more private material gains, and a reduction in the relational nature of our societies. We are drawn to greater consumerism and are less willing to live with paradoxes and questions of our own mortality or reflect on meaning of our lives. The tragic cost of BaM is the deep sense of isolation; in spite of a longing for intimacy and a need to experience our interconnectedness.[16] Attending to the other, and cherishing the other, as many traditions assure us, is the beginning and the only way perhaps towards a spiritual journey.

Several moments in a GRC can be deeply spiritual and this can happen in many events and spaces – moments when you feel awash with tenderness for the members, where you experience there is no difference between your happiness and that of others. There is a particular word in Tibetan that exemplifies this – the word is *tsewa* – the tender warm and open heart, is the fundamental basis of spirituality and human well-being. *Tsewa* is a radical concept – it expresses itself as kindness, compassion, generosity, resilience, tolerance, mental clarity, and courage. When people lose their natural connection to *tsewa*, they become cold-hearted, greedy, cynical, and withholding. It requires a great deal of work to cultivate *tsewa* as it extends to all life – humans, animals, and nature.

One of the spaces, among others, where we have tried to work with spirituality in conferences in Group Relations India, has also been what we initially called the yoga event, but more recently called the Mind Body Spirit event. Yoga, we felt, was one of the ways, but there were others like music, meditation, silence, embodying and holding space for the dissolution of boundaries without it being a terrifying experience. Our ability to experiment with this space came from a need to clarify for ourselves why such an event was important and relevant to a GRC. Without this, we ran the risk of the yoga event being reduced to feeling good and relaxing, but not integral to working on spirituality in an experiential way in the conference. The realisation that we had not clarified enough about why the yoga event in a GRC came to me when I was on the staff of a Leicester conference and there was a discussion there among staff about the place of the yoga event in that conference.[17] It struck me then that in India, we had perhaps not challenged ourselves enough on our rationale, as yoga was culturally more acceptable in India.

J.D. McClatchy, the extraordinarily gifted American poet and polymath writer said "Love is the quality of attention we pay to things." GR offers the opportunity to experience love in this way. It is not the self-serving pandering love of establishing one's specialness and uniqueness which often encourages people to be more fragile and needing safe spaces, wanting more and more appreciation, unable to work with their role in the system, and finding it difficult to work with reality or accept delayed gratification in order that tasks can be tended to.

The move from self-centeredness to other-centred-ness implies a radical paradigm shift that has elements of the political and the spiritual in it. I believe that the hardest to eliminate or even reduce is our narcissistic investment into the self, and even more so the view of a "self" – and that is perhaps one of the reasons why we fight shy to make a clearer commitment to the dimension of the spiritual in our work in GR.

To conclude, I am convinced that GR work is as relevant today as it was when initiated. I am even more convinced that the political agenda of transforming the world is not possible without the spiritual agenda of transforming oneself. The two are intertwined and both are necessary. I call for a greater role of the political and the spiritual in GR as I believe it can only make our work stronger, more human, and more real.

Notes

1 Grateful to Ganesh Anantharaman, Marijke Torfs, Swathi Seshadri, and Tanuja Viswanath for their comments to the chapter.
2 Marijke Torfs, who was then International Coordinator of Friends of the Earth International, the world's largest grassroots environmental network.
3 The Occupy movement (2011–2012) was an international socio-political movement inspired partly by the late-2000s financial crisis and subprime mortgage crisis and the Arab Spring. Protesting against social and economic inequality and the lack of "real democracy" around the world, prime concerns were how large corporations (and the global financial system) control the world in a way that disproportionately benefited a minority 1%.
4 GRC: identity, authority, leadership – resistance, self-empowerment, and transformation in organisational and social systems – 2003 – sponsors: Learning Network and Dappu

> Exercising Leadership in a Gendered World – Exploring gender relations in groups and institutions – 2007 and 2008 (HIDF)
> Exploring & Managing Differences in Groups & Organisations – 2009 and 2011 (HIDF)
> Leadership for Transformation in Self, Groups and Systems – 2012 and 2013 (HIDF/GRI)
> Transforming Systems – Exploring the place of compassion in the exercise of leadership – 2015 (GRI/HIDF)
> Knowing and Not Knowing – Exploring intention and risk in self and systems – 2016 (GRI/HIDF)
> The Courage to Lead: Exploring dynamics of collaboration and dissent – 2017 (GRI/HIDF)
> Meeting the Other, Meeting Oneself – Fear and longing in working with difference (2018) (GRI/HIDF)
> Knowing and Not Knowing – Exploring intention and risk in self and systems – 2019 (GRI)
> Shorter workshops:
> Gender & Authority – Expanding capacities for personal authority in work roles – 2005
> Listening to the Unconscious – Over 12 such workshops have been offered between 2007 and 2019
> The Brahmin in the Mind: Exploring the nature and dynamics of caste and constructed hierarchies in oneself, groups, and society – 2016

5 our colleague Gouranga Chattopadhyay first presented his idea of purity and pollution being the ingredients of the 6th Basic assumption in this workshop.
6 At Group Relations India, while we are nearly 6 years old, we have apart from our annual GRCs, online study groups, a workshop on listening to the unconscious, workshops to further learning such as Furthering Learning about Small Groups; Task Role System; The Brahmin in the Mind; staff dialog spaces and a triennial called Koodam where we present and explore our current thinking on GR and its application.
7 Bernard Gertler's paper presented at Belgirate 2015 alludes to this too, and I very much appreciate his sending me his draft paper.
8 I refer to the sophisticated frameworks of Mahayana Buddhism here only because of my own familiarity and engagement – but this would apply to other forms of eastern spiritual traditions/philosophy, for instance, various streams of Hindu philosophies and practise.

9   The three core insights of the Buddhist tradition are the facts of impermanence, of suffering, and of non-self. The first of these refers to the truth that all phenomena, without exception, change; the second recognises that all experience is structurally incapable of yielding lasting satisfaction; and the third points out the awkward truth that we are not quite what we take ourselves to be.

10 This has gone to great or should I say absurd lengths such as mindfulness as the way to ensure America's military security and defence! "Healing America: How a Simple Practice Can Help Us Recapture the American Spirit." Congressman Tim Ryan says "When we bring mindfulness into the military, we help to enhance the greatest resource we have to ensure our own security and defense, something more powerful than any high-tech weaponry: well-functioning, high-performing human beings who have refined situational awareness."

11 Neo-colonisation is visible, for instance in the context of the anti-immigration policies and right-wing populism of many western governments, separating the economic refugees from the people who flee violence, as if seeking a better life is not a valid reason for mobility.

12 Swathi Seshadri.

13 To do away with illusory comfort is a reasonably Buddhist view actually, about what helps human beings. Unlike Freud, the Buddha is quite optimistic about what human beings can aspire for and achieve!

14 Bion's O – an aspect of mysticism that Bion quite openly referred to in later years, is perhaps closer to Christian mystical theology and also the Upanishadic idea of Brahman – may be a legacy of his early years in India and influence of Indian Hindu philosophy.

15 Our "this is me" story is like a raft that we are unable to let go, even when we have reached the other shore.

16 I would like to acknowledge Ganesh Anantharaman for this insight.

17 I do know that my colleagues in the Tavistock Institute, particularly Eliat Aram and Rachel Kelly and now Leslie Brissett have been committed to incorporate yoga and through that the mind-body-spirit connection in the Leicester conferences and Eliat has spoken of and written about the connection between leadership and compassion and the place of love. These are important steps.

References

Chattopadhyay G (1999), A Fresh Look at Authority and Organisation: Towards a spiritual Approach for Managing Illusion, pg 112, in *Group Relations Management and Organisation*. Eds: French, R and Vince R, Oxford University Press.

Gertler B (2019), Has the World Changed? Has Group Relations Changed? – Considerations of the Group Relations Movement in a Postmodern World, pg 28, in *Doing the Business of Group Relations Conferences Exploring the Discourse*. The Group Relations Conferences Series, Vol V. Eds: Aram E et al, Routledge.

Gertler B and Hayden C (2015), 'Uneasy on the boundary: reflections on culture and effectiveness of group relations conference work in the USA 1965-2012' in *Group Relations Work, Exploring the Impact and Relevance Within and Beyond It's Network*. Vol IV. Eds: Aram, E, Baxter, R, and Nutkevitch, A, Karnac.

Lawrence G W, Bain A, and Gould L, (1996), *The fifth basic assumption,* Free Associations 6:1 (No. 37).

Chapter 5

A Call to Consciousness on the Unknown Known of Dominance

Basic Assumption Authority and Basic Assumption Identity Behavior in Group Relations Conferences

Zachary Green and René Molenkamp

This chapter was originally written in advance of the 2020 global coronavirus pandemic and the worldwide civil unrest relating to the matter of Black lives. The intent of an earlier version of this piece continues to hold value but was written in the voice of a conciliatory invitation to new level of consciousness in group relations practice. The urgency of the moment just prior to publication of this volume permits some additional thoughts to underscore the applicability and relevance of these words. While initially offered as a set of implicit considerations for passive contemplation, should it remain only as such, then we as authors stand complicit in perpetuating a kind of collusive silence and violence that fails to acknowledge how our own work as practiced is far too often an (unconscious) enactment of supremacy in the guise of the study of authority.

At root, the actual underlying call of this chapter is to a reckoning. The true focus is a cautionary one where the basic message is that group relations practice, especially in conference life, runs the risk of becoming a relic if greater consciousness about the perpetuation of a dominance discourse is not faced (Skolnick & Green, 2004). Having betrayed our own origins in the treatment of trauma and the application of our work to social justice causes, group relations may have become psychoanalytically sanitized and neutered of its activist essence. The authors share a concern that group relations at times becomes a regressive and thereby oppressive reification of its colonizing and enslaving cultural roots; reveling in dominance through its seductive shadow with the propensity to perpetuate supremacy (hooks, 1994; Kendi, 2016).

In group relations conferences, we readily interpret a dynamic, especially those related to dominance, as unconscious processes that are a function of the "temporary" institution, often forgetting that this temporary institution is a mirror of the "institution" of the world in which we live (Bion, 1961; Armstrong 2005), including dynamics of dominance and their toxic outcomes. This intellectual mesmerization is a sleight-of-hand that serves as a defense against the painful awareness that our method may actually be

DOI: 10.4324/9781003261483-8

an enactment of dominance. As such, we live into a kind of solipsism where group relations cannot see its own offense. When we promote excessive regression, when we engage in denigration through interpretation, when we activate trauma, are we not responsible for any enduring harm that comes? Our current practices create the conditions for plausible deniability as a social defense to keep unknown what is already known.

One challenge for us to consider is our collective role in how some group relations practices are reductionistic enactments of systemic oppression that is rooted in dominance if not supremacy (Brazaitis, 2004). We see it in the rigidity of role stances that become caricatures of authority devoid of humanity. Another challenge is to begin earnestly to explore and understand how the study of unconscious processes can become a tool for dominance and denigration of the "other" when such considerations are left unexamined. We posit that group relations becomes an extension of supremacy when such study sharply denies the call to a greater collective consciousness—often in the form of a broader spirituality—another unseen known that predates and permeates any psychoanalytic concept of unconscious.

Finally, this chapter proposes that as currently practiced, group relations has created for itself two more elements of basic assumption life. The intent is not to challenge the core elements of the tenets of the classic assumption mentality first presented by Bion in *Experiences in Groups* (1961), and elaborated upon by Lawrence, Turquet, and others (Turquet, 1975; Lawrence et al, 1996; Hatcher Cano, 1998). Our focus is on the paradoxical experience of individuals in groups that has no contemporary name. As such, Basic Assumption Authority and Basic Assumption Identity reflect the currency of this particular era in human history. The fundamental tension between those who are granted the conferred right and power to do work on behalf of the group, formally and informally, and those who declare autonomy to name their own experience and claim their own voice independently and in coalition in response to perceived power is volatile (Smith & Berg, 1987). We see this tension on the streets as protests. We see it in nations through the rise of populism and resurgent nationalism. We see it evidenced in the inequities and disparities of current economic systems. We see it in group relations practices and conference life that mirror these trends. The belief that we in group relations are somehow not subject to such forces, especially when they remain largely beyond conscious awareness, is at best naïve (Strauss, 2009) and may well be what makes group relations practice a source of dominance and supremacy expression.

The Invitation

The invitation to the unknown known is expressly one to the realms of human consciousness that may be operative in conference life. Variously thought of as the akashic field, Vedic holism, second-tier consciousness, and simply spirituality, these disparate and related concepts reflect ancient and contemporary expressions of what is presented here as collective consciousness. In 2009, Group Relations International embarked on an ambitious quest, inviting prominent members of our global group relations community to attend the first Collective Consciousness Conversation (CCC). This event was not a conference. As the invitation stated, we sought to offer a space to co-create *a connective collective.* What emerged in those days in the Netherlands was an expression of creativity and the emergence of something we experienced as novel in the group relations ecosystem.

Our premise and aspiration were to create the conditions to explore a different way of approaching leadership. In the invitation, we wrote of a task that was:

> *... to learn how we can explore as yet perhaps hidden potential and work with that which is already indigenously known so that we can live and work more effectively, collectively and responsibly to find a different way—one that invites us to consider who we may yet become, what we can contribute, and how we can become co-creators of...constructive action in the world.*
> Collective Consciousness Conversation Invitation (2009)

Group Relations International remains very much grounded in the study of unconscious system organizational processes, including attention to the exercise of authority and the emergence of leadership. We are also rooted in a social justice orientation (Molenkamp, 2020). It is our perspective that all group relations work shares an origin story based in classic early interventions in the United Kingdom that were assuredly social justice in nature. Nonetheless, some feel that being so explicit about social justice is a romantic notion inconsistent with group relations approaches where an unabashed Kleinian lens on regression and deprivation are viewed as the essence of our collective work.

Group Relations International also actively attends to the role of spirituality in our work. Silent retreats, which are indeed derived from practices in the Jesuit traditions, and meditation that is more aligned with the dharma than with more secular mindfulness interventions are commonplace in our work. It is our view that there are realms of the unknown that are known to each of us in different ways. Indeed, attention to unconscious process as the only kind of "unseen" that can influence our behavior in social systems seems to us to be the kind of hubris that fails to take into view the vastness of the ocean and the endless of the evening sky and still feel awe and wonder. In short, GRI is only partially about sponsoring conferences. And when we do, they are on themes such as "On the Matter of Black Lives" or "Hierarchies of the Collective: Mind, Body, Spirit." We also work closely with a community-based leadership program, the RISE San Diego Urban Leadership Fellows program. One of its core experiences—simply known as "The Spiral"—is a variant of the large study group. Through RISE young professionals and social advocates primarily from communities of color gain access to our language and way of work and adapt the learning into projects to address issues such as immigrant rights, affordable legal services, human trafficking, educational equity, systemic racism, police reform, and mass incarceration.

Another GRI effort, Youth Empowerment Services, conducts retreats for incarcerated youth from such communities. These retreats blend large group sessions with other awareness-raising social technologies. This group relations adaptation includes meditation and yoga to help these young people develop greater capacity to cope with and speak to the trauma that is far too commonplace in their lives. Through these complementary methodologies, we observe that these young people are better able to speak to the chaos in their lives as well as take greater responsibility for the consequences of their maladaptive behaviors on others. In terms of the spirituality focus, we offer monthly webinars through our Sacred Inclusion initiative. In these sessions, topics from a variety of spiritual traditions are explored through facilitated virtual dialogue that is akin to the small study group. Rather than members or associates, GRI has a global network of co-creators who propose innovative approaches to learning. Generally speaking, so long as these efforts are grounded in group relations either in theory or practice and have a social justice or spirituality focus, we have supported such efforts.

Our story actually has its roots in a conversation in the backyard of Lamis Jarrar following an international group relations symposium at the University of Maryland in the late 1990s that pre-dated Belgirate. Group Relations International formally launched with the CCC held in 2009. Through this event, we focused on three areas:

- Connection
- Collective Consciousness
- Constructive Action

These three areas will serve as the basis of exploration in this chapter. We seek to offer a better understanding of how these constructs are used and what they offer us about the challenges and opportunities that may well be at or near the core of our work in group relations.

Connection

Our invitation was extended with the belief that there is a critical mass of divergent voices who speak in a similar language about ... Our aim is to provide space where the commonalities may be found and a new language for our collective experience can begin to be discovered: a space for collective inquiry into the rhythm of leadership waiting to emerge ...

Collective Consciousness Conversation Invitation (2009)

We believe we are approaching a new area of inquiry about the role of connection and consciousness in the group relations realm. We were not the discoverers but were early explorers of the intricate implicit link between authority and identity (Turquet, 1985; Skolnick & Green, 2004) and continue to see this study played out daily in every meeting we attend as well as across social media. Our growing concern is that the current state of much of the exploration of authority and identity has become akin to the shadow side of basic assumption behavior (Freud, 1930; Bion, 1961). The inherent task avoidance takes the form of "as if" reductionistic naming of identity to replace the real work of exploring the unique meaning and intersectional expression of authority and identity in any given systemic context. In short, even in group relations work, we may be a party to perpetuating systems of dominance and oppression through our own narratives that presume our way of working and knowing offers a "right" path (Volkan, 2001). This orientation is at best odd given how beyond group relations circles, traditional group relations efforts are too often misunderstood, denigrated, and rejected. Those positions of formal authority outside of conference life are known to sharply question the utility of such experiences, especially when conferences result in casualties (Taylor et al, 2004). Much of the rest of the world operates far more in black and white terms.

Basic Assumption Identity

We propose Basic Assumption Identity as a contemporary expression of classic dependency, pairing, and flight-fight formulations (Bion, 1961; Tchelebi, 2017). It is our perspective that BA ID also is differentiated from oneness, me-ness, and we-ness though sharing some resonance with this proposed addition to the basic assumption pantheon. The exploration of identity as also having basic assumption elements met early resistance in our group relations conferences. The first director of a conference with the name "Authority and Identity," was challenged by mentors and seniors in group relations work about whether there was a need to distinguish identity thematically from the more traditional study of authority and organizational life. In the United States, in the last decade of the 20th century, there was a surge of black, female, and gay conference directors. The dynamics that emerged in these conferences reflected the social identity of these directors and yielded reflections of the study of authority that varied from the hegemony of such study of unconscious processes under white male and presumably straight directors. What came to be more central was the role of race, gender, and sexual orientation in how members understood their experience and how staff took up their roles (McRae & Short, 2010). In one residential conference with a gay and black director, same-sex attractions and identities other than white were privileged currency in terms of the recognized exercise of authority and emergence of leadership. While such world turned-on-its-head learning was vital in terms of offering voice and view-point from groups often rendered more token-like in their presence, these conferences have also helped open group relations work to new populations.

The unintended consequence of the rise of authority and identity was a large exodus of straight white males from group relations work, particularly in prominent east coast centers of the United States. Along with the concurrent establishment of the International Society for Psychoanalytic Study of Organizations, conference life was left to gays, blacks, and women in some group relations centers. With ever-diminishing numbers of white, straight men at the helm of conferences, the exploration of identity became a normative part of conference work. Yet, as with any other kind of dominance discourse, the "as if" nature of the study of unconscious processes soon followed unchallenged. Basic assumption in all but name was born in the behavior of conference staff and began to be projected, albeit unconsciously, onto members.

It is particularly painful for the authors to acknowledge the presence of this basic assumption behavior, given our roles in introducing the study of identity as an inextricable companion to the study of authority. Yet, in practice, Basic Assumption Identity behaviors can be seen in many a group relations conference wielded as an essentialist reductionism used as a complicit foil of differentiation. Akin to "we-ness," in Basic Assumption Identity, a social identity construction operates as if there is solidarity and singularity to understanding such identity (Hatcher Cano, 1998; Hopper, 2003). The sharpest evidence of the presence of BA Identity is when a signifier of a social identity is named for oneself or another and all further exploration of the nature and meaning of that identity, especially in a larger conference dynamic, ends. A collusive "as if" stance is taken whereby any attempt to offer alternative interpretations to behavior or being is met with aggression and rejection meant to foreclose what may be otherwise exposed. There is an implicit threat to those who share a constructed identity of their loss of the group identity should they begin to differentiate and deviate from the chosen narrative (Helms, 1993; hooks, 1994; Volkan, 2001).

BA Identity behaviors are most commonplace as a defense against learning on the staff side of the boundary. These behaviors are most problematic when members are met with tones of contempt in consultations. The impact of this dynamic is played out when those who are seeking to learn about the relationship of identity to authority are dismissed, denigrated, and shamed for not knowing what they did know (Sampson, 1993; Hafsi, 2006; Sue & Sue, 2013). Basic assumption behavior is seen in rigid and essentialist identity formations that are accompanied by corresponding chosen constructed narratives. Any verbalizations or behaviors that blur the lines of some perceived match with how an identity is held are rejected, if not ridiculed. One such example is when staff reference someone as being a "gay white male" or "lesbian cisgender female" and presume an underlying understanding of an unconscious dynamic through these delimiting and defining labels. Implicit meaning is attributed to identity without exploration (Erikson, 1964; Erikson, 1997). As such Basic Assumption Identity is operative.

Basic Assumption Identity is based in binary thinking and dualistic divides. Absent attending to the inconvenient complexity of intersectionality and unique variants in social identity, Basic Assumption Identity fills in the gaps with reductionistic caricatures (Crenshaw, 1989). It celebrates blocking those with *any* representation of socio-historical oppression from assuming formal roles of authority, essentially demanding an owning of privilege irrespective of the reality of the lived experience of the person in role. The challenge in this formulation of Basic Assumption Identity is when it is considered in relationship to its companion hypothesis, Basic Assumption Authority, and thereby also challenges the foundation of group relations life itself.

Basic Assumption Authority

The central tenets of authority and its study related to unconscious process are beyond refute. Social systems forces can be readily understood to be at play in human interactions in groups. Questions about boundary and role in terms of task consistently reveal "as if" behaviors that impede efficiency and effectiveness in organizations. It can be readily argued that one major contribution to our understanding of human systems is in the power of group relations as means and methodology to study the inherent challenges of our responses to and exercise of authority (Bion, 1961; Wells, 1995; Green & Molenkamp, 2005).

When we look at the etymology of authority, we learn of the early French origins of the term. Tied to the Scriptures, *autorité* referred to the use of a passage, book, or quotation to settle an argument. It later came to have a meaning related to advice, influence, and command. Rooted as well in the word "author," authority is also linked with being the progenitor, specifically a father and creator that brings forth increase—one who makes provision for things to grow. As such, the pronouncement at many a group relations conference that authority simply means "the right to do work" is consistent with the historical basis of its expression (Rioch, 1971).

When we look closely at the origin of authority and how it has come to be used in group relations life, we also see the seeds of its basic assumption variation. Interpretations offered in group relations conferences are technically hypotheses about what a system is doing as it is doing it. Aimed at revealing something of the unconscious, such consultations are open for study but are imbued with power by the corresponding emphasis on the study of authority. Basic Assumption Authority is present when authority becomes blurred with autocracy. In conference life, it becomes rather easy for regressive pulls to ego to emerge and for those with delegated formal authority to take on their roles from a stance of dominance (Armstrong, 2005). Consultations decidedly reflect Basic Assumption Authority behaviors when dynamics such as contempt for members and their learning, seduction, and betrayal in interpretations, and defense of abusiveness that seeks to preserve power and biased status quo are present (Kahn & Green, 2004). Basic Assumption Authority is particularly pernicious when these dynamics are evident in combination and thereby exponentially expressed and experienced by members. Yet, the self-sealing nature of some staff work means that the impact of such dynamics can go readily undetected and the learning that may be revealed is concealed; ultimately assuring that toxicity and shadow within the system can remain denied (Jung, 1968).

Basis Assumption Authority is a form of work avoidance that denies one's role in perpetuating dominance and confuses the study of authority with supremacist authoritarianism. Basic Assumption Authority is seen in the adept interpretive jargon and prolific rhetoric of hypothesis generation, creating a collective hypnosis where no one notices the self-projection. In Basic Assumption Authority, the interpretive field becomes lodged in others who then carry the consequences of being burdened by unmetabolized dominance beyond the bounds of the moment (McTaggart, 2008).

At its root, Basic Assumption Authority is a form of unconscious domination that projects its shadow and shields itself from reflection and examination. The boundary between exploration of a dynamic and exploitation of a collective is lost (Kahn & Green, 2004; Krantz, 2019). More specifically, Basic Assumption Authority is a vehicle through which individual narcissism as well as systemic oppression find expression. It is seen in the denigration of others. It permits racist, misogynist, and xenophobic perspectives to flourish unchecked. It allows abuses of power in the name of the study of authority. It denies its presence in what it perpetuates. It leaves victims of psychological violence and casualties of unconscious collusion in its wake. It is distant and distinct from what it does through chosen self-serving and mutually reinforced narratives that conceal as much as they reveal (Kendi, 2016).

Basic Assumption Authority is a dark and largely unexamined element of group relations life. Yet, we know that there are more than a few members who walk away from conferences still carrying toxic projections for which we take no responsibility for having activated. By definition, the study of the unconscious is self-sealing, but we often fail to attend to the substance of the wounding in the name of learning. In recent years when recruitment to conferences has been challenging and making offering the events marginally viable, far less attention is given to the readiness and capacity of some in the membership to participate in such study. Proceeding without such caution is also a reflection of this same Basic Assumption Authority and the level of the group relations global community (Freud, 1930). As with all other forms of basic assumption life, we can no longer abdicate responsibility for being progenitors of our own creation. Our power is in our words.

Collective Consciousness

We are beginning to believe that group relations work has an untapped responsibility in these contentious and divisive times to ask and make more available an exploration of 'what is it that we share.' We are calling on all who are consultants in our varied group relations organizations, irrespective and perhaps beyond identity, to work with paradox. In other words, how might we continue to hold a mirror up to the often dire, lived reality of such identity-based dynamics while not succumbing to the reductionistic divisiveness in which such illusory social constructions are embedded. We are turning to sources to inspire our thinking and augment an experience that thus far seems largely ineffable and inaccessible ... We are seeking to discover a felt-known which we believe is 'there' and 'present' but does not yet offer its name. We believe this experience exists in all of us in a manner that is far greater and more vast than what we currently reveal in group relations as unconscious process and the study of systems ... Right now we call it 'spirituality' or 'consciousness' but even such terminology has been rendered largely meaningless through its contemporary use — and is inadequate, pre-emptive and delimiting; a short-hand attempt to bring reification to the boundless ... we are just beginning this inquiry and may not yet even have the essence ...

Collective Consciousness Conversation Initiation (2009)

Practices and processes that make the unconscious conscious are hallmarks of our group relations orientation. We are skilled at operating in the elusive realm of the "here-and-now." Yet, there is a fundamental question of whether making the meaning of words, feelings, behaviors, defenses, and systemic patterns conscious is the same as bringing people to consciousness (Laszlo, 2007; Cannato, 2010; Molenkamp, 2012). The short answer is "no" or more likely, not yet.

In our GRI efforts, we place a great deal of emphasis on what we call a "Cycle of Noticing" (van Linge & Green, 2010). In this model, we identify at least three levels of noticing: perception though senses, resonance of affect and meaning, and intuition of the field. Most of the interpretive work in group relations conference life does an exquisite job of helping people to open their eyes and touch their hearts. We also provide similar transformative interventions by making the unspoken and the unseen audible and visible even in the face of unconscious basic assumption life and in various manifestations of task avoidance. Combined, our group relations approaches provide potent insights about the self and system. Yet, it is not our experience that the pool of meaning that emanates from the field and may include what most would call "spiritual knowing" is understood as part of our tradition.

The exploration of consciousness involves more than what is within and is likely located beyond the "here" of the "here-and-now." Such work is also more than day-to-day "right to do work" of authority. Beginning with what is best known as the collective unconscious (Jung, 1968), the study of consciousness may well be found in the infinite nature of the interconnections of systems. As we see it, group relations practitioners are adept at making available the kind of unconscious process characterized by the shadow and murky kind of unconscious—a dark realm of projection, denial, primal competition, regression, envy, and rivalry. What happens when we dwell in such places is an oblique celebration and continuous re-traumatization in an abyss of toxicity and torment—a kind of enduring dance with Thanatos and Hades. In thinking about a recent group relations experience, what is affirmed is Eros without Agape—lust without love—conflict without compassion. In this regressive space, indeed there is learning—there is always learning. Yet such learning is also accompanied by the self-sealing narrative that precludes us from looking further than our chosen narratives related to the interpretation of unconscious processes. If we were to do so, there is the prospect that we will notice at the edge of the field how we are agents of perpetuating a kind of hegemony that shields each of us from the discovery of the divine within and between all of us; a kind of reverence not inherent in any faith tradition or spiritual practice (Laszlo, 2007; McTaggart, 2008). Our current propensity as group relations practitioners thus makes processes conscious while keeping consciousness at bay.

By consciousness, we mean a field of knowing that the ancients and mystics and shamans and indigenous referenced as the encounter with the universe. In our current group relations practices, we make efforts to put a boundary around the boundless (Green & Molenkamp, 2015). Our collective interconnectivity is reduced and denigrated in a far too facile manner. Our way of managing the emergence of such consciousness is to label its essence as a kind of alternative fact and dismiss its meaning by calling it "basic assumption oneness" (Lawrence, 1996). Certainly, the dangers of groupthink and group polarization are well documented, but what we dare to call an error is the presumption that seeing oneness in a conference or consultation to an organization may also include having a blind eye to those moments when a group or system may be operating "as one" (Katzenbach & Smith, 1993; Wilber, 2001). Great sports teams, symphony orchestras, high-performing executive teams, theatre ensembles, jazz musicians, and first responders are at their best when they operate as one. When we are the audience to an orchestra that brings a great symphony to life, when the musicians are performing as one, we are also elevated into an ineffable air and filled with awe.

We know this feeling. While we recognize it as feeling that may well be beyond words, we are not able to deny its presence. Our invitation is for all of us to begin to explore and become more present to that essence. If we do not, we will be no different from the masses of what Robert Kegan and Lisa Lahey (2009) write in *Immunity to Change*. We have a competing commitment to a calcified way of working that renders us rigid in the face of new knowledge. Instead, our preference for the predictability of authority as we understand it and routinely see it manifest is reverenced. Our practices beg the question of how much of what we do is out of our own unconscious need for control and defense against learning anew. If such a hypothesis has even a remote hint of validity, it is not too far of an extrapolation to suggest that we also act in ways that seek to cast some illusory control over the unconscious. Not only do we say this is our practice, but the authors also believe our real challenge is the more pernicious potential that our interpretations in their current form are little more than the imposition of narratives that perpetuate status quo structures and echo the oppressive contexts in which we are all embedded—an inevitable and likely unavoidable collective parallel process that does nothing to alter, let alone transform, the underlying dominance discourse.

Consider the basic tenets of time, task, and territory—the basics of boundary formation.

Looking at time, we routinely and often rigidly privilege *cronos* clock time over the *kairos* moment. We say that this boundary is to create a safe container for the unconscious processes to emerge (Bion, 1970), but we fail sometimes to see that we are also the ones that are contained. That we, in the name of the task—as an artifact of formal role, continue allegiance to authority. We do not see the boundaries, the territories we allocate, as arbitrary. Our shared narrative is that such boundaries serve as aides to our interpretation of what the members are doing, leading (sometimes) to useful hypotheses. But where in most of our hypotheses are the references to the conditions we set that were a pre-determining delimitation of the experience?

Then there is the task. We decree that the task of a conference is "clear" and optimizes freedom for learning. What we fail to consider is that our presentation of the task lacks the precise boundaries that are elsewhere in conference life tightly held. Our language is wrought with ambiguity and reflects our rhetoric and rings with jargon that has specific autistic meaning. The seduction and betrayal of members presents itself in the seemingly perverse delight far too many group relations consultants take in the predictability with which the members of a given conference moment fail to adhere to the task. Members are met with contempt and are psychologically admonished for their ignorance, which we then become free to interpret as the insistence of the members to defy authority.

What we create as group relations practitioners is gaslighting of the most ghastly form. We blame the members for not understanding a task that is in our language for which there is no translation, for the purpose of learning over which we are the arbiters and interpreters of what is made available. Through interpretations in what we determine is the "here and now" of what we say is unconscious, we consult to make conscious what must be conscious enough for us to access it in the first place. As such, our allegiance to the task is also a form of arrogance through which we presume to know the unconscious when what may be at hand is little more than self-projection.

Connection

What we as authors are calling us all to consider is how we can disrupt our worldview by allowing ourselves to encounter a shift in self-narrative, which shifts all other narratives in the group relations global community. Otherwise, all we will continue to do well is protect our work though placing the conference in the language of being a temporary institution, creating an *as if* scenario that attempts to disaggregate conference experience from the larger societal context. We are fond of speaking of how the world comes into the conference but attend with less curiosity about what we export into our world—the two-thirds of members who come to a conference once but never find their way back to our precious offerings. One personal example involves a conference offered to the Kellogg Leadership Fellows nearly 20 years ago. Given some ongoing relationships with select fellows, some of us who were on staff of those conferences are privy to being informed of how the experience continues to influence that system. At each of their reunions, the conference continues to be a subject of some heated debate. One faction continues to characterize the conference as having been a slathering of toxicity that contributed to divisiveness while others in the same cohort champion the conference as the most important learning in their entire fellowship, pivotally enriching their leadership development at that time and to date. While we could readily term this kind of response as a kind of splitting, what gets lost is the responsibility those of us who were on staff may have to those who do not "get" what our work produces or the fact that these members are in the world sharing a narrative about the destructiveness of group relations conference life.

Recently, in a conversation with a fellow university instructor about group relations work, her disdain included a rejection and repudiation of what our work causes. The number of times she has dealt with students unable to integrate the experiences, only to be met with our form of abdication—by saying that a conference is a temporary institution, felt to her to be an irresponsible denial of the very real ongoing psychological disruption such experiences can yield. She particularly found it disingenuous to speak of and taking credit for lasting transformative learning from conferences without owning the trauma that can also result when group relations work succumbs to projective processes that leave more than a few members "walking wounded" from the same type of experiences. Her biggest critique was that group relations work, given its admitted power, is anything but temporary in its effect and is not uniformly positive in what it renders in the lives of those who are less psychologically minded or developmentally prepared for what such learning activates.

Recent advances in research on emotional intelligence may need to be taken to heart. In terms of the self-awareness dimension, Scharmer (2007) wrote that most of us think of ourselves as being self-aware when easily one-third of us are assuredly not perceived that way by our colleagues. Citing research by Tasha Eurich, Scharmer points to how this gap in self-awareness on business teams drops productivity by as much as half. Though many of us are psychoanalytically trained, have worked for years as organizational consultants, or studied these issues in academic settings, there is an implicit question of whether most of us can we say that we meet the self-awareness test in the eyes of our colleagues. Many group relations practitioners have been on a conference staff where the blind spots, our own and those of our colleagues, were especially broad and pernicious to the point where dynamics persisted on the side of boundary unworked through the end of the conference—and beyond. Projection of unworked unconscious issues can be transmitted and left unmetabolized in the membership: this is made murkier and darker as exported unresolved conflict from the consulting staff that some members then carry as unconscious trauma. There is no suggestion of some malicious intention when such things occur, but the impact remains, at least in part, our unacknowledged responsibility. Currently, our work to make unconscious processes conscious falls quite short of bringing people to consciousness when seduction and betrayal may be the more normative dance.

The point is that at each conference, we must find our roles anew and then make them our own as we take on the task of consulting to unconscious processes in human systems. It would be a mistake to assume previous conference roles will make this automatic (Green & Elson, 2015). By analogy, consider how the actors in a television series do not always fully inhabit their roles when the show starts. Is it too great an extension to believe something similar happens with us in conference life? Yet while we are making and taking our roles, we are still offering interpretations of the unconscious process of the group. But if our role boundaries are not fixed, surely the boundary of the task and thereby the container has greater permeability than we would prefer to recognize. We suggest that we import our experience into such moments to reduce the impact of this permeability.

Consciousness

The central inquiry of this offering is whether the work of making unconscious material conscious is the same as bringing people to consciousness. In our estimation, there is a vast difference between these two considerations, creating an opportunity for us to look at our work in group relations with more potential fullness. In this context, consciousness is the felt known; an experience of an essence that has substance through our interactions with one another. It is the energy, vibration, and being of not only each of us but indeed the stuff of the universe. The New Age spiritual teachers are fond of thinking of each of us as embodied expressions of universal consciousness. Stardust that takes a form that we call life. Our premise is that these teachers are not too far off. As mystics of a fragment of this realm, we take aspects of this pool of knowing and help people to discover the meaning and nature of things unseen. The New Testament of the Christian Bible says that this kind knowing is the essence of faith:

Now faith is the substance of things hoped for, the evidence of things not seen.
Hebrews 11:1

The nature of meaning of what such thinking may have to offer an emboldened group relations community ready to broaden our work into the next century is the question at hand.

Community

In the book, *The Different Drum,* M. Scott Peck (1998) uses principles from group relations and even references Margaret Rioch to offer an argument on what constitutes what he terms true community. In his argument, he points to how the journey of a collective though pseudo-community and emptiness into this true community often requires processes that are found in group relations conference life. Perhaps we have an opportunity to learn what our community may yet become.

Conclusion

This chapter is an invitation to a larger conversation—a conversation that began with the CCC in 2009 and continues into this moment. It is our hope that an authentic dialogue about what group relations continues to be and may yet become will be taken up through consideration of these words.

References

Armstrong, D. (2005). Names, thoughts, and lies: The relevance of Bion's later writing for understanding experience in groups. In R. French (Ed.), *Organization in the mind: Psychoanalysis, group relations and organizational consultancy* (pp. 10–28). Karnac.
Bion, W. R. (1961). *Experiences in groups.* Tavistock Publications.

Bion. W. R. (1970). *Attention and interpretation*. Tavistock Publications.

Brazaitis, S. (2004). White women—protectors of the status quo; Positioned to disrupt it. In S. Cytrynbaum & D. Noumair (Eds.), *Group dynamics, organizational irrationality, and social complexity. Group relations reader 3* (pp. 99–116). AK Rice Institute.

Cannato, J. (2010). *Field of compassion: How the new cosmology is transforming spiritual life*. Notre Dame, IN: Sorin Books.

Crenshaw, K. (1989). Demarginalizing the intersection of race and sex: A black feminist critique of antidiscrimination doctrine, feminist theory and antiracist policies. *The University of Chicago Legal Forum*, 140:1 139–167.

Erikson, E. H. (1964) *Insight and responsibility*. Norton.

Erikson, E. H. (1997). *The life cycle completed*. Norton.

Freud, S. (1930). *Civilization and its discontents*. Hogarth.

Green, Z., & Elson, E. (2015). Leadership and the third space. Working paper. https://doi: 10.13140/RG.2.1.4258.0648. Group Relations International.

Green, Z., & Molenkamp, R. (2005). Boundary, authority, role and task: BART method of organizational analysis. https://baddfa7d-5c43-4bec-b3f5-eefad7099302.filesusr.com/ugd/a50107_ebe83be1ff374b408cd39ef407fab110.pdf. Group Relations International.

Green, Z., & Molenkamp, R. (2015). Beyond BART: Analysis at the level of the field. https://baddfa7d-5c43-4bec-b3f5-eefad7099302.filesusr.com/ugd/a50107_9134592ec6c540e8b9cb2c2aa7d4bd57.pdf. Group Relations International.

Hafsi, M. (2006). The chemistry of interpersonal attraction: Developing further Bion's concept of "valency." *Memoirs of Nara University*, 34: 87–112.

Hatcher Cano, D. (1998). Oneness and Me-ness in the baG? In P. B. Talamo, F. Borgogno, & S. Nerciai (Eds.), *Bion's legacy to groups* (pp. 83–94). Karnac.

Helms, J. E. (1993). *Black and white racial identity: Theory, research, and practice*. Praeger.

hooks, b. (1994). Seduced by violence no more. *Outlaw culture: resisting representation*. Routledge.

Hopper, E. (2003). *Traumatic experience in the unconscious life of groups: The Fourth Basic Assumption: Incohesion: Aggregational/Massification or (ba)*. I:A/M. Jessica Kingsley.

Jung, C. G. (1968). *Man and his symbols*. Dell Publishing Company.

Kahn, W., & Green. Z. (2004). Seduction and betrayal: A process of unconscious abuse of authority by leadership groups. In S. Cytrynbaum & D. Noumair (Eds.), *Group dynamics, organizational irrationality, and social complexity. Group relations reader 3* (pp. 159–182). AK Rice Institute.

Katzenbach, J. R., & Smith, D. K. (1993). *The wisdom of teams: Creating the high-performance organization*. Harvard Business School Press.

Kegan, R., & Lahey, L. L. (2009). *Immunity to change: How to overcome it and unlock potential in yourself and your organization*. Harvard Business Press.

Kendi, I. X. (2016). *Stamped from the beginning: The definitive history of racist ideas in America*. New York: Nation Books.

Krantz, J. (2019). Leadership, betrayal, and institutional integrity. *Organizational and Social Dynamics*, 19:1 112–120.

Laszlo, E. (2007). *Science and the akashic field: An integral theory of everything*. Inner Traditions.

Lawrence, W. G., Bain A., & Gould, L. (1996). The fifth basic assumption. *Free Associations*, 6:1 28–55.

McRae, M. B., & Short, E. L. (2010). *Racial and cultural dynamics in group and organizational life: Crossing boundaries*. Sage Publications.

McTaggart, L. (2008). *The field: The quest for the secret force of the universe*. New York: Harper.

Molenkamp, R. (2012). The field. https://baddfa7d-5c43-4bec-b3f5-eefad7099302. filesusr.com/ugd/a50107_720f16a0cee34e2b8cf737c9362f3689.pdf. Group Relations International.

Molenkamp, R. (2020). Group Relations International. https://www.grouprelations. org/post/group-relations-international. Group Relations International.

Peck, M. S. (1998). *The different drum: Community making and peace*. Simon and Schuster.

Rioch M. J. (1971). "All we like sheep" (Isaiah 53:6): Followers and leaders. *Psychiatry*, 34:3 258–273.

Sampson, E. E. (1993). Identity politics: Challenges to psychology's understanding. *American Psychologist*, 48:12 1219–1230. https://doi.org/10.1037/0003-066X.48. 12.1219

Scharmer, C. O. (2007). *Theory u: Leading from the future as it emerges*. Society for Organizational Learning.

Skolnick, M., & Green, Z. (2004). The denigrated other. Diversity and group relations. In S. Cytrynbaum & D. Noumair (Eds.), *Group dynamics, organizational irrationality, and social complexity. Group relations reader 3* (pp. 117–130). AK Rice Institute.

Smith, K.K., & Berg, D.N. (1987). *Paradoxes of group life: Understanding conflict, paralysis, and movement in group dynamics*. Jossey-Bass.

Strauss, G. (2009). Learning from experience. The two group relations meetings in Belgirate. In E. Aram et al (Eds.), *Adaptation and innovation, volume II*. Karnac.

Sue, D.W., & Sue, D. (2013). *Counseling the culturally diverse: Theory and practice* (6th ed.). John Wiley & Sons.

Taylor, F., Kuriloff, P., & Smith, K. (2004). Anatomy of a casualty. In S. Cytrynbaum & D. Noumair (Eds.), *Group dynamics, organizational irrationality, and social complexity. Group relations reader 3* (pp. 183–209). AK Rice Institute.

Tchelebi, N. (2017). Taking Bion "back to basics": Let us stop counting "oneness" as the only basic assumption mentality. *Organizational and Social Dynamics*, 17:1 50–71.

Turquet, P. M. (1975). Threats to identity in the large group. In L. Kreeger (Ed.), *The large group: Dynamics and therapy* (pp. 87–144). Karnac.

Turquet, P. M. (1985). Leadership: The individual and the group. In A. D. Colman & M. H. Geller (Eds.), *Group relations reader 2* (pp. 71–88). Washington, DC: AK Rice Institute.

Van Linge, A., & Green, Z. (2010). The cycle of noticing. https://baddfa7d-5c43-4bec-b3f5-eefad7099302.filesusr.com/ugd/a50107_934753cd8c484c23a1466caf236c746e. pdf. Group Relations International.

Volkan, V. D. (2001). Transgenerational transmissions and chosen traumas: An aspect of large-group identity. *Group Analysis*, 34:1 79–97.

Wells, L. J. (1995). The group-as-a-whole: A systemic socioanalytic perspective on interpersonal and group relations. In J. Gillette & M. McCollom (Eds.), *Groups in context: A new perspective on group dynamics* (pp. 50–85). Addison-Wesley.

Wilber, K. (2001). *A theory of everything: An integral vision for business, politics, science, and spirituality*. Shambhala.

Chapter 6

A Nomadic State of Mind

In Search for a Place to Live

Coreene Archer

The invitation offered by the opportunity to reflect on the provocative title "The place where we live – a space for Group Relations" allowed consideration and reflection on the process of trying to enter the Group Relations canon and examining whether there is space within it that pushes the boundary or challenges the rules. This is a personal journey which is explored through the shifting lenses and overlapping fractals, considering the different dimensions and struggles of the journey. How many of the challenges I encountered are par for the course or unique to my experience?

For most of my career, I have been a professional nomad. I moved from place to place, role to role searching for something to hold me beyond the novelty of newness and the process of learning "how we do it here". The person I am, was largely hidden and unknown, mostly by choice; it did not feel safe to reveal myself, aspects of my identity and humanity to more than a few close colleagues. At the time, I didn't know I was searching for something deeper or more complex and challenging. I bumped into the longing for more, for depth, and for growth. Or perhaps, it bumped into me. I did not find group relations methodology via systems theory or psychoanalysis. I entered via management and curiosity. Once I had entered the arena, I found answers and new questions.

The definition of place, in this chapter, found amongst the eight definitions available was the following:

> a portion of space designated or available for or being used by someone;
>
> a right or privilege resulting from someone's role or position.

This resonated and allowed for exploration of the concepts within the title and to consider whether it is professionally possible to find a place to live?

The aim of this chapter is to explore and address two ideas:

How does one occupy "a portion of space designated or available for being used" especially if the space has not been used that way before? Through the lens and experience of developing group relations conferences

DOI: 10.4324/9781003261483-9

for young people, I reflect on the process and challenges presented whilst seeking to create something new with an established methodology. Was the space comfortable or uncomfortable and what rights are embodied or challenged in the act of creation? This links to my second area of exploration.

As a black woman, having been told several times that I am privileged, defined as "a special right, advantage or entitlement" according to the dictionary, but a word that is not normally associated with black people, or with women, I had no connection to the word, or to the meaning. It does not describe my journey to date. My experience of trying to do something new, has felt more like breaking ground, conjuring the picture of something demanding and/or difficult. However, I do recognise that the opportunity to try and do something new may not be so common. Perhaps my experience of creation is not unusual, that, in fact, it is both a privilege and a challenge. This observation has caused me to ponder; Is it possible for race and privilege to comfortably co-exist in an individual? Does it enable the possibility of taking up a role to do new things?

Starting Out

The first place that we live is our childhood home. It should be a place of safety, joy, and growth; a place to try new things and to thrive. Home can also be the place where we develop our most wonderful and our most painful memories. These are the things that shape us.

Professionally, I have found my home at the Tavistock Institute and unexpectedly, it has become "the place I live". It is a place of joy and growth, it is a place that I can try new things and to thrive. It has been a place where I have had wonderful and painful experiences. It is with this frame in mind that I will explore the development of a group relations offer for young people (18–26 years old), called Launching Young Leaders (LYL). We have run LYL several times, in adapted formats and each time it has embodied both the wonderful and the painful.

LYL is the offspring of the Leicester Conference. It has the same genetic markers: it attracts an international audience, which came as a surprise for a one-day event. It draws on the original design elements: large group; small groups; intergroup and role and application groups. It also has some new elements, a theory segment, and other systems or group-based exercises. It has a small staff of three or four consultants, one who also takes up the role of Director. There has been a maximum attendance of 15 participants but we could accept more, the groups are smaller, lighter but use the same approach and have the same methodological aims. In his paper *The Leicester Model*, Eric Miller states these succinctly when he says this event is "devoted to experiential learning about group and organisational behaviour, with a particular emphasis on the nature of authority and leadership" (Miller 1989). The major difference is that the focus of LYL is on young leaders. Those who are just entering the world of work or taking up their first leadership role. It is an opportunity to explore and reflect on group process, the impact of authority, how roles are given or taken and to engage with the unconscious, often amongst this younger demographic, for the first time. For the majority of participants, they have not thought about these issues before.

A Bit about Role

The first conference that we ran, I took up the role of Director and although I had the title, I didn't own it. Originally, I had conceptualised the programme as being led by an established or at least an experienced director. I am an experienced consultant and manager and I have run teams and projects, but I have not taken up the role of director. At the Tavistock Institute, there are several members of staff who have taken the director role, so there was a strong choice and I hadn't included myself in the list. It wasn't until a colleague challenged me, by asking why I wasn't directing the conference that I started to think about taking up the role. It is only as I write this chapter, I realise that I am also one of the young leaders, stepping into an unfamiliar space.

As we prepared for the conference or by then, thinking about the programme and the elements it would contain, I unconsciously made my role and place in the programme less significant; I would say "I am running a workshop" or "leading the team". Both points are true, but perhaps the underlying concern was that I was at that point, I hadn't stepped into the role or taken the seat. My caution could also be related to my understanding of the power of the work and that in using the "Tavistock Approach" people can be taken to a place of depth. I felt but had not fully stepped into holding the responsibility for their experience.

The other concern that I was holding was related to the question of tradition. Miller summarises the weight of responsibility when he states "*Ascribed to me, therefore is a symbolic role as custodian of the tradition*".

Although I do not hold the idea of tradition lightly and deeply value what it represents, there is a weight inscribed in the word that resists change. It inspires thoughts of whom and what have gone before and perhaps, the forbidding image of the Tavistock forefathers, who resembled psychologically the faces in Mount Rushmore – big, heavy, and white, that made me feel more cautious, slower to enter the space. The names of these heavyweights: Bion; Turquet; Miller; Menzies Lyth; Bridger, individuals who have changed and influenced the methodology and who I felt watching me like the members of a judgemental family.

The space of tradition is complex, because it is filled with expectations that belong to others, both in the past and in the present. It often takes the form of an organisational dynamic or the mantra "that's not how we do it here". Crossing into this territory feels risky, more like breaking through ice, than stepping up. For me, innovation was the pathway that made it possible to enter the space and yet somehow held me back. I had to find my role and my place within the work, to do something new. Debra Meyerson describes this approach as being a "tempered radical" which means existence in a space of tension. The strategy is "to recognise modest and doable choices in between such as choosing their battles, creating pockets of learning and making way for small wins" Meyerson (2001).

The Concept – What I Wanted to Do and What It Became

My starting point was engaging with the history of the approach. I considered that historically, the group relations methodology is used amongst more mature and established people. The idea of this conference was that it would be aimed at young people approximately aged 18–30, and although a new audience, the link would be that they would be at a point of transition. This age range has been selected on the basis that this is a pivotal point in the young lives of participants, a time when they are reflecting on who they are and how they find their place in society. The anticipated outcomes of the conference were that it would help participants, particularly those who are disadvantaged and disaffected, to see themselves and the world in a new light.

Initially designed as a residential event of three to five days, creating a space for the emotional and psychological movement or growth that could be achieved during this period will be significant. The conference would be supported by follow-up groups in the form of peer mentoring or coaching in order to avoid destabilising the psychic frame of the members, and to embed the learning. The format of this support structure was designed to be open and subject to agreement by members. The conference aimed to attract approximately 25 members, with the objective of helping participants think about themselves in relation to their communities, giving them opportunities to experience themselves as citizens. The thinking behind this aspect of the project was twofold: creating space for alternative roles to be "taken up" allowing participants the chance to see themselves in a different way; and to help them to "unhook" themselves from historic and sometimes toxic emotions. The experiential process amplifies personal reflection and encourages the exploration of individual and group dynamics and engagement, creating the opportunity for each member to consider how they are both experienced and perceived. As the membership of the conference would be drawn from a diverse selection of young people, it would allow exposure and cross-fertilisation of ideas and experiences, highlighting not just differences, but similarities. The aim was to create an opportunity for this new younger participant to find a bridge into the world of work and reflect on their understanding of authority, role, and organisation.

I thought about the conference a lot. I kept thinking and tweaking, trying to create a perfect conference, a flawless start. I looped around ever-decreasing circles, changing and adjusting small points until eventually, I was pushed to do more that "polish" my idea, but to be brave enough to run the event. I accepted that to deliver this event successfully would be a "small win".

The first conference was run on 21 July 2017 with the theme of "Exploring Authority, Role and Impact" – with the subheading of "For young people who want to make a difference". In selecting the theme, I was keen to retain roots in the Leicester Conference and the exploration of authority and role as key elements in Tavistock thinking. The addition of the word "impact" felt necessary. I wanted to make the connection to the idea of making a difference, for all the young people who were thinking about trying to have an impact on society; and picking up on recruitment trends that suggest young people feel strongly about social responsibility and how organisations engage with the issues. When I think about the selection of these terms, I can connect with my own desire to make a difference; to positively engage with the lives of the young people who we met during this process and to all the other lives that they would subsequently touch. In noticing my own connection to change, I also recognised another unconscious dynamic. The date I chose for the event, 21 July, was my deceased father's birthday. By selecting this date, I was unconsciously making a connection with my biological father (and I was very much a daddy's girl), perhaps in order to feel that a least one of the "fathers" looking down on me was supportive and positive.

The first conference that we ran looked quite different from the initial design. We stopped using the term conference, replacing it with workshop so that it wouldn't be misleading to an audience who were expecting an event where people sat around and listened to others speaking, deliberately choosing something more interactive and hopefully accessible to a new audience. Gone was the residential element, which didn't seem to fit with the day and the demographic. It became a one-day workshop that was based in Central London. The elements were similar to the previous design and the aims were the same. I felt as though I had "let some air out" of the design in order to take this first step. I finally took up the role fully of director and selected my team. We finalised the programme. Fifteen young people applied to attend and we prepared for the day.

When the day was over, I remember feeling completely elated. I felt that I had achieved my goal. I had run an event that fulfilled my desire to work with a younger community, and from the feedback, it had been a success. The participants said that they had learnt from the experience and that many felt they had grown. There was a part of me that was relieved to be able to tick the box and mark the endeavour as complete. A colleague who was part of the team asked when we would be running the next one, I didn't have an answer, but it was clear to him that I wasn't that keen. He pressed me for reasons to understand why.

Reflections

Dumas (1980) states *"The presence of black women in leadership positions takes on highly significant meanings in organisational life"* and goes on to suggest that *"she is invested"* with particular stereotypes; a nurturer; or aloof; or angry. Robert Livingstone echoes this analysis in his research and suggests that black females in senior leadership are largely ignored until something goes wrong, and then they are expelled from organisational life. Why is she expelled? Perhaps because she recognises that she is the outsider and slips into a defensive position very easily, maybe too easily. Reni Eddo-Lodge (2017) expands on this and states *"there is such stigma attached to speaking up and being a woman, let alone speaking up, being a woman and being black … the angry black woman cannot be reasoned with. She argues back. She is not docile, sweet or agreeable"*.

Although over 30 years apart, there is truth to the words of Dumas (1980) and Eddo-Lodge (2017) for which there is still evidence and impact today. Pulling together the LYL event was very difficult. I felt like something of an organisational curiosity, as I tried to grapple with the ideas of tradition, methodology, and change. I did have some support throughout, but I largely worked on my own and I was unsupported in a number of ways. Fortunately, or unfortunately, I was used to working on my own, so I just worked harder. There seemed to be an expectation that I would know how to launch the event on my own, and somehow the expectations silenced me. I found my way through. I worked largely outside the organisation with external colleagues and then with a new member of staff when she joined, who helped me, which I greatly appreciated. Without knowing it, by working this way, I was creating a "positive self-definition" which helped me to keep the momentum going. I wasn't sure that I wanted to do it again, but I was persuaded to and I am glad I did – although the journey is still a difficult one, it has created a space for new interpretations and opportunities to emerge.

The workshop has now been run five times with the addition of a shorter version which introduces a few ideas and is run as two half-day virtual workshops. It has not been a process that is free of problems. We have discussed the development of each new workshop, reflected on the impact of the programme on the participants and supported each as they desired. Each workshop has evolved and we as the staff team have worked through the dynamics associated with hierarchy and race. My role as director is now established which is evidenced by previous staff members asking me whether they are due to be involved in the next one. Systemically, the growth in my confidence in the director role and overall design has been matched by the development of the workshop as attendance numbers have tripled.

The question of whether it is possible to inhabit a place of privilege in organisational life as a black woman is a paradoxical one. The definitions of the words place and privilege can be expressed in the same way; a position or right, however, they are understood socially in a very different way because rights and positions are given or taken. A phrase that is often used in relation to role: as a role can also be taken or given and often come with complex and unexpected challenges. Therefore, for me to respond to the invitation in the title to identify "the place where I live" it is the word "live" that becomes operative, and the place that I live is in the work. It for me is a place of creativity and exploration. A place of challenge and growth, but the road is not an easy one. The unconscious highlights things amongst colleagues and peers that are sometimes painful to see and hear, all of which are in service of the work; and the work is the improvement of society.

Dumas (1980) states "*The black woman leader is often torn between the expectations and demands born of her mythical image and those inherent in her official status and tasks in the formal organisation*" because it questions who has the right to do certain things and encoded in that perspective is that some are more fortunate than others, or more accurately, are expected to behave in certain ways. Gilroy (2004) referencing W. E. D. Du Bois describes this as double-consciousness or twoness, which he describes as feeling the different aspects of your identity (being black and a (wo)man) – being seen through the eyes of another and I also think through our own eyes. Are we willing to face our darkness in order to bring our best to the world? To the work? To the place we live.

In this chapter, I have explored two ideas; how does one occupy "a portion of space designated or available for being used" especially if the space has not been used that way before? And is it possible for race and privilege to comfortably co-exist in an individual? Does it enable or hinder the possibility of taking up a role to do new things. To do this, I have explored the experience of developing group relations conference for young people, reflecting on the process and challenges presented whilst seeking to create something new with an established methodology. I made the connection between the development of my role as director alongside the emergence of a space for new leadership amongst younger people.

References

Dumas, R.G. (1980) Dilemmas of Black Females in Leadership. *Journal of Personality and Social Systems*, 2:1, 3–14.

Eddo-Lodge, R. (2017) *Why I Am No Longer Talking to White People about Race.* Bloomsbury.

Gilroy, P. (2004) *After Empire, Melancholia or Convivial Culture.* Routledge.

Meyerson, D. (2001) *Tempered Radicals: How People Use Difference to Inspire.* Harvard Business School Press.

Miller, E. (1989) *The Leicester Model,* Tavistock Institute Occasional Paper No 10.

Chapter 7

Co-Constructing a Society That Promotes Life

An Exploration of the Unconscious Dynamics in Radicalisation Processes

Joan Roma I Verges, Sandra Carrau Pascual, David Sierra Lozano, and Jaume Benavent I Guardia

Purpose

Every time a terrorist attack occurs, "The place where we live" changes inevitably, and on many levels. The cities that have experienced these events are no longer the same as they were before, both literally and symbolically.

Not being able to understand the reasons behind such irreversible acts creates insecurity with respect to "the outside world" and makes us question what it was that led young people, who were supposedly integrated into "our" country, who were considered to be fellow citizens, to carry out such irreparable acts. In the end, these actions and their reactions can consolidate the experience of threat of the "outside world", as represented by "the other" and so eliminate the possibility of a "creative game" in Winnicott's "place where we live".

Using the systemic approach and socio-analysis, we will analyse the lived experience after Barcelona and Cambrils' jihadist terrorist attacks of 17 August 2017. In doing so, we intend to explore a hypothesis that could shed light on the dynamics that may be generating this sudden process of radicalisation among European Muslim youth. We will also consider how other groups could make use of these radicalisation processes in order to justify their drift.

The Terrorist Attacks in Catalonia (August 2017)

On 16 August, an explosion occurred in a house in Alcanar (province of Tarragona) in which one person died (Abdelbaki Es Satty) and another person was injured. In the afternoon of 17 August, a young man drove a van down Les Rambles in Barcelona, indiscriminately running over pedestrians. Thirteen people died at the scene from their injuries, while one woman died a few days later in hospital. Another young man was stabbed to death when the perpetrator stole his car in order to make his getaway. In the early hours of 18 August, a group of young terrorists attacked citizens with knives in Cambrils (province of Tarragona) and were shot down by the Mossos

DOI: 10.4324/9781003261483-10

d'Esquadra (Catalan police force). All five terrorists were killed, along with a woman who was run over by the terrorists as they tried to flee. Some 72 hours after the attack on Les Rambles, a woman in the town of Subirats (Catalan county of Alt Penedès) spotted one of the young terrorists on the run and alerted the police, who shot him dead after hearing him cry out "Allah is great".

The subsequent investigation confirmed that the terrorist attacks had been perpetrated by a jihadist cell composed of 12 people (11 young Muslim men between 17 and 24 years old from the town of Ripoll, under the leadership of the Imam of the same town, Es Satty).

One of the most shocking aspects for Catalan society was that the Ripoll youths were considered to be well integrated in this small town of 11,000 inhabitants. They had all been schooled there; had jobs there; and one of them had even been born in Catalonia. Such was the degree of familiarity with the young terrorists that even the media frequently used their first names when referring to them: Younes, Said, etc.

This assumed a very deep, catastrophic change in Catalan society and in particular in Ripoll, as described in a letter sent by Raquell Rull, a social educator who had worked with the youths from their childhood until their teenage years, on 22 August:

> "I'd never had such a strong feeling as this one, because it's not rational; it doesn't come from something that you see is bound to happen or that forms part of life. It comes from another place I can't even describe".

Without a doubt, the deepest effect of a jihadist terrorist act is the fuelling of fear and mistrust between "us" and those who destroy the "place where we live" together. A mass demonstration held the day after the attacks attempted to resist these feelings as protestors repeated the chant "I'm not afraid" (#notincpor).

Despite collective demonstrations, defensive behaviours can continue operating as a result of our anxieties. This lands us in "fight mode", where the immigrant person is perceived as an enemy, being Muslim or however they may be labelled, or alternatively in flight mode, wanting to turn the page as quickly as if nothing had happened. This was felt just as strongly a year after the attacks, New information was published in the media alongside stock footage, and the population of Ripoll expressed their anger with the media for recreating these lived events once again.

Terrorist Attacks as a Symbol and Symptom

Just like any catastrophic event that alters the normal functioning of a human community, terrorist attacks could be treated factually – thus, we could try to re-establish the community's day-to-day functioning and alleviate the destructive effects that the attacks leave behind. This, however, could also be a symbol or symptom of something intangible that has extensive-reaching effects on co-living in the community. From a systemic perspective therefore, the growing radicalisation among European Muslims who end up becoming perpetrators of attacks "on their own doorstep", could be understood as an expression of an individual but also as a symptom of a collective unease.

According to the description that Byun-Chul Han gives on the current "performance society", we find increasingly that consumerism and productivity dictate how we relate to each other in the world. The Super-Ego repressor is substituted for an idealised Super-Self, living as if it were free, but deep down it is subjected to the results lived as the only fruits of its performance.

Thus, confronted with failure, a series of self-produced and self-blaming violent dynamics are generated. Within this context, frustration grows more and more generalised, and along with it arise many forms of self-rejection and self-exploitation. This could go a long way to explain the main ills of modern Western society; depression and burnout.

It is within this context of productivity, that life becomes an individual survival course, where collectively we may be co-creating a culture of slow death. This is a culture which has damaging effects on the "losers", who find themselves having to compete on uneven playing fields. The same, however, applies to the supposed "winners" who may be in constant state of unfulfillment, as they fear they can always do more.

It could be therefore that narratives which in other circumstances wouldn't have followers, gain force as a means of struggle by individuals against a society that, at its core, doesn't foster happiness. Despite not rationally seeing benefits, it could be that perpetrating terrorist acts were, unconsciously, an avenue of expression of a feeling of emptiness and unease, ultimately converting the acts themselves into a counter-cultural symbol.

We say "counter-cultural" because we can read a terrorist attack as an antidote to current Western tendencies: they are unproductive acts (going in favour of destruction and against constant growth). They require few resources in order to make a great impact (contrary to materialism). They are a claim to a feeling of a transcendental life (against material output); they offer the return to being part of a community (contrary to individualism) and they allow for working in solidarity and on behalf of the collective (the very essence of dying for "Muslim brothers").

Could it be, therefore, that these processes of growing radicalisation were a symptom of a social malaise and a radical expression of something that resists death within this "performance-based society"?

If this is the case, what kind of "place where we live" are we co-creating that causes some of "our" young "ones" to find themselves feeling as if they are becoming "the other" and acting out in such a radically and irreversible destructive way against "us" and ultimately against "themselves"?

"One of Our Own" (Belonging to a Common Space)

In her letter following the attacks, Raquel Rull described the youths, suddenly converted into terrorists, with the following words:

> "These kids were just like all the others. Just like my children, they were kids from Ripoll (...) Just like the kid who says hello and lets you jump ahead of him in the supermarket queue, the kid who doesn't know where to put himself when a girl smiles at him".

This sentence shows us how, in a society that aims to be inclusive, we may tend to generate a fantasy of uniformity for ourselves; that "we are all the same". And this "being the same" may be based on specific parameters which, as soon as they define us, other differences also present between "us" are excluded.

It is this uniformity tendency that Sennett (1972) describes as *"mixofobia"*, "that desire to be similar, as a way for men to avoid the necessity of looking deeper into each other. And in this way, make life in common more tolerable and not have to make the effort to understand, negotiate and reach agreements, which is what coexistence in diversity requires".

If Sennett's (2001) "mixofobia" does indeed exist in our communities, this could create a divide between people who feel legitimised being who they are in a common space, and others who live in a subtle exclusion, with the consequential dissatisfaction, fragility, and vulnerability that is generated within these dynamics.

These unconscious images of "them" and "us", and the associations that come with these images lead to the attribution of social roles; the immigrant people are seen as the "eternal new arrivals" or "the pleasant guests"; while the host population takes on the "normal" identity or that of "the eternal property owner", among other roles.

As Erikson (1959) mentioned, despite the feeling of having an individual identity, one could be forced to define oneself by an external identity. The processes of "racialisation" of which there is now a growing awareness, and a growing critique.

This is what Mostafà Shaimi demonstrates in the newspaper ARA (2 September 2017) in describing how Catalan public television used sentences that subtly excluded some social groupings:

> "The citizens of Barcelona embrace two young men from the Muslim community" or "The citizens of Ripoll with the presence of the Muslim community have condemned terrorism".

Do they mean that members of the Muslim community are not citizens? Are they sure that those men feel themselves to be representative of a Muslim community?

Obviously within a context that unconsciously manages the differences in the ways described above, resentment is generated and reactive identities easily appear, counter to the "dominant culture"; the discontentment that young European Muslims could feel and which jihadist groups know how to recognise and channel for their political interests. Radical groups that capitalise on some avenues created by Western societies through religious communities: mosques and imams. They offer a pathway to rid themselves of resentment in a vengeful way, whilst at the same time trying to defend a collective cause.

Who Am I? (Multiple Identities)

Wafa Marsi, a 31-year-old woman who was a neighbour to some of the youths of Ripoll, recounted in the Catalan newspaper ARA on 12 August 2018 her lived experience as a Catalan Muslim woman:

> "I was schooled in Catalan, I think in Catalan, but at certain times your family tells you, 'Remember you're a Muslim', while your group of mates tells you, 'You're a Moor'. So one day I put a headscarf on to understand who I was," she explains.

This experience demonstrates the difficulty some people of immigrant origin can have in holding more than one community identity; an experience that becomes more negative when one of the cultures does not have social prestige, illustrated in the case of being referred to as "mora" (a derogatory term used to refer to immigrants of North African origin) in Catalonia as well as in Spain.

We know that having emigrated to a country considered richer and more developed and with better opportunities and so on can often lead to a sense of inferiority. Furthermore, we know that the colonial unconscious, the host culture for the immigrant, can feel very dominant at the moment of entry and taking up a role. So much so, as Sennett points out, that even on attaining a certain level of financial security, an immigrant still cannot attain the associated social status that would normally come with this.

Therefore, people of immigrant origin can feel themselves under constant scrutiny, feeling the need to earn their place, and not feeling themselves to have done so by social standards, even when they have rightfully proven themselves in this respect.

All in all, our hypothesis here would be that people of immigrant origin may often feel themselves to be defined externally by the negative identity of being "from neither here nor there".

An identity constructed from a negative standpoint could imply that any personal projects can only be expressed only negatively, whilst simultaneously idealising the majority.

This sensation of being "neither, nor", while imagining that others have a more clear and unique identity, may generate feelings of envy, and where there is envy, it becomes easier to activate the impulse to destroy that which we feel we cannot have. This hypothesis is reinforced by Zizek (2015) when discussing the lack of religious fundamentalism of terrorists (in this case, the Paris terrorists) who seem more driven by the urge to destroy Western life than by any feeling of being in possession of a truth that must be disseminated.

Two ways that an individual might project the negation introjected by living with a "neither, nor" identity include destroying what they envy by symbolically removing the envied identity, by constructing an alternative identity in its place (that of "infidels"), or also by removing it physically.

This impulse for destruction also involves self-destruction. The process of radicalisation involves eliminating the insufferable tension of ambivalence or empty identity in order to become a jihadist, and finding a sense of purpose in a suicide which also results in the deaths of others. This also explains the action carried out and widely disseminated by ISIS whereby radicalised youths burn their passports, in a ritual named "a no return path".

The Family Legacy: Conscious and Unconscious

We know that every emigration experience incurs pain; a loss of what we left behind; places; friends; family members; memories. The Ulysses Syndrome usually has more intense effects on children who have emigrated, and who are unable to make sense of the loss they suffer. Emotions such as these are usually heightened in adolescence by the difficulties faced at this vital stage, as we will explain in more detail later on.

As León Grinberg and Rebeca Grinberg explain, people who have to emigrate experience stress throughout the process for all sorts of reasons: separation; doubts about loyalty and the values that make up the superego; persecution anxiety due to the culture shock involved in coming into contact with the new and unknown; depression due to mourning the abandonment or loss of parts of the self and confusion about distinguishing between the old and the new.

Faced with the aforementioned culture shock of emigrating, people can develop certain defence mechanisms in order to survive which can range from idealising their host culture while directly rejecting their culture of origin, to creating a restricted space for themselves, seeking protection by enclosing themselves in the community that shares their culture of origin. These are ways in which to allow oneself to survive the process of adaptation, but do not allow one to work on one's experienced emotions.

In this sense, we might think that these emotions, repressed as they are due to the necessity of adaptation and the lack of space in which to develop them, could be transmitted as an unconscious legacy to further generations, despite these new generations having been born into the new culture.

We know that for children, family emigration has a series of knock-on effects such as feelings of responsibility and debt for to the sacrifice their parents have made. On one hand, this could make children more focused on their cultural identity of origin. Alternatively, they may be more inclined to hide their migrant origin, undervaluing their family's cultural identity (and as such, denying part of themselves). Alternatively, they may unconsciously feel that they will never completely be "from" the place they were born and may see themselves as second-class citizens or even guests in their "own home".

On the other hand, the patriarchal culture of Muslim origin families is a more conscious family legacy than the one mentioned above. With this in mind, we could ask ourselves whether male children might perceive their father to have failed in his role by having to emigrate at all. They might also question their father's role in relation to the women of the family whom, if they have to enter the world of work, may have a more active and public role than their own culture might expect from them.

Our hypothesis is that young males from patriarchal families, such as the Muslim one, grow up aspiring to a rigid ideal of masculinity that substitutes the dominance of the father, while searching for a successful male role model in whom to project themselves.

These sons might see themselves as "doubly second-class citizens" and might find in the Imam figure a strong masculine role model that transmits an unambiguous message, without the contradictions that they experience at home. The Imam may also become a channel for their own capacity of agency, which they feel they lack. This could also indirectly replace that of their parents, who are possibly seen as overly obedient or passive.

Similarly, there may be a desire to recover a feeling of power experienced in other eras. This is also implicit in the resurgence of fascism in Europe and the nostalgia for historical moments of superiority and could serve as a justification of Al-Andalus through the virtual creation of a Caliphate on behalf of radical Islam.

In the case of Ripoll, the Imam would have served as a catalyst of the widespread discontent, which had already been expressed in the form of interest in Jihadi culture from members of the Ripoll group (Reading from writings, following their messages on social media, and so on).

If it were not for a social system with unconscious dynamics that allowed them such a significant role, these indoctrinating figures would act with much more difficulty.

We should therefore not allow the stereotype of the evil Imam, an adult that corrupts youngsters, to distract us from identifying a much wider social dynamic and impede us from recognising the depth and extent of the phenomenon. Even more dangerously, overlooking this could impede us from acting along other lines.

Youth Transitional Stage and the Emptiness of Ideals

As we described at the beginning of the chapter, the radicalised youth of Ripoll were between 17 and 24 years old. The majority of youths who have committed these kind of terrorist acts in Europe previously fit into this age range. They are young people at a transitional stage of their youth, in which the ideals of infancy are destroyed and need to be substituted for new ones.

This is an intense time of de-idealisation and re-idealisation, or as Winnicott (1958) describes, it is the step from "pot au noir" towards a new "potential space" in which to play creatively again.

In de-idealisation a young person might feel empty, bored, depressed, and unable to find meaning in life, and may have a tendency to under-value themselves. At the other extreme, in re-idealisation they feel elated; passion; elevation of themselves; the hunger for a new and creative world coupled with a search for meaning; and the fantasy that justice and truth will prevail.

In these moments, the subject has to re-appropriate their own person, as if they were shedding their own skin to find a new one. Suicide attempts in this vital stage could be interpreted as a form of taking one's life before feeling dead or rotting away.

For some, this transition becomes more difficult and they experience it as a secret and unforeseen torment, making them more easily recruited for terrorism and also more difficult for authorities to anticipate and detect.

Jihadism therefore, with all its marketing actions, addresses this age group (known as *millennials*) with a positive image of its cause, and with *mujahidin's'* friendly faces. Some marketing images mimic popular video games, whilst kind *YouTubers* explain how to make homemade bombs easily. In such videos, victims are made to appear unreal, preventing feelings of empathy towards them. What's more, social media allows these potential audiences to be reached under the guise of major *hashtags,* transmitting these terrorist images as something popular and familiar. These are communicative acts that are controlled with the same precision as terrorist ones, giving rise to the term *transmedia* terrorism.

For young people, who tend to feel alone during this transitional phase, a new jihadist identity may allow them to numb their anxiety during this vital transition, perhaps giving them a sense of omnipotence in times of depression and an opportunity to accelerate the process of constructing a new self. To this end, these new radicalised youths change their names and acquire new habits rapidly.

This idea is in keeping with reports made about the Ripoll youths, commenting that their friends stopped greeting them almost overnight. They changed their habits of drinking and going out at night and seemed to become much quieter. This seemed to give some satisfaction to the youths' parents, who perceived them to have a greater sense of purpose, reporting; "they had stopped drinking alcohol and they went to the mosque more".

Even so, while such youngsters are seduced by ideas of jihadism, thinking they have found authenticity and a quick way to recover their capacity for agency, fundamentally what they are doing is becoming automatons, imitating other individuals as new heroes to copy, all the while losing their own individuality.

It is this process of erosion of individual identity and becoming "like the others" that makes radicalised youngsters difficult to identify through institutionalised services. This adds to the importance of incorporating other perspectives that may come out of the frameworks that we are aiming to outline in this chapter.

Islamic Identity as Salvation and Healing

With all this said, while the West attempts to prevent attacks, generating policy protocols in order to identify radicalisation processes in schools, Islamic leaders are getting to know how to capitalise on the Western system's current weakness.

They offer a universal doctrine as an avenue of healing, a welcoming community, and a cause for which fighting is worthwhile.

As Vidino[1] mentions, access to Islamic identity gives youngsters a sense of prestige, as opposed to a feeling of being second-class in their own habitat. The process of radicalisation is seen as an entry into "a prestigious school, which is highly selective; not accepting just anyone". It is a school based on its own interpretation of Islam, which permits the filling of an existential void with a political cause and allows youngsters to feel distinguished and special in a chiefly secular culture as Europe. This Western culture supposedly offers them a host of opportunities, but in practice offers them nothing.

Through radicalisation, these youths can avenge themselves against a society that they feel to be unjust and can allow them to acquire a more assertive identity than that which their parents might have had to assume through over-adaptation.

The new radicalised identity values the afterlife over the present one, and so the risk of death has more value. At the same time, individuals feel protected by something greater than themselves, whether that be God or "Muslim brothers". "Islam" means not only "submission" but also a state of healing once a danger has been overcome. Therefore, as described in detail by Benslama, Muslim identity can be stronger than a cult and more toxic than a delusion, due to a psycho-social state aligning itself with a historical reality of political oppression and war, which lends support to the representative narrative where of the myth of Islam.

As Pius Alibek[2] points out, the mosques from where these youngsters are being recruited by charismatic Imams do not represent the population of the Muslim religion. Due to its complexity, the Koran is open to many different interpretations, and in these mosques, an aggressive and self-interested interpretation of the Koran is made.

Radical interpretations of Islam define massacre as an act of moral purification of the unholy in the eyes of God. The "kamikaze", following Benslama,[3] is an idealistic example of a puritan, renouncing the enjoyment of the present life (viewed as impure) and thus ascending to a paradise of total pleasure, devoid of prohibition.

It is not strange, therefore, that purveyors of such ideals can attract youngsters with a high sense of responsibility and commitment, as Rull, the social educator described Younes Abouyaaqoub (one of the Les Rambles terrorists). As such, radicalised youths require discipline and deep commitment to the cause; to avenge the historical wrongs inflicted on Islam. It is in this very way that ISIS recommends the historic wound be acted upon through bodies of young recruits, turned into avengers "chosen by God". They would be the chosen ones who would transgress human law in the name of God's law, in doing so, making themselves pure. Both purification and repentance are said to be the fundamentals of Islam.

Co-Constructing a Society That Promotes Life, Not Death

If we go beyond the pain and wounds that jihadi terrorist acts have had on the community, we may be able to interpret the meaning of this phenomenon in more depth and for society as a whole. We might then build a significantly more complex image of the societies considered "the receptors".

A systemic point of view emphasises the relationships that are established between groups, from the perspective that everyone is different, not only those considered as "the other". As such, all groups can use the concept "us" and simultaneously the pronoun "them" towards themselves.

With such strong focus being placed on young radical jihadi groups, we would hope that their existence is not used to conceal or justify other young radical groups with far-right and fascist tendencies with the implication that these ends are more "ours". This certainly should not prevent careful, in-depth exploration of the bases for the growth of these similarly violent phenomena.

We should also highlight the relationship between the creation and manipulation of fear in contemporary societies, "Fake news" is increasingly being found to be used by various countries to generate these type of climates that lead to distrust between ourselves.[4]

As John Carlin[5] remarks: "If I achieve to create fear, in five minutes I can sell hate, in three minutes racism, and on top of that all the other types of discrimination I want".

This climate of fear can be seen in the preventative measures taken by Catalan police in schools, and in the comments made by some neighbours in Ripoll a year after the attacks saying, "I cannot look at them now like before" (referring to their Muslim neighbours). To combat this community groups like "Som Ripoll" (We are Ripoll) are trying to work on recovering the sense of community lost among the local population.

Against these emotional and defensive reactions, extensive work is required of us. A revision of unconscious images in relation to "the others" with which we as community workers, teachers, the immigrant population, the native population, administration, the media, and so on is required. We must learn to understand the different conscious and above all unconscious contributions we are making, as well as discovering what we can do proactively to co-construct a liveable "space in which we live" for everyone.

As Bauman[6] foresaw, "The challenge that currently presents itself to us [those of us that want a society that promotes life] will be to learn to live together with our differences, despite the self-interested attempts to destroy this possibility".

Notes

1 Vidino, L. (2007) "The Hofstad Group: The New Face of Terrorist Networks in Europe". *Studies in Conflict & Terrorism.* 30:7 579–592.
2 Alibek, P. (24 August 2017) https://www.vilaweb.cat/noticies/pius-alibek-acabes-pensant-que-ningu-no-vol-liquidar-estat-islamic/ *Vilaweb*
3 Benslama, F. (2016) *Un furieux désir de sacrifice. Le surmusulman*, Seuil.
4 *To stress the point*: the previous information published by reliable sources such as the newspaper "El Público" (7/18/2019) and not refuted by any institution affirms that the Imam of Ripoll was an informer for the Spanish "CNI" (National Intelligence Centre), that would have maintained contact up to quite shortly before the attacks. The refusal by The Spanish Congress to set up Investigative Committee and the refusal by the CNI to supply information have done nothing but increase fear and distrust in the community.
5 Carlin, J. (2018) Revista "La Maleta de Portbou", núm.13 septiembre–octubre, 2018 https://lamaletadeportbou.com/conversacion-hakan-gunday-john-carlin/
6 Baumann, Z. (2006) "Confianza y temor en la ciudad: vivir con extranjeros", Arcadia.

Bibliography

AlSayyad, N., Castells, M. (eds.) (2003) *¿Europa musulmana o euro-islam?* Alianza Ensayo.
Bion, W. R. (1961) Experiences in Groups and other papers. London, Tavistock Publications.
Bion, W. R. (1966) "Catastrophic change", *Bulletin of the British Psychoanalytical Society*, N°5.
Bion, W. R. (1970) Attention and Interpretation. London, Tavistock Publications.
Erikson, E. H. (ed.) (1959) *The Lifecycle Completed*, W. W. Norton.

Lesaca, J. (2017) *Armas de seducción masiva: la factoría audiovisual de Estado Islámico para fascinar a la generación millennial*, Ediciones Península, Spain.

Napoleoni, L. (2004) *Yihad: cómo se financia el terrorismo en la nueva economía*, Ed. Uranos, Pluto Press.

Sennett, R. (2001) *Vida urbana e identidad personal*, Ediciones Península.

Sennett, R. (1972) *The Hidden Injuries of Class*, W. W. Norton, Ediciones Península.

van Hulst, S. J. (2006) "The Netherlands. Ministry of the Interior and Kingdom Relations. Violent Jihad" in *The Netherlands: Current Trends in the Islamist Terrorist Threat*. The Hague: General Intelligence and Security Service.

Ward, C, Bochner, S, Furnham, A. (2001) *The Psychology of Culture Shock*, Routledge.

Winnicott, D. (1958) Collected papers: Through Paediatrics to Psychoanalysis. London, Tavistock Publications.

Winnicott, D. W. (2006) *Realidad y Juego*, Gedisa.

Zizek, S. (2015) *Islam y Modernidad*, Herder.

Chapter 8

In the Shadow of Envy

Shame in Group Relations Conferences

Ellen L. Short and Janice K. Wagner

> Shame is the most powerful, master emotion. It's the fear that we're not good enough.
> —Brené Brown, Daring Greatly (2012)

The experience of envy occurs frequently in group relations conferences. Envy's close ally, shame, is less often acknowledged in conference work despite the understanding of envy by some psychoanalytic theorists as a defence against shame. Both envy and shame can be problematic and toxic social emotions that may lead to destructive, aggressive attacks, withdrawal, avoidance, and hiding in the case of shame.

Shame is implicated in the intergenerational transmission of trauma and abuse in families, communities, organisations, and institutions that embody multiple aspects of oppression (e.g. racism, sexism, classism, heterosexism, homophobia, xenophobia, etc.). It is a difficult emotion to identify and work with because of its instinct to be hidden, and yet identifying, uncovering, and processing shame has the potential to loosen pathogenic elements in systems, thus enabling more effective group and systemic functioning.

Group relations conferences are temporary institutions where participants learn through experience about authority relations and dynamic social systems. Shame may emerge as participants attempt to cope with concerns about competence, not knowing, or "getting it right." Additionally, shame may emerge as the unknown becomes known and participants begin to recognise their role in unconscious projective processes where unconscious aspects of self are projected onto or into others. These same dynamics often occur among the conference staff as parallel processes to participants' experiences.

This chapter will explore emotion and specifically the experience of shame in group relations conferences. Conference experiences of the authors along with responses to a brief questionnaire on shame that was sent to GRC colleagues will be used to illustrate some of the ideas presented in this chapter. We will also highlight the "shame of learning in public" in a multicultural

DOI: 10.4324/9781003261483-11

counselling and group dynamics course in a graduate program as an analogue to the experiential learning that takes place in group relations conferences.

A Narrative of Shame

I was the team leader of the LSG and, along with three other consultants, we consulted to a membership of about 80 individuals. The group was comprised of three unique cohorts of adults from different professional development training tracks.

During the second back-to-back LSG, the membership was agitated and anxious about the task. Some members of the group were making suggestions to move themselves to a part of the room adjacent to the arrangement that the team and I had designed.

As the membership assembled, an attractive white male participant seated just across from me (a Black woman) looked at me and winked. At the same time, a row of white male members in the back of the spiral stood up to rearrange themselves in another part of the room.

At that moment, I felt a range of emotions, from fear and anger to embarrassment. I was shaking and my heart was pounding as I imagined the large group dis-assembling and leaving the room. I worried about what my colleagues might say about me, sure they would see me as a failure. I also was aware that, in keeping with the learning task of the conference, it would be important to interpret the members' behaviours in terms of their relationship to me, the team, and the director. In my mind, I thought that I needed to make a bold consultation, and that I needed to prove my mettle as a GR consultant in the more provocative Group Relations tradition.[1]

I offered the following consultation to the group: I said something to the effect of, "The membership has put forth one of its members to flirt with me, while others are moving to rearrange their chairs," and using language that was provocative, sexual and profane, I expressed confusion about whether they (the members) were trying to engage me erotically, or whether they were trying to mess with my authority and that of the Director who had authorised me and the staff to arrange the room for their learning.

Everything stopped at that moment, and then, in an aggressive manner, members began to question who was it that winked, as if tracking down a predator. I tried to reinforce the notion that no one member was responsible for this, but rather the behaviours represented something about the group-as-a-whole. Members began to explore possibilities for what it might mean that the group may have challenged the authority of the consultants, and what it might mean that a white man had potentially challenged the authority of a Black woman. As the consultants left together at the end of what was a very powerful and intense session, my colleagues said to me, "I wish he had winked at me ...," with what felt like admiration.

This large group seemed to set the stage for an equally compelling IE, where two small groups of white men occupied two different territories in prime spots, while a group of queer people of colour was left without territory. It was a dynamic conference, but with some very painful moments for learning that stemmed from the dynamics of the LSG and the IE. Members hinted that they might make complaints to their program heads about the language; some also expressed the belief that they, the members, had been at peace with one another before the conference stirred things up for them. I feared they were going to tell on me.

At the closing plenary, the membership was angry. They sat silently glaring at the staff but did not want to speak about what they had experienced or learned. One member scowled at me and then said contemptuously, "You know what happened!" I could only respond with a rather weak entreaty to "say more about their experience so that it could be better understood" and suggested something about "the hatred of learning." Despite the negative expressions, one member, an African American male, came up to me at the staff-member social and said that this was the best conference he'd ever been to because the issues that emerged in the conference felt real for him and relevant to his own experiences in the world.

Later in a casual conversation with a colleague, I learned that my consultation had in fact caused a stir with the program director because of the language I used, and I felt ashamed.

To call this experience the "hatred of learning," as we often do in group relations conferences, does not describe the complex set of emotions and interactions that occurred over the course of the conference. The experience of shame and its derivatives were, I believe, instrumental in both opening up and closing down possibilities for staff and member learning. Shame is *always* present, but rarely acknowledged or named. As a colleague stated quite emphatically, "... Is there any way to do this work without feeling shame?"

Certainly, as I reflect on my own experience of that conference, I can see that an experience of shame is threaded throughout the conference—from my first reaction of feeling challenged by the membership, to my response of wishing to live up to imagined ideals of my GRC "elders-in-the-mind," to the probable reaction of the membership in discovering something painful about their unconscious participation in the social inequalities and attitudes that emerged and were on display in the conference, to a host of other possible experiences that may have emerged, but were neither acknowledged nor discussed. These difficult, shameful, and disturbing experiences appeared to threaten the identities of some while validating reality for others. The aggressive and, some might say, vulgar consultation might even have threatened the program's reputation and brought shame upon it.

In group relations conferences, we tend to look at basic assumption behaviour as a defence against psychotic or social anxieties that arise in groups, even though anxiety itself is often a reaction to the emergence of hidden and uncomfortable feelings, like shame or anger, for an example, (Malan, 1995).

Emotions are a basis of human empathy, attachment, and learning.

> *… emotions are not inner states that we experience only individually or that we have to decode in others, but instead are primarily shared states that we experience through inter-bodily affectivity, often without verbal articulation. We refer to these processes … as "moving through and being moved by." … meaning making comes from moving in the world and being moved by it, when we move each other, we participate in each other's meaning making.*

(Boston Change Process Group, 2018)

They suggest that an implicit process of "trying on" others' attitudes and orientations towards self and other in the world leads to a push and pull to "integrate the others 'take' on the world with one's own" take, ultimately leading to an increased capacity to "participate in human relationships in increasingly fluent and flexible ways by moving through the experiences of others." This process allows us to better cooperate and collaborate with others at home, work and community. My colleague, Dannie Kennedy, often describes the process of staff joining at a GRC as 'the staff trying to find each other' (Danielle Kennedy, personal communication, August 2018), and this sounds very much like a process of "moving through and being moved by each other."

The social emotions of sympathy, embarrassment, guilt, pride, jealousy, envy, gratitude, admiration, indignation, shame, and contempt are complex emotions that require relationships with other people. They serve a communicative function interpersonally and socially, signalling opportunities and warning of threats: facilitating, or frustrating the process of collaboration and cooperation.

Envy of course is a painful emotion that is generated by social comparison. Andrew Morrison (1996), an analyst writing on shame says that envy "diverts shameful feelings of our own inadequacies [real or imagined] and meager accomplishments by focusing on someone else's good fortune and or achievements." In other words, envy may conceal shame, *and* envy isn't the only emotion or expression of unacknowledged or unbearable shame; contempt, anxiety, anger, indifference can also reflect a defence against shame.

Bion, whose work with groups has influenced the development of the group relations model, never mentioned shame directly, as his work was more focused on group development that occurred in the absence of the object. When thinking of the shame state, it is very much about the experience of holding the presence of the object in mind, and of the experience of being seen or unseen by the object (Cartwright, 2017). Our consultations centring around how the director and their surrogates are being taken in by the group, may diminish or even ignore the group's experience of being seen by that authority (fantasied or otherwise) and what that experience may mobilize in it.

We might say that shame is all about authority – our own internal sense of authority as measured by who we are versus who we want to be, and the external authority of the environment as we are seen, *"in the eyes of others"* (Heller, 1982). In conference life, this might be expressed through authority relations between member and director, member to member and member to self, and of course among the staff and director.

There are good reasons for avoiding the of exploration of shame; it is painful at multiple levels. In shame, the self sees itself as defective, inadequate, weak, or vulnerable in the eyes of one's ideal self or other. The sensation of searing, burning, mortification, and paralysis are some of the bodily sensations that accompany the shame affect. Blushing, averted eyes, slumped body, and head down are the more observable physical manifestations of shame, while silence, withdrawal, and indifference may also be behavioural indicators of shame. The shame state can impact one's ability to think and process information. When one feels shamed, it is the experience of being completely exposed and naked, while wanting to completely disappear. Shame is an emotion that disrupts the social bond, bonds that are required for collaboration, cooperation, and survival. Thomas Scheff (2000) states, "... shame figures in most social interaction because although members [of society] may only occasionally feel shame, they are constantly anticipating it ..." The social and evolutionary function of shame seems to be to make sure that we don't get kicked out of the tribe by promoting conformity to cultural, community, and organizational norms and behaviours, and authority, and it can maintain various social arrangements (Heller, 1982; Rukgaber, 2018; Scott, 2011). Conditions of social inequality and oppression can induce shame leading to negative health outcomes (Peacock, Bissell & Owen, 2014).

In response to our questionnaire asking consultants to share an experience of shame in a GRC and to make meaning of those experiences, a senior female consultant shared this experience:

> *During the opening, the Director ... failed to introduce me and went on to the person sitting next to me. As he finished his list of introductions I leaned over and looked in his direction and said to him in the presence of the entire staff and membership, that he seemed to have left me out in his introductions. I was aware of feeling surprised, bemused, then confused, and finally, shamed ... an experienced very senior woman in the membership shouted out that something had happened that needed to be addressed—that the Director had ignored a senior woman consultant on the staff and made her invisible ... At no time during the conference did this get addressed except in the membership ... It now occurs to me that the Director was angry at me and that his anger resulted in forgetting that I was sitting in the staff lineup; thus he forgot to call my name, and effectively made me disappear. It is of course very possible that his own anxiety at managing this very first opening event affected his own sense of competence.*

Shame as a normal, or useful signal is bearable and has a regulatory function, promoting self-control, reflection about one's relationship to the other, and connection.

> *Another consultant shared an experience in which sensitive information shared by a member during a role analysis group was used by the Director of the conference to make a suggestion to the member that he get therapy and the member took offense to this and then confronted the consultant, believing they had shared confidential information with the Director. The consultant felt momentarily ashamed but notes that it helped them "to understand the experience of shame as a powerful and sudden signal rather than something one should act on. Had I excused myself, which is what I wanted to do immediately to reduce my sense of vulnerability, I might have needlessly confirmed the member's worst interpretation and also gotten myself in a terrible mess ... But to the extent I can help myself to not-act on the impulse of shame, I can allow the other to interpret whatever he or she wants and deal with the consequences, without de-skilling myself and 'keep thinking while under fire.'"*

Helen Block Lewis (1978) made a significant contribution to the study of shame when she observed that resistance to change in analysis was due to the presence of unacknowledged shame and guilt in the analytic situation. She viewed resistance as a "social transaction" that "always represents some emotional truth about threatened affectional bonds ..." This brings to mind observations shared by Ed Shapiro (2016), in his essay on Learning from the Director's role when he wrote of the *mutual vulnerability of the authority boundary* and noted that acknowledging the vulnerability of authority *requires recognising the need for the "other," and opens the possibility of love, hatred, envy, sexuality, fragility, and loss of role.*

Shame plays a such significant role in our human endeavours and given its role in mediating and regulating authority relations and promoting or inhibiting collaboration, we would be wise to broaden our attention to the presence of shame as a signal that could inform our learning about the vulnerabilities that exist and that impact one's ability to take a role. We talk about the concept of "negative capability" as the capacity to tolerate uncertainty, and to that, I would add that our work could also move us towards a capacity to tolerate shame long enough to learn from it.

Shame and Learning in Public: School Settings

Although shame literature exists in relation to therapy and psychoanalysis, as a construct, shame has in recent years been introduced and explored in popular culture through the work of researcher and professor Brené Brown. Brown (2013), whose research focuses on vulnerability, empathy, and shame, defines shame as "the intensely painful feeling that we are unworthy of love." Specifically, she defines shame as, "A sense that we are bad, unworthy of love, acceptance and belonging," which reveals a focus on the self. She distinguishes guilt from shame by stating that guilt is characterised as a feeling of having done something wrong or inconsistent with oneself (e.g. "I did something bad"). Brown describes shame as a universal experience for all genders and believes that people receive societal messages that are organised and fuelled by gender. Additionally, she believes that shame is highly individualised, personal, and culturally defined.

Shame as an emotion is integral to the human experience and learning in public is often the site of shame experiences. Learning in public is an experience that most individuals have throughout the life span and most often, this occurs in childhood, in school settings. Brown's (2013) shame research shows that many participants reference having had shame experiences in school and she states, "School is a very tender place for shame experiences."

Jude Walker (2017), who identifies shame as both an impediment and catalyst for transformation in adult educational programs, cites shame as a "core part of the learning and educational experience." According to Walker, we don't talk enough about shame. Walker believes that we bring our "existing shame and shame triggers as learners and educators into the classroom and each learning encounter." She also believes that learning and listening can be impeded by feelings of shame but it can also influence students to learn more.

Both Brown and Walker believe in the importance of surfacing, exploring, and actively working with and through shame experiences. The presentation that my colleague Janice Wagner and I did at Belgirate VI focused on shame in group relations conference work. My portion of the presentation focused on my teaching of two courses in which shame is often prevalent. The following portion of this chapter will focus on both courses and aspects of shame experiences related to adult learning, as well as recommendations for best practices for constructively working with shame in group relations conferences.

I teach graduate counselling students who are training to become licensed mental health and school counsellors and marriage and family therapists at a university in New York. Two of the courses that I teach are required: CSP 660A: Group Work and CSP 659: Counselling in a Pluralistic Society. Our students are adults, primarily Women of Colour with diverse racial, ethnic, and socio-economic backgrounds but joined in their collective desire to become professional counsellors.

CSP 660A: Group Work

This course has a didactic and fieldwork component; the fieldwork consists of 10 weeks of small experiential group work in a fishbowl configuration and application of the group relations model. The small groups are facilitated by one or two Teaching Assistants (TAs) hired by me who have successfully completed CSP 660A and have experience in group relations theoretical practice and application. The TAs are alumni and working professionally in the field of counselling. They receive feedback from me at the end of each class and supervision once a week. The small groups occur during the first half of the course; the second half of the course requires students to co-facilitate their own small groups among their peers in the class. Students are continuously reminded that the small experiential groups are for training and not therapy groups. Each small group session is followed by a large group discussion of what occurred in the groups. When the students co-facilitate their own groups, they are graded on their application of any group theory they choose, as well as their learning about group stages, boundaries, authority, role, and task (BART) (Green & Molenkamp, 2005). Two textbooks, ten journal entries (read only by me and the TA's), and a final paper are required. One of the textbooks is co-authored by me (McRae & Short, 2010).

Initially, the students' curiosity surfaces when I inform them that although their focus might be on leadership, the course is designed to deepen their experiences of being a group member, which is essential for becoming a competent group counsellor. Their anxiety becomes palpable when I inform them that neither the TA's or I will provide topics for them to discuss and instruct them to be authentically who they are in the group sessions and discuss whatever they wish to discuss. They are repeatedly asked to focus on: (1) their member roles, (2) group-as-whole functioning, and (3) the here and now. Students receive points but are not graded on their participation in the small experiential groups for the first half of the course; they are graded for co-facilitation of their groups during the second half of the course.

Shame surfaces immediately at the start of the small group sessions. The students' experiences of shame involve learning in public, being observed by their peers, the TA's, and by me as their professor. As is natural for graduate students, they are very concerned about doing well in the course, but they are at first unclear about what this means. This confusion and anxiety usually continue for several weeks despite my and the TA's repetition of the instructions and assurances that what they're doing in the groups is good and productive work. Their longing to be given a topic by me and/or the TA's also surfaces during group sessions.

Thus, shame feelings arise due to anxieties about performance and their challenges with dependency. Another aspect of shame is connected to observation by me and their peers, which leads to competition between groups and increased feelings of shame about having competitive feelings. This is especially salient because women of diverse cultural backgrounds are often shamed and punished for openly engaging competitively with each other in societal contexts. A final aspect of shame is related to the students' realisation that being in the here and now and making connections with each other and the TA's in the group sessions is much more difficult than they anticipated. In other words, they enter the class thinking that they know about groups because of their past experiences in/with them but quickly realise how much there is to learn about the power of groups and the complexity of group dynamics.

The students' shame experiences can be most readily identified in their small group work, in which they struggle with identity fragmentation, splitting, projection, and projective identification processes, as well as all forms of basic assumption functioning (Bion, 1961). Shame feelings are also documented in their journals, which are often used as repositories for expressions of curiosity, longing, frustration, anger, and wonder—feelings that they're often fearful of expressing openly in their small groups. A phrase that often signals shame is that they *don't feel comfortable* in the small groups. A fantasy often expressed in the journals and group sessions is that everything would be perfect if only their Professor or the TAs would "give them a topic" to discuss, or, would "tell them exactly what to do" in their small group sessions, which is indicative of the group relations model's pull for members' dependency needs and feelings of deprivation.

My choice to implement the group relations model in CSP 660A: Group Work is based on its focus on didactic, observational, and experiential learning. As an African American woman professor who is teaching mostly female graduate counselling students, who are also primarily Women of Colour, there are dynamics related to race, culture, gender, and authority that must be recognised and openly explored for new learning. Also embedded is the thread of shame experiences which often become an integral part of the students' processes of learning. Overall, I believe it's important for the students to "sit" in the spaces of discomfort and not knowing in their learning processes. These experiences often serve to enhance their self-awareness of their vulnerability and strength as counsellors-in-training who will be working with clients who are experiencing life challenges and crises.

CSP 659: Counselling in a Pluralistic Society

CSP 659 is a course that focuses on theories of identity development in multiple domains and multicultural counselling theories and competencies. The nature of biases, prejudices, oppression, and discrimination and their effects are also investigated in this course.

Walker (2017) states that shame can occur in formal and informal educational moments when an individual learns about social inequalities in their collective history related to racial-cultural group privileges. Most of the students in CSP 659 are individuals of colour from diverse ethnic background; the levels of learning and the potential for feelings of shame are complex due to race differences and similarities, immigration statuses, colourism, language fluencies, sexual orientation, age, and other aspects of intersectionality.

Additionally, CSP 659 is essentially a reparative course, which means that it exists, educationally, to teach students about the damage done in the fields of psychology and counselling to women and populations of colour. Thus, this course focuses on aspects of systemic shame and guilt that are embedded in the teaching, practice, and research of counselling and psychology, historically.

The required textbook for the course, *Counseling the Culturally Diverse: Theory and Practice* (Sue & Sue 2016), focuses on (1) White supremacy, institutionalised racism, and the damage done to women and People of Colour in the US, (2) between race racism and within race/interethnic prejudice and the internalisation of White dominant cultural values/beliefs (colourism, classism, etc.), and (3) anti-semitism, sexism, and homophobia. Needless to say, the textbook and lectures tend to make the students feel uncomfortable emotions.

Assignments focus on students' reading narratives of individuals' life experiences of oppression, discrimination, and resilience. Students are also required to write about their own experiences. For example, after learning about microaggressions, they are asked to write about microaggressions they have been victimised by and that they have perpetrated upon others and/or witnessed. Shame feelings that occur for them when doing these assignments involve their heightened awareness of the impact of race and culture and deeper levels of understanding about the ubiquitous nature of privilege and institutional racism.

A salient characteristic of most of the students in our counselling programs is that although they have strong desires to become counsellors, they may have never been in counselling or therapy. This is often due to in part to cultural taboos and fears of counselling that they may have. Moreover, they're not mandated by our department to seek counselling as graduate students. Feelings of shame can surface when students recognise the paradox of wanting to be a counsellor without having experienced the challenging role of being a client.

Shame and Transformative Learning

The literature that states "While shame has the potential to eat away at our souls, it constitutes a desired rejection of a part of ourselves (Kaufman, 1985; Kristjansson, 2014) that has the potential for us to become better people" (as cited in Walker, 2017). Walker cites that, "Shame can lead us to listen, reflect, and restrain. Shame can be a positive force for learning, not just something to overcome: Shame can be a catalyst for transformative learning" (p. 367).

In both courses described above, aspects of shame are embedded in the students' processes of learning. However, their shame experiences often lead to transformative learning. For example, in CSP 660A: Group Work, transformative learning occurs when the students realise the importance of groups in their lives and they begin to understand their member roles, starting with their family constellation, more clearly and deeply. Learning the power of group dynamics as well as the intricacies of boundaries, authority, role, and task (BART) (Green & Molenkamp, 2005) helps them in the development of their professional identities as counsellors-in-training and future change agents in the systems they will work in. In CSP 659, transformative learning occurs through shame experiences related to legacies of harm done in the fields of counselling and psychology and the students' desires to become multiculturally competent and to counsel their clients ethically and empathically. Transformative learning also occurs in relation to their own intersectional identities and recognition of their victimhood, their potential to harm others via their own biases and prejudices, as well as their ability to engage in reparative work, personally and professionally.

Shame and Learning in Public: Group Relations Conferences

Group Relations Conferences provide its members with a temporary institution that can facilitate learning about the salience of group life and systemic functioning. Members' learning often takes place in public; in small, large, and intergroup sessions. Plenaries and role and review groups further support members' learning by allowing them to reflect, process, and speak openly about their experiences. Shame experiences can be an integral part of the GRC experience for members due to the intensity of emotions felt; defence mechanisms are activated, anxieties and fears of the unknown related to boundaries, authority, role, and task as well as conscious and unconscious processes are all fodder for the emergence of feelings of shame. The impact of shame in GRCs in various contexts has also been written about by group relations practitioners (Brazaitis, 2004; Kahn & Green 2004; McRae, 2004; Rosenbaum, 2004; Short, 2007; Skolnik & Green, 2004; Taylor, Smith & Kurlioff, 2004), among others.

Shame at GRCs is also experienced by staff members in their interactions with their peers on consultant and administrative staff. Staff also learn in public in dual roles: as consultants to the members in various group settings; and during staff meetings. Consultant staff members may contend with idealised projections from the members, for example, that they are omnipotent, which, if internalised, can impede their ability to recognise and own their vulnerabilities, anxieties, and fears and may lead to feelings of shame. More experienced consultant staff members may struggle with feelings of shame related to unrealistic expectations of their expertise; less experienced consultants may likewise struggle with feelings of shame about being less seasoned in group work. Shame and guilt may become enmeshed, as well as envy and competition. Consultant and administrative staff may idealise the director; these projective processes can impede the director's awareness and ability to recognise their own challenges in role. These dynamics will be embedded in the temporary institution of the GRC and must be explored to enhance member and staff learning.

Recommendations for Working with Shame in Group Relations Conferences

GRCs present many opportunities for shame to emerge, be recognised, and worked with by members and staff. It is imperative that directors of GRCs recognise that these temporary institutions function as containers that embody multiple aspects of learning in public for staff and members.

Pre-conference work among the Directorate often presents opportunities to explore and discuss instances of shame that occur in the planning, design, and overall containment of the GRC. Making space for this type of exploration and discussion can be important for conference staff work. Once the GRC begins, the Directorate can assume responsibility for introducing the topic of shame to the staff during the first staff meeting. This type of discussion can be facilitated by the Directorate's sharing of their pre-conference experiences with shame in their work together.

The Directorate can model and support consultants to heighten their awareness of their own shame experiences, which may help them to recognise members' feelings of shame throughout the GRC. Administrators have a unique role in boundary management between the members and staff and may have a systemic valence to contain shame. Consultants' recognition and sensitivity to members' shame experiences as well as their own may allow them to create spaces for the exploration of shame during various events of the GRC. This may be especially important during the Role and Application Groups when members are supported to reflect on their experiences in the GRC.

Although not designed to be therapeutic, GRCs do have the potential to enlighten members and staff about the complexities of systemic shame and group life in the places where we live.

Note

1   In my experience, the initiation into the community of group relations consultants often involves informal storytelling about esteemed elders of the tradition and their escapades as well as their provocative in-your-face consultations that are often of a sexual and/or aggressive nature.

References

Bion, W. R. (1961; 1989). *Experiences in groups and other papers.* Tavistock Publications, Routledge.

Boston Change Process Study Group. (2018). Moving through and being moved by: Embodiment in development and the therapeutic relationship. *Contemporary Psychoanalysis*, 54:2, 299–321.

Brazaitis, S. J. (2004). White women: Protectors of the status quo: Positioned to disrupt it. In S. Cytrynbaum, & D. A. Noumair, (Eds.). *Group dynamics, organizational irrationality, and social complexity: Group relations reader 3* (pp 99–116). A. K. Rice Institute for the Study of Social System.

Brown, B. (2013). *Men, women & worthiness. The experience of shame and the power of being enough.* Audible Audiobook. Sounds True, Inc.

Cartwright, D. (2017). A Bionian formulation of shame: The terror of becoming one's self. *Psycho-Analytic Psychotherapy of South Africa*, 25:2, 1–40.

Green, Z. G., & Molenkamp, R. J. (2005). The BART system of group and organizational analysis: Boundary, authority, role and task. www.academy.umd.edu/tle/BART.

Heller, A. (1982). The power of shame. *Dialectical Anthropology*, 6:3, 215–228.

Kahn, W. A., & Green, Z. G. (2004). Seduction and betrayal: A process of unconscious abuse as authority by leadership groups. In S. Cytrynbaum, & D. A. Noumair, (Eds.). *Group dynamics, organizational irrationality, and social complexity: Group relations reader 3* (pp 159–181). A. K. Rice Institute for the Study of Social Systems.

Kaufman, G. (1985). *Shame: The power of caring.* Schenkman Books.

Kristjansson, K. (2014). Is shame an ugly emotion? Four discourses—Two contrasting interpretations for moral education. *Studies in Philosophy & Education*, 33, 495–511.

Lewis, H. B. (1978). Resistance: A misnomer for shame and guilt. In D. S. Milman & G. D. Goldman (Eds.). *Techniques of working with resistance* (pp 209–225). Jason Aronson Inc.

Malan, D. H. (1995). *Individual psychotherapy and the science of psychodynamics (2nd ed).* CRC Press.

McRae, M. B. (2004). Person-in-role implications in taking up the directorship. In S. Cytrynbaum, & D. A. Noumair, (Eds.). *Group dynamics, organizational irrationality, and social complexity: Group relations reader 3* (pp 225–237). A. K. Rice Institute for the Study of Social Systems.

McRae, M. B., & Short, E. L. (2010). *Racial and cultural dynamics in group and organizational life. Crossing boundaries.* Sage.

Morrison, A. (1996). *The culture of shame.* Jason Aronson Inc.

Peacock, M., Bissell, P. & Owen, J. (2014). Shaming encounters: Reflections on contemporary understanding of social inequality and health. *Sociology*, 82:2, 387–402.

Rosenbaum, S. (2004). Group-as-mother (GAM): A dark continent in group relations theory and practice. In S. Cytrynbaum, & D. A. Noumair, (Eds.). *Group dynamics, organizational irrationality, and social complexity: Group relations reader 3* (pp 57–79). A. K. Rice Institute for the Study of Social Systems.

Rukgaber, M. S. (2018). Philosophical anthropology and the interpersonal theory of the affect of shame. *Journal of Phenomenological Psychology*, 49, 83–112.

Scheff, T. J. (2000). Shame and the social bond: A sociological theory. *Sociological Theory*, 18:1, 84–99.

Scott, S. (2011). Uncovering shame in groups: An exploration of unconscious shame manifest as a disturbance in communication within the early stages of an analytic group. *Group Analysis*, 44:1, 83–96.

Shapiro, E. R. (2016). Learning from the director's role: Leadership and vulnerability. *Organisational & Social Dynamics*, 16:2, 255–270.

Short, E. L. (2007). Race, culture and containment in the formal and informal systems of group relations conferences. *Organisational and Social Dynamics*, 7:2, 156–171.

Skolnik, M. R., & Green, Z. G. (2004). The denigrated other: Diversity and group relations. In S. Cytrynbaum, & D. A. Noumair, (Eds.). *Group dynamics, organizational irrationality, and social complexity: Group relations reader 3* (pp 117–130). A. K. Rice Institute for the Study of Social Systems.

Sue, D. W., & Sue, D. (2016). *Counseling the culturally diverse. Theory and practice* (7th ed). Wiley.

Taylor, F. N., Smith, K. K., & Kurlioff, P. J. (2004). Anatomy of a casualty. In S. Cytrynbaum, & D. A. Noumair (Eds.). *Group dynamics, organizational irrationality, and social complexity: Group relations reader 3* (pp 183–207). A. K. Rice Institute for the Study of Social Systems.

Walker, J. (2017). Shame and transformation in theory and practice of adult learning and education. *Journal of Transformative Education*, 15:4, 357–374.

Section 3

Issues of Practice and Methodology in Group Relations

Introduction

This section begins with a chapter by Diane Forbes-Berthoud, et al, that is based on a panel presentation. "Polyglossia or Babel: Working across Languages, Traditions, and Identities in Group Relations Conferences" examines three innovative or experimental GRC's from the perspective of how or whether the language we use in GR facilitates communication ("polyglossia") with others who are new to it or don't share it, or whether instead, it creates confusion and misunderstanding ("babel"). The clearest example of the latter are the accounts of a GRC held at the Art Institute of Chicago with a dual directorship design. The description of the Israeli conferences and the GRCs on Black Authority arguably reflect more polyglossia.

The chapter by Fabio D'Apice, John Wilkes, and Barbara Williams, "Exploring Differences in The Places Where We Live", describes a series of workshops they developed "for creatively exploring cultural experiences and differences that link our past, present, and future. These workshops (one in the US, and three in Canada), apply a storytelling (ST) event embedded in the Group Relations model in the Tavistock Tradition. The goal had been to creatively explore experiences of difference, how they shape identity, and how they manifest in workplaces and society".

In their chapter, "At Home At Work and Vice Versa: Exploring the dynamics of dual/special relationships in group relations conferences and organisational life", Katherine Zwick and Seth Harkins report on the results and implications of research they conducted with AK Rice Institute members who have served on GRC staffs. They report on a questionnaire answered by 78 respondents as well as twelve interviews with "US-based conference directors" with an average of four decades of GRC staff experience. The chapter focuses on what they call "dual, multiple and special relationships", which they find to be pervasive and largely unexplored.

"LFA: When Action is not the opposite of Thinking: Living in a temporary community as a space for experiential learning", by Luca Mingarelli, et al, is an update of the work of Robert Hinshelwood on Learning From

DOI: 10.4324/9781003261483-12

Action (LFA), workshops that reflect "the Therapeutic Community development in the UK and in Italy, the development of community care in Italy, and the Group Relations tradition of experiential learning in terms of methodology". (Unlike in the US, therapeutic communities in Italy refer to facilities for the chronically mentally ill.) They explore the challenges of using GRC elements in these workshops.

Chapter 9

Polyglossia or Babel?
An Exploration of Authority, Innovation, and Identity in Group Relations Conferences

Diane Forbes Berthoud, Patricia Kummel, Janice Wagner, Schmuel Erlich, and Jack Marmorstein

Debates about innovation, experimentation, and change are nothing new to Group Relations. Not only have they been hashed out in events and publications through Belgirate conferences and AKRI Dialogues, but they have also engendered conflict and controversy in Group Relations organisations worldwide. What has emerged over the years is a diverse array of conferences with the potential to move our discussions forward. More recent conversations with directors of these experimental conferences have revealed emerging data and experiences that could chart a different course through old debates. In organisations such as the Tavistock and A.K. Rice Institutes, approaches to the study and experience of authority and leadership are fraught with tensions around rigor, excellence, legitimacy, and Group Relations tradition.

The work presented on this panel integrates innovative and creative approaches to Group Relations, and creates new opportunities for dialogue and research. Polyglossia, distinct varieties of the same language or multiple languages that exist alongside each other, could describe the current state of Group Relations. Others, however, may describe this state of difference as Babel, wherein people with distinct languages experience confusion and the inability to work across boundaries to accomplish a collective task.

This panel explores the following research questions: What can we learn about conference work across differences by thinking of them as encounters between languages? These languages–both the conscious and unconscious – represent the ways we communicate. Do they include the languages of self and other, of the familiar and the new, of the old generation and the young one, or of one culture/tradition and another? Assets of socio-cultural practices, as taboos, norms, and values, and as idioms and vernaculars that mark identity and difference, languages are, in essence, a place where we live. Languages and modes of understanding and experience that are a part of recent Group Relations Conferences (GRCs) are diverse and fascinating: languages of the body and movement, of recovery from addiction, political conflict and activism, art and performance, of social identity and identity politics, and many others. What happens when the language of Group

DOI: 10.4324/9781003261483-13

Relations meets *other* tongues, that is, different models of knowing, studying, and experiencing? And how are the task, study, learning, and experience affected? And what do we learn about Group Relations in the process and what potential remains yet untapped in our development and expansion of Group relations theory and practice?

Of course, Group Relations theory has already contributed a profound insight into the encounter between the native and the "foreign", between self and other. Axiomatic to all Group Relations work is the idea that every encounter with external otherness is also an encounter with internal otherness (and vice versa). Indeed, we posit that the Group Relations community's anxiety about conversing outside itself – across the language barrier – has its origin in conversations that we have not been able to have within ourselves.

The panelists explore frameworks and their experiences of distinct and diverse GRCs: A conference that was literally multilingual (conducted in English, with a membership of native German or Hebrew speakers) is also the one where words took on the most political charge. The accounts of the encounter between the language of art and art direction, versus the language of Group Relations and conference directing focus on how things go in unanticipated directions when translation between these two languages isn't well negotiated. And a conference that centred the study and experience of Black authority while integrating innovative design and structural elements.

"Brave Enough to Listen, Safe Enough to Hear" GRC Conference at the School of the Art Institute of Chicago, May 2017

Patricia Kummel

In November 2016, I was contacted by Leigh Ledare, an artist who had attended some GRCs. He wanted to hire me to organise and direct a three-day GRC that he would film. He intended to use video of the Large Study Group ("LSG") in an art exhibit planned for the autumn of 2017 and winter of 2018 at the Art Institute of Chicago. I was very excited by the possibility that group relations work would be introduced to a wide audience through the art exhibit and had fantasies of recruiting captains of industry, government, religious, and community leaders in Chicago to participate in the conference. Mr Ledare said he would introduce me to some of his patrons, who might be interested in learning more about group dynamics work.

Over a weekend in May 2017, a GRC was filmed in its entirety at the School of the Art Institute of Chicago. I was the Conference Director and Leigh Ledare was the Artistic Director. We had negotiated a dual directorship, with each Director overseeing the work of their team and consulting regularly about work across the work team boundaries. The stated dual task of the conference was to film/study the effect of the camera on human subjectivity and social relations, "... to convey the power and complexity of the experience of being in relationship in our society", while introducing GR technology to the conference members. Mr Ledare agreed to give the film of the conference to AKRI to use for educational and training purposes by the AKRI consultant training program.

Seduced by the possibility of being seen and having our work validated and accepted as useful beyond the usual venues, we (the staff) found ourselves in an intergroup event with the film crew, led by Mr Ledare, vying for the hearts and minds of an inexperienced membership. Would they speak in our language or the language of art? Would they support the conference structure or rebel against it? It did not seem possible for the GR consultants to understand the artists, nor for the artists to understand the GR language and culture. Several conference members were old friends or work colleagues of Mr Ledare; five were experienced AKRI members living in Chicago. All conference members had been vetted by Mr Ledare, who had insisted on doing all the recruitment alone, ostensibly to prepare each recruit to join a GRC that would be filmed. Not surprisingly, this had a great impact on the loyalties of the membership. Throughout the conference, the staff struggled to secure the boundaries of the institution and maintain our reflective and interpretative stance while responding to the artist's expressed desire for footage in which the membership spoke about the camera's impact on its experience in the conference.

Before the third of four LSGs, Mr Ledare came to the staff room to request that he be permitted to go into the LSG room and stand by the window where he could be filmed in relief. My thought was of a Christ figure. He assured us he wasn't planning to speak; he just wanted his presence to spark the members' thinking about the cameras. I noted that the cameras had been referenced frequently, throughout the conference, in all events. I pointed out the purpose of the LSG was to explore what was occurring in the LSG in the moment. He said that, as the conference funder, he had the right to come into the space to "push things along". As a compromise, I suggested that he sit in the LSG room with his team, the film crew. After further negotiation, he agreed not to stand in relief, to stay in a chair by the film crew, and not to talk. Based on Mr Ledare's expressed concern, I asked the LSG consultants to focus the membership on the presence of the cameras and their impact. After the session, the LSG team reported that Mr Ledare had abided by our agreement. The team also reported having consulted to the cameras.

Exactly 15 minutes before the end of the fourth and final LSG, without any further discussion, Mr Ledare walked into the middle of the LSG, sat down in an empty chair, and began talking. The consultants were unable to speak about his action from a systemic standpoint; they used personalised language of assault and attack. While the consultants expressed outrage, most of the members expressed delight that Mr Ledare had joined them. Any feeling of anger on the part of the membership was directed largely at the consultants for reacting so rudely to Mr Ledare's actions. Mr Ledare took the position, supported by most members, that this was his art project, so he should be permitted to do whatever he wanted in the name of art. Two experienced GRC members walked out of the LSG, indicating that they no longer felt able to work, given Mr Ledare's boundary breach.

Looking back, it seems obvious that the Artistic Director was posing a direct challenge to the authority of the Conference Director. If the staff had consulted to the competition between the directors and the question of whether two leaders can collaborate to successfully create and run an organisation or if one must annihilate the other, perhaps the membership would have felt safe enough to explore the complex authority structure and the challenges it posed to accomplishing the tasks of the organisation.

In my Director role, I found it extremely difficult to speak, much less hold the task during the Closing Plenary that followed the conclusion of the LSG. I felt violated on behalf of the institution. After introducing the Closing Plenary, I attempted to join the expressed experience of a member who spoke of feeling shut down; I said that I felt I had just experienced a sort of rape but, since we were no longer in a here and now event, I did not feel able to speak to it. Members expressed shock at my use of the word "rape" and focused on my language, rather than working to speak about their experience of the conference. In retrospect, finding a more systemic, less triggering way of describing my experience might have resulted in a more measured consideration of conference dynamics and their significance for our learning.

Instead, it seemed as if a fight that had been simmering all weekend, then broke out, with people speaking over each other, shouting, raising, and waving their hands. Efforts by staff to redirect members to reflect on their own learning had limited effect, even as consultants spoke about their own learning. I'm not at all clear about the extent to which staff retained its authority. I know that whatever took place was at great emotional cost to at least some of the staff as we tried to manage the container of the conference to the end.

Looking back, I believe that Mr Ledare had been containing much of the competition between the film crew and the consultants as well as the wish we all held for attention and the ambition to have a successful final work product. There had been an incident as the staff was preparing to enter the Opening Plenary that Mr Ledare did not address at the time, but that seems to have coloured his attitude for the duration of the conference and beyond. A member of the film crew had asked if I needed him for anything and I had indicated I did not. I was distracted by the imminent start of the conference, had no actual idea why he was speaking to me and only vaguely recognised him as part of the film crew. Apparently, the crew member took my words as permission to absent himself from the Opening Plenary. In subsequent interviews associated with the showing of his film, Mr Ledare claimed that the Conference Director had violated boundaries and over-stepped her authority by "dismissing" the film crew from the Opening Plenary. Mr Ledare claimed the Conference Director had acted to diminish his authority and demote him to a lesser level of authorisation. Perhaps if I had redirected the crew member to the Artistic Director, tensions would not have escalated so quickly between the Conference Director and the Artistic Director. But it appears more likely that another incident would have revealed the competition and division between us.

How much of the split can be attributed to poor communication across varying languages (art *vs.* Tavi), or to conflicting goals (creating a film with a dramatic arc – something Mr Ledare acknowledged was a concern in an interview with The Box dated 7/29/19 *vs.* holding a GRC focused on member learning), and related issues of competition and ambition, is unknown but it is probably a combination of all of the above. Had the staff spoken to its ambition, shame, ambivalence, excitement, and uncertainty over this risky, unusual venture, we might have been able to hold our task and boundaries and retain our authority as the conference managers.

This collision of two worlds, art and group relations, is suggestive of challenges that many organisations face to be both creative and innovative while also maintaining tradition and structure. It raises warnings about the losses and/or damage that may be incurred when one or the other becomes the foremost primary task. It makes clear the importance of clarity of intention and words: efforts to communicate must be ongoing, even when attempts seem futile. Owning our own feelings of ambition, shame, and frustration, even while performing tasks to accomplish a project is necessary to keep the lines of communication as clear as possible. And acknowledging the language differences and the need for translation, as well as the validity of both languages and goals is essential, even when it feels impossible.

Polyglossia or Babel: Belgirate VI

Janice Wagner

Risk and Opportunity – reporting on a GRC filmed at the School of the Art Institute in Chicago, May 2017.

Patricia Kummel invited me to work with her on this conference that promised to be "big" in that it offered an opportunity to be part of the filming of a GRC in its entirety for an art/film project of a successful New York artist who has attended GRCs and was interested in the model as project for studying social dynamics. I would agree that the spare, limited props in a conference of unrelated individuals charged with studying their behaviour invite a certain dramatic intrigue. This conference appealed to me for a number of reasons, but primarily it would be an opportunity to do work in a setting that represented prestige in the art world, while doing work that is endlessly fascinating and provocative in terms of what one can learn about the intrapsychic, interpersonal and systemic dynamics over the course of a weekend. I would be lying if I did not acknowledge the appeal of being invited to do something special and potentially transformative for my career, nodding to that part of me that desires to be seen, valued, and validated. This was just too good to resist and herein lies at least one of the risks.

We walked into a situation that our imagination failed to conjure, or that we chose to ignore in our eagerness to do something novel, creative and exciting. I was assigned the role of Small Study Group team leader. While most of the conference was filmed, including the staff work, only the LSG would be used for the art exhibit and film for the public, so this allowed the Small Study Groups to be somewhat relieved from the artistic pressures of the LSG. All the filmed material was to be used for training purposes though neither staff nor members signed a release for the use of the material with a training institution, and only the members signed releases with the Artistic director of the film prior to the conference.

From the moment we met the professional camera crew with their expensive equipment and their utilitarian black jeans and black t-shirts, we were in another world. The setting was an industrial, concrete building with high ceilings and student artists and artworks all around. The Artistic director who had been present for pre-conference phone calls disappeared once the conference started and did his work with his crew. (Let me pause here to say that my fantasy of a photographer and his subject is that the artist must work with his subjects forming an emotional bond in a way that inspires trust and respect to the point that subject feels comfortable revealing their vulnerability in front of the camera and to this point, I would imagine a certain seduction that occurs between the photographer and their subject. In the case of the conference, I believe that the conference staff may have felt abandoned by the photographer/artistic director as the conference got underway, inspiring confusion, disappointment, and finally, rage when the Artistic Director failed to collaborate with the staff and essentially abandoned the staff as the conference got underway.) The conference took on the flavour of an inter-group event between the art crew and conference staff, especially when the absent art director showed up for a conversation with the conference staff accompanied by some of his camera crew during the Institutional Event seated on the other side of the aisle, as it were. We continued to work as if it were a conference, growing increasingly anxious when the Artistic director failed to work with us and communicate consistently until he was unhappy with how the LSG was developing under the camera's eye. This was when the conference appeared to explode and the vulnerabilities around conference planning and collaboration became consequential.

The experience of this conference, as an intergroup, provided an opportunity for discovering, or rediscovering important group relations practices and processes that we took for granted. First, there is the recognition that despite the fact that each conference is considered a temporary organisation, there is a structure, or at least a set of predictable rituals, events, and processes in so-called traditional GRCs that can feel institutionalised as has been said by many, most notably Eric Miller. These institutionalised practices lead to certain assumptions about members and staff roles and relationships and how the unfolding events of a conference are interpreted.

I left this conference with a few questions and observations from the experiences that may be useful for future work.

1 It seems obvious now, but it is of utmost importance to articulate and document the contract for the work one is to undertake. The practice of contracting has been a given between directors and their staff, and between conferences staff and members, as articulated in the brochures that members are given to describe the events, and it becomes even more crucial, or as crucial when working with institutions or entities external to the group relations staff. That requires appreciation or knowledge of the institution we are working with, and them of us and how we work. I don't think that we fully understood what we agreed to participate in. This seems to be a failure of imagination on our part at best, an unconscious collusion in rebellion against the authority of a formal group relations organisation. I note that there was relief that this conference was not sponsored by a formal group relations organisation, providing a kind of freedom from a certain accountability along with the prospect and possibility of more creative work. I am left wondering about the extent to which one has to step away from a formal organisation in order to do creative work, or rather, how does one do creative work within the confines of a formal group relations organisation?

2 The Artistic director recruited the members and did a phenomenal job, though we don't know what he said to the members. This raised a question about the type of institution that is created when the Artistic director attracts and recruits the members and excludes the conference director and administrators from the process? Were we consulting to his organisation, or co-creating a unique organisation? Of course, this was the Artistic director's project and he had the most to gain or lose, so it would make sense that he would have a large hand in this, but was this a red flag about his lack of trust or failure to authorise the Directorate to enrol a full conference, or was it just a more practical solution to the problem of recruiting for GRCs? In any case, the issue might have been addressed earlier on in the work. Did we understand, as A. K. Rice outlines in his monograph, *Learning for Leadership* (1965), that

"the conference institution is made up of two major subsystems: pre-conference recruitment-the import system which produces the members; and the conference programme ..." p. 28? I had not given thought about the significance of pre-conference recruitment as part and parcel of the institution that is created in a GRC and what the work of this sub-system might tell us about the relationship and relatedness of membership to staff and to the conference as a whole.

3 Reviewing the film and seeing what happened in the LSG was enlightening as it revealed an observable recording of the group process, at least through words and images, that differed from the truncated and filtered report from the LSG team, highlighting how much what is reported in here-and-now events is an interpretation of events, which may or may not best represent the member experience, which left me wanting to consider other ways to "survey" the members in the here and now events to get their version of what happened.

4 GRCs study authority relations and we had a dilemma around the authority of the Directors' of this conference. The Artistic director hired the conference director to hold a GRC, but as noted, he also recruited the membership. At what point would it have been appropriate to use our authority to put a pause on the conference when it appeared to be off task? This decision was not taken, nor was an interpretation offered about the conflict with authority because we were caught up in an emotional experience that left us reactive versus reflective, I think, losing our roles more frequently and for a sustained period of time than is usual from my experience.

5 When going into the dark, as this experience was sometimes experienced, one is challenged to remain flexible and adaptive while adhering to the task ... this was our dilemma.

6 And finally, this was a conference experience filmed almost in its entirety and the meaning of this fact, could not be fully appreciated until after the film was made and left forever open to the interpretation of others giving new meaning to the concept of there and then, for an experience where the here and now is studied. I believe this fact provoked a great deal of anxiety that perhaps could have been contained better with clarity around authority, boundaries, roles, and contract i.e., Group Relations 101.

Nonetheless, this was an exciting conference probably for all the mistakes and encounters with the unknown. For the above reasons, I would recommend that we make an effort to take on these kinds of risks or opportunities, for the dual purpose of deepening our understanding of what we do traditionally, by discovering the strengths and vulnerabilities in the model, and developing a greater capacity for adaptation and flexibility in our thinking about authority and systems psychodynamics. Only through engagement with the world can we evolve and develop innovative work. For many of you, this is probably not news.

All of us were stirred by this conference and as contentious as it was, most except the administrative staff probably would do this again in a heartbeat.

If one of the goals of this conference was to bring this work more into the world, then we do have some evidence that the film has led to the development of another conference. Two Art students saw *The Task,* the title of the filmed LSG and were inspired to attend a conference at Teachers College. They obtained a grant through the University of Pennsylvania to develop a GRC which happened in the winter of 2019.

Polyglossia or Babel: Notes and Reflections

Schmuel Erlich

1   We are dealing in this panel with the place and function of language, especially as it pertains to the GR tradition and practice. As I am a psychoanalyst, I approach this question from the perspective of the special place of language in our psyche and functioning. In this view, the most significant part is played not by the spoken language, which must be conscious, but by the language of the unconscious. This language finds expression in communications such as dreams, slips of the tongue, performed acts, character traits, symptoms, etc. It becomes a question not so much of the language spoken but of the language one listens to.

2   My second point involves the use of language as a boundary and the part it plays regarding the issue of authority. I am basing my observations on my experience in GR conferences, in both the Tavistock model and our adaptation of it in the German-Israeli conferences.

   a   In the title of the latter – leadership and/or authority are not mentioned. But as I have noted in my plenary presentation, these terms seem to have dropped out in quite a number of conferences described as GR. There is a change in the language, the question is how to understand it. Is it that these issues are no longer important, or that other issues have become more dominant? The changed terminology has important implications that need to be heeded.

   b   In OFEK's international GRCs, the language issue became a boundary issue. English was designated as the conference language. In a way, it reflected an aspect of colonialism, as these conferences were started by and with the help of the Tavistock Institute. The use of English was taken religiously, bowing to the British authorities. It resulted in strange situations, as when a group and a consultant spoke the same language, but "had to" speak English, and not adhering to this was interpreted as a boundary violation. Later on, with growing autonomy, the rule was changed to: English is the conference language "except when all present speak same language ..." I think this demonstrates the function of language as a boundary and an authority issue.

c   Language is, after all, supposed to be a bridge, a means of communication and contact. What happens when you meet the Other across the language barrier? The meaning of terms, of words depends on and reflects the cultural context that gives them meaning. E.g. authority, leadership. Another example: In the third German-Israeli conference in Bad Segeberg, Germany, neutral words that designate a space, a room, or a leader (such as Lager, Raum, Fuehrer) took on heavy associative meaning for the Israelis, for whom it conjured up concentration camps, "living space" and Hitler.

3   The orthodoxy of Group Relations Language: The orthodoxy in which it was adopted in the early Israeli GRCs (see above). It becomes something enshrined in language, and therefore the danger of becoming frozen and fossilised.

4   Language is also a space for meeting, and an area in which diversity and divergence can exist.

5   Finally, language as a definer of national identity – the experiences with Polish and Palestinian participants. In two different conferences, Polish and Palestinian members formed groups based on the need to speak their own national/personal languages. In both instances, this was done in a way that set them up as an opposition to the conference institution: the Polish group met clandestinely outside the territories, while the Palestinian group met within but isolated itself from the rest of the conference. Both instances underline the need for safeguarding a national identity by coming together around language as well as opposition to authority.

The Psychodynamics of Black Authority: Reflections on Innovations in Design, Decision-Making, and Approaches in Group Relations Theory and Practice

Diane Forbes Berthoud

On the Matter of Black Lives, a non-residential GRC, was designed to study the authority of Black people, with the stated the task: *to explore the unconscious elements of leadership, authority and identity in human systems with particular focus On the Matter of Black Lives.* Authorised by Group Relations International and RISE San Diego, the conference took place in the wake of the so-called post-Obama era and was conceived during the

2016 US presidential election season, fraught with political strife amidst the rise of critical political and social movements such as #MeToo and the Black Lives Matter. The conference was developed and offered with an all-Black staff. It was the second of its kind, with the first conference, *Authority and Identity: An African American Perspective,* being offered in the mid-1990s in Washington, DC. It was, at that time, one of the largest GRCs in a decade, which may have signalled a deeper curiosity and willingness to explore unconscious processes influencing the exercise of Black authority.

Theoretical and experiential perspectives on the second conference became part of a 2019 Harvard University book project, *Race, Work, and Leadership in the 21st Century: Learning about and from Black Experience,* which explores how race matters in people's experiences of work and leadership (Roberts, Mayo, & Thomas, 2019). In that chapter, we discussed critical events from the conference to elucidate the complexities of our experiences studying Black authority. We offered a framework to understand the psychodynamics of Black authority and discussed the implications for the study of leadership and authority (Forbes, Taylor, & Green, 2019).

This chapter, based on the presentation from the 2018 Belgirate meeting, lies at the intersection of the second and upcoming conference on Black Authority. For the third time in two decades, we will turn our attention to Black authority in a group relations context, explore connectedness across and within systems, application of conference learning to other contexts, and examine the relatedness between conference learning and larger socio-political and psychological dynamics. The impending conference will occur in another election year in the US (2020), amid complex and deeply entrenched psycho- and political dynamics. The focus of this discussion is on authority, the integration of intersectionality, structure and process, and the ways to apply and integrate group relations practice in conference life focused on Black authority. I'll briefly present a model and lessons learned in the organisation and planning of a GRC focused on Black authority.

Group Relations work as it intersects with work and people's organisational experiences reveals a set of lenses and perspectives, languages to make sense of our organisational experiences of leadership and authority. Developed in the early to mid-20th century, group relations theory drew on the work of scholars such as Bion (1961), Klein (1946), and Wells (1985, 1995). Taken together, their work has offered an enduring and complex interplay of frameworks that inform systems and psychoanalytic approach to groups, focused on the interrelatedness and influence between individuals and groups, and groups as systems. Their work has centred tensions around authority relations, belonging, anxiety, roles, and leadership and built a foundation for GRCs that have traditionally explored authority relations. These conferences have typically paid little attention to identity-based analyses or impacts in their formulation and execution; the influences of culture, race, gender, and other related constructs were rarely explored.

More contemporary Group Relations scholars and practitioners, however, have studied these intersections and impacts of cultural, ethnic, age, racial, sexual identity and orientation, and the ways in which negative stereotypes, societal scripts, identities, and group dynamics can complicate unconscious and conscious group dynamics. Their collective work offers a systems analysis that contributes to a more complex and nuanced understanding of groups and organisations as systemic factors such as authority, roles, leadership, power, and interpersonal relations, intersect with identities (Green & Molenkamp, 2005, 2015; McRae & Short, 2005, 2009).

Early work integrating an intersectional approach to Black authority was scarce (Dumas, 1980). Forbes (2002, 2009, 2017) has offered an intersectional approach to leadership that integrates gender, class, nationality, culture, and other social identities to build on work that approached race and gender as mutually constituted systems of relationships, particularly those that impact Black women's group and organisational work. As we continue this work to develop group relations and study Black authority more intentionally, I offer the following questions:

1   What is the future of Group Relations and what is the place of Blackness in its construction and transformation?
2   How/where is Blackness situated in Group Relations theory and practice?
3   What new directions can we forge as a Group Relations community?
4   How can we innovate and create new pedagogies and methods in Group Relations theory and practice that actively integrate identity and leadership?

Figure 9.1 summarises our experiences and learning from the most recent conference as well as other experiences of/with Black authority: Generations/ Generativity, Sentience/Privilege, Marginalisation/Alienation, and Black authority archetype. These themes represent unconscious, tangible, and salient dynamics and frameworks that affect and inform our work in the study of Black authority (Forbes, Taylor, & Green, 2019).

The second conference had a racially and ethnically mixed membership, which was comprised of predominantly women and people of colour. Members ranged in age from 20+ to 80+ and were of varying gender identities and sexual orientations.

Generations/Generativity speaks to dynamics of tensions and movements around process, authority structures, and norms across generations, and the ways in which diverse family, regional, and faith backgrounds intersected with the experience across generations. *Sentience/Privilege* addressed complications of task, relationship, desire, and significant and formative relationships that collided in an already complex undertaking of the study and experience of Black authority. *Marginalisation/*

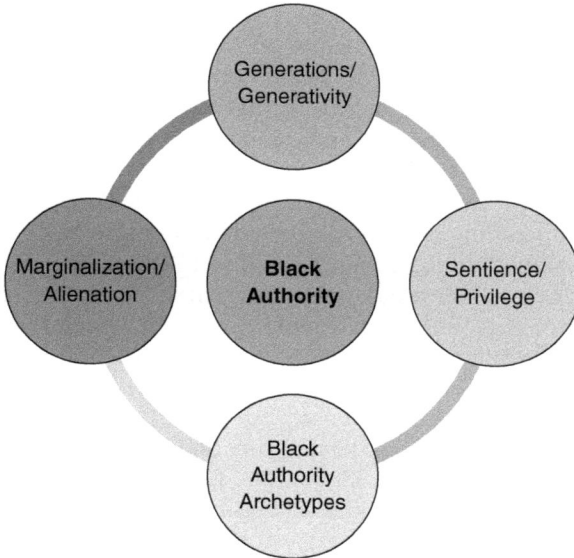

Figure 9.1 Cycle of Containment: Responses to Black Authority

Alienation – captured the complexities of authorisation and deauthorisation in and out of authority roles as Black, leaders, followers, and participants throughout the conference. Previous work (Dumas, 1980; Wells, 1985, 1995) addressed aspects of these historical, psychological, and organisational conundrums of oppression and authority. *Black Authority Archetypes,* a theme that was evoked in and through unconscious processes, centres on pervasive stereotypes and images (Mammy, Sapphire, etc.) that intersected with the learning and processual experiences of the conference (see Forbes, Taylor, & Green, 2019).

Between offering the second and third conferences which I will direct, the *generations/generativity* spectra will continue to guide the process for production and preparation for the upcoming Black Authority conference. First, ancestry and identity are central components of African Diasporic ethos and cosmology; Blackness and constructions of race and ethnicity are inextricably linked to identity and history – past, present, and future. As there is little explicit focus in Group Relations on race and authority, we will seek to generate new knowledge, innovation, and approaches that will inform and challenge traditional thinking and practice in the study of authority through the continued exploration of Black authority. Generativity is also closely tied to succession, a theme about which the previous conference director was concerned. The staff, therefore, consisted mostly of junior to mid-level staff members, twice the number of senior staff. The hope was to offer training and development opportunities for them to learn and study in a complex and unusual environment, since no other conference had this explicit focus, and other conference directors had not often included many people of colour on their staffs. The dynamics, however, of having a mostly inexperienced staff were almost uncontainable. The management team later grappled with how the next conference might be staffed, and what we would be needed to ready the next generation, given the new historical and sociological complexities of race, particularly in the United States. The lessons for the upcoming conference included attention to the generational dynamic in and with the selection of staff. While there is no set formula, as director, I hope to strike a balance among three groups: more senior, mid-level, and junior staff, and there would be a mentor and development model that cascades throughout the system, wherein junior staff would be paired, as a consultant-in-training, with more seasoned staff for consultations and check-ins throughout the conference.

I hope to lead with some understanding and a deeper exploration of *differentiation, diversity, and authority,* thus facilitating processes with staff to deepen members' learning and strengthen the conference enterprise as a whole. Black Authority, Blackness, and indeed, Black peoples represent complex and nuanced experiences and backgrounds across multiple contexts, including in Group Relations work. Therefore, any serious study of Black authority will require a strong commitment to diverse and inclusive perspectives about positionalities that include diverse socio-economic classes, immigrant groups, regional, occupational, sexual orientations, gender expressions and identities, linguistic histories, cultures, and others. Such an examination can make for a complicated and enriching group relations study of authority. How the conference will be staffed, what I write in the opening statement, how the conference is framed and contextualised are all intended to explicate Blackness, Black authority, and authority relations more broadly.

Based on our collective discussion as a conference directorate, I will incorporate the lessons learned in future conferences that call for closer attention to the balance across various levels of staff experience; focused work on containment, the understanding of complex dynamics of race, history, and the study of the here-and-now, as well as our collective work in this area that can be transformed into rich and engaging learning. Consideration will also need to be given to the role of elders in the work, given the importance of seniors in Black culture, history, and cosmology. Potential areas of study and conference themes that future research could explore are the complexity and intersections of Black authority, colonisation, and integration of Group Relations, which has been borne out of a European tradition, yet adopted and integrated by peoples of colour (including Black, Latinx, indigenous, and other groups) that have been impacted by colonialism.

Panel Conclusion

Across the various conference experiences and designs discussed, some common elements emerge related to the tensions and complexities in the encounter of difference, the other, and contemporary modes of knowing and studying Group Relations. One conference integrated art and technology, and non-Group relations staff as part of the system; another centred Black authority and Black lives, with an all-Black staff, while exploring innovations in design and structure; another ventured into complicated national, historical, linguistic, and psychological boundaries in a conference with Israelis and Germans. Taken together, our work integrated innovative and creative approaches to Group Relations study and practice, and collectively challenged us to re-imagine authority, leadership, and followership, in a milieu of diverse and complex systems.

References

Bion, W. R. (1961). *Experiences in Groups and Other Papers*. Tavistock Publications.

Dumas, R. G. (1980). Dilemmas of black females in leadership. *Journal of Personality and Social Systems*, 2:1, 3–14.

Forbes, D. A. (2002). Internalized masculinity and women's discourse: A critical analysis of the (re)production of masculinity in organizations. *Communication Quarterly*, 50:3–4, 269–291.

Forbes, D. A. (2009). Commodification and co-modification: Explicating Black female sexuality in organizations. *Management Communication Quarterly*, 22:4, 577–613.

Forbes, D. A. (2017). An Integrative Analysis of Diversity and Discourse in Women's Leadership. In C. Cunningham, H. Crandall, & A. M. Dare (Eds.), *Gender, Communication, and the Leadership Gap* (pp 201–222). Information Age.

Forbes, D., Taylor, F., & Green, Z. (2019). The Psychodynamics of Black Authority – Sentience and Sellouts: Ol' Skool Civil Rights and Woke Black Lives Matter. In L. Roberts, A. Mayo, & D. Thomas (Eds.) *Race, Work, and Leadership: New Perspectives on the Black Experience* (pp 291–310). Harvard University Press.

Green, Z., & Molenkamp, R. (2005). The boundary BART system of group and organizational analysis: Boundary, authority, role and task. Retrieved from https://www.it.uu.se/edu/course/homepage/projektDV/ht09/BART_Green_Molenkamp.pdf

Green, Z., & Molenkamp, R. (2015). Beyond BART: At the level of the field. The BART system of group and organizational analysis: Boundary, authority, role and task. Retrieved from https://www.grouprelations.org/ssg-readings

Klein, M. (1946). Notes on some schizoid mechanisms. *International Journal of Psychoanalysis*, 27, 99–110.

McRae, M. B., & Short, E. L. (2005). Racial-cultural training for group counseling and psychotherapy. *Handbook of Racial–Cultural Psychology and Counseling. Training and Practice*, 2, 135–147.

McRae, M. B., & Short, E. L. (2009). *Racial and Cultural Dynamics in Group and Organizational Life: Crossing Boundaries*. Sage.

Rice, A. K. (1965). *Learning for Leadership*. Karnac Books.

Roberts, L., Mayo, A., & Thomas, D. (Eds.). (2019), *Race, Work, and Leadership: New Perspectives on the Black Experience*. Harvard University Press.

Wells, L., Jr. (1985). The Group-as-Whole Perspective and Its Theoretical Roots. In A. D. Colman & M. H. Geller (Eds.) *Group Relations Reader 2* (pp 109–126). AK Rice Institute.

Wells, L., Jr. (1995). The Group-as-a-Whole: A Systemic Socioanalytic Perspective on Interpersonal and Group Relations. In J. Gillette & M. McCollom (Eds.) *Groups in Context: A New Perspective on Group Dynamics* (pp 49–85). University Press of America.

Chapter 10

Exploring Difference

A Group Relations Adaptation

Fabio D'Apice, John Wilkes, and Barbara Williams

Introduction

No matter where one looks in the news, every day, you will find something about difference, about being different and protests about the injustice, this difference has attracted: indigenous resistance, violence against women and trans persons, anti-racism movements, LGBTQ+ groups, Black Lives Matter, discrimination because of disability, discrimination due to mental illness, the Irish Traveler ethnic group, Trump's travel ban on Muslims, and much more. As never before, perhaps, this is the place where we live.

What sense can be made of these experiences, in society and in organisations, of being different, of the difference of the Other and differences at large? Most importantly, rather than perpetuate these differences in discriminatory or violent ways, is it possible to explore these dynamics in a meaningful way? Over the last few years, we have offered workshops for creatively exploring cultural experiences and differences that link our past, present, and future. These workshops (one in the US, and three in Canada), apply a storytelling (ST) event embedded in the Group Relations model in the Tavistock Tradition. The goal had been to creatively explore experiences of difference, how they shape identity, and how they manifest in workplaces and society.

The three authors live in different countries, have very different life contexts and histories: we are different in age, gender, cultural history, education, and class. When we first met, we were drawn to each other and we discovered we shared a particular concern about the heteronormativity that seemed embedded in many of the events we had participated at the International Society for Psychoanalytic Study of Organisations (ISPSO), the Organisation for Promoting Understanding of Society (OPUS), and at Belgirate. We were curious about the absence of younger members and 'racially different' members or people with disabilities.

We wondered, what made for the predominance of a certain 'membership' (without devolving into simplistic identifications) within these international spaces and whether there might be room for 'difference'.

DOI: 10.4324/9781003261483-14

As Group Relations Consultants, we believe in the experiential learning opportunities that Group Relations Conferences (GRC) offers to study one's own behaviour and that of others and the group as it happens in real-time. Further, in the unique environment of a GRC, hidden aspects of one's motivations, behaviours, defences, identifications, and ways of narrating one's self are brought to light in an accelerated learning experience which can enable a deeper understanding of oneself, leadership and followership, and can further one's own leadership capacities, and the leadership potential of others. However, our experience has been that whilst GRC design and the quest for the unconscious dynamics might facilitate 'naming' and 'identifying' differences, its focus falls short of adequately exploring them and making them meaningful.

We continued to explore our mutual curiosity and concern, deciding that the best way to pursue this was to form an online reading group with each other. We then met regularly for two years looking for socio-analytic articles about difference, theories of meaning-making and unconscious processes in groups and organisations. We read widely: from the Tavistock Clinic Series publication exploring new dimensions in social defences against anxiety to Lacanian perspectives on language. Ultimately this led us to a proposal to offer a brief Tavistock-inspired workshop with a specific focus on 'difference'.

With colleagues in NYC, and supported by Kathleen White, we offered a half-day workshop there in 2017 with 16 members, all of whom were experienced in the group relations methodology. In terms of the social context of which we were part (in the UK, the US, in Europe, and in Canada), we each felt the impact, in different ways, of the seismic changes in the political and social forces operating in the Western World. The Inauguration of President Trump the week before our NYC workshop had an impact on the members, raising even more fears and anxiety around race. In that workshop, telling stories of difference came to be central.

The learning that took place then inspired our next three annual workshops to explore difference using traditional Group Relations elements with several adaptations, including the use of ST.

Different cultural contexts would impact how and what differences were explored in a difference workshop/conference. Working with a recognition of how different socio-cultural contexts might affect the exploration of difference, and with our Group Relations investments, we became fascinated with ST as a mode of learning and working with unconscious processes.

In our reading group, we were deeply affected by Kathleen White's (2002) paper 'Surviving Hate', in which she tells the story of her own experience of racism, hatred from others, and her own, self-hatred. And in the reading group, we shared our own 'stories' of hatred, shame, love, and fear. We became fascinated with ST, so much so that we wanted to experiment with it as a method for 'exploring difference' and how that might be incorporated into a Group Relations workshop: difference in terms of race, gender, sexuality, age, class, and nationality. We believed ST might add an important dimension to GR methods – but weren't sure how. We had experienced it as a powerful tool for us in creating connections, building meaning in the realm of differences, and enabling here and now understandings and wanted to see if others might as well.

Certain 'stories' seemed to garner more attention. Was this related to the social context in which the stories were told? To identities in the room and the identifications that were being mobilised? How were our own identities and identifications, as the conveners, being called upon and ignored? Was the emphasis on some differences reflecting current and often urgent societal tensions? To what degree would a focus on difference and its complexities highlight some and not others?

The authors, having experienced ST as a powerful tool for creating connections and building meaning in the realm of differences, integrated it into workshops. Yannis Gabriel (2000) quoting Polkinghorne (1988) writes about ST and narratives:

> *Narrative emerges as the privileged form of sensemaking, as "the primary form by which human experience is made meaningful."*
> (Gabriel, p. 15, Polkinghorne, p. 1)

Although Gabriel writes about ST and organisational change, we find his ideas helpful in deepening our understanding of how and why stories work the ways they do to deepen meaning-making. We are also aware of the risks that stories create their own 'truths' from which it is difficult to explore differing perspectives.

In this chapter, we describe our design as well as the theories that we made use of in designing and implementing the workshops, the themes that have been emerging which touch on the unconscious material that arises when there is a focus on 'difference' and conclude with our thoughts about next steps. This work has been primarily developed in working with Barbara Williams' group relations network in Toronto (Insight for Community Impact – ICI).

Design – Telling Stories and the NYC Experience

The task for the initial event in NYC was to 'explore the difference' among the members. The design included two small study group (SSG) events intended to focus on the here and now experience. What happened in fact was that members shared and continued to share memories in which they experienced their own differences with each other.

The stories in the NYC event were very varied and visually rich, connected historically and structurally to past and current political or cultural issues in the US and focused predominantly on 'race', despite a range of other differences that might have been explored: gender, sexuality, class, religion, or age – all of which were readily apparent in the room. We noticed, none-the-less, that this ST did create a sense of a shared experience and connection of 'being different' even as specific identifications of race coalesced in the room. But attention and work in the here and now were much more difficult to sustain and in NYC ST seemed to preclude the possibility of working in the here and now. Was the propensity to 'tell stories' a defence against the anxiety of exploring real, complex, and perhaps painful differences in the room? Could there be none-the-less, some utility in using stories and here and now events together? What mode of consultation would be needed in each of these different events?

Exploring Difference Workshops in Toronto 2017, 2018, 2019

Group relations events in Toronto are activities undertaken by a network of professional and social justice organisations called Insight for Community Impact (ICI). It is a network, that for 6 years has offered a variety of GR events: a 5-day more traditional GR conference, several week-end conferences on authority and irrationality, SSG training and a regular consultant practitioner training for consulting to GR events and for learning to take up an interpretive stance for leading networked organisation and co-ordinating community projects in Toronto. The ICI work has been actively supported by James Krantz, Danielle Kennedy, and Kathleen White. After our experience in New York, the Difference Workshops have become a 2½-day annual offering for ICI.

ICI works through an acknowledgement that there are, along with individual psychical histories, social, historical, and economic differences which shape how each of us come into contact with ourselves, each other, and a group. These are differences which disadvantage and oppress some while advantaging others. In a country like Canada, with its history of colonisation and racisms, ICI believes that its current ways of talking about difference are ineffective and ritualistic. These ways of talking rely on discourses of 'equity, inclusion and diversity' (IED). But at a community level and in organisations and institutions, these discourses associated with social justice[1] have not helped making deeper contact with others so that the structural differences which lead to oppression which affects us all can be addressed in new and perhaps different ways. It has been a learning process for ICI to know how the theme of 'exploring difference' works in 'the community': does it neutralise structural oppression? Does it provoke the exploration that feels so necessary now to building the capacity to confront these issues?

Can the theme invoke what ICI has been calling 'curious regard' for how individuals are different and how they might be the same (Keith, 2010)? Is it a working proposition, a defence, the dream of the director, the ICI community, or all of the above?

ICI is committed to working together to explore how differences have, in the past, precluded accomplishing 'things' together: work, campaigns, leading, following, building vibrant communities. The goal is now to explore what can be done 'differently' in the here and now.

The Importance and Limitations of the GR Design

In the three difference-workshops in Toronto, and learning from our NYC experience, we incorporated a ST adaptation into traditional GRC elements: small and large study groups and application groups. In this section, we examine the design and its adaptations including how the ST adaptation has worked and some of its limitations.

Within the Tavistock tradition, the group relations 'conference' structure according to Correa et al (1981) quoted in the Group Relations Reader 2 (Coleman & Geller, 1985), is intended to:

> *form a temporary learning institution, in which members are relatively free to study through experience as well as conceptualization, the covert dynamics within the groups, the political mechanisms between groups, and the impact of authority and its exercise on the individual, the group and the institution.*
>
> (p. 288)

We want to indicate several important variations from this conceptualisation in the Toronto setting:

* Not a temporary learning institution: as members work with and/or know each other and have on-going relationships in the various organisations from which they come, the conference or workshop environment is more 'on-going' in nature;
* Freedom to study: while this is the ethos of the difference workshops and there is freedom to explore and learn, there is more interpretative attention to difference and social justice than to authority;
* The impact of authority: relates not only to the figures who 'hold' formal staff authority but importantly to other members who might in work settings hold authority roles; as well as to authoritative ideas and discourses of equity, inclusion, and diversity which 'hold sway' over how members have learned to navigate the 'truth'.

There are some design variations between the three difference-workshops, but for the purposes of this article, we will focus on the 2019 workshop.

The Workshop Design for the 2½-day event made use of traditional GRC elements: SSG = small study group in the here and now; LSG = large study group in the here and now, Review and Application = opportunities to review the workshop experience and explore an 'outside dilemma'. The 'adaptations' to the Tavistock methodology include the *Large Story Telling (LST) and Sharing Dilemmas* (SD) in the following sequence over the 2½ days:

Friday evening	Saturday	Sunday
Welcome and Introduction	SSG	LSG
Storytelling	LST	Review and Application
Sharing Dilemmas	SSG	Review and Application
	LSG	Closing and Review
	SSG	

Storytelling and the Exploration of Difference

For the three years that we have been designing and staffing *Exploring Difference Workshop*, we have offered an opportunity for members to 'tell a short story' of their experience of difference. In the 2019 Workshop, we used the LG event, immediately following the opening Welcome to invite these stories. The Welcome itself, provided by Barbara Williams as the Director, referenced the significance of the usual University venue which sits on 185 acres of prime downtown real estate originally purchased from the Mississauga Indigenous Community in 1787 for objects like gun flints and hats. It was then formally purchased by the British Government for an additional 10 shillings in 1805. This land acknowledgement is one of the 2015 Canadian Truth and Reconciliation Recommendations and an important Indigenous practice – to 'recognise' the original ownership of the land'. The director's welcome, her presence as a white woman signals a coloniser 'history' with which members will begin to contend.

We then ask members to share short stories of 'difference' – a moment when they felt 'different'. We have found that this invitation sets the stage for members to begin to think about and attend to the 'differences' which they have experienced in the past and begin the difficult work of exploring and sharing these in the present. Sometimes the stories are from a more distant past, sometimes they are very current – and in every case, they are 'present' and 'alive' in the room as they are shared and re-experienced. We do not consult to this event but rather allow members to make use of the time to 'tell their story'.

Frequently, racialised[2] members, those who experience 'being raced' structurally, culturally, and socially, will tell stories of their experiences of discrimination or racism from an 'other', sometimes members tell stories of religious discrimination or anti-gay discrimination. These stories expose the pain of feeling excluded, belittled – in some cases physically threatened or harmed – or barred from opportunities. But at the same time, they speak to a desire to sustain a sense of self in relation to the other.

There are long-standing connections between ST and psychoanalysis (Brooks, 1994, Gabriel, 2000, Brown & Humphreys, 2006) in which the importance of narration has been explored. Narration offers a way of making and re-making meaning and creating containing knowledge for the self. Ferro (2006) writes extensively about the central ways in which stories 'tell ourselves' about ourselves. Following Ferro's (1999) work on psychoanalysis and ST, we also see the narrative process as a way of enabling the member to situate her or himself in this process of noting a difference, or giving voice to it in the presence of others – and while it may have been repeated other times (or never), this new telling constitutes a fresh review of the experience.

Grosz (interviewed by Henley, 2013) tells of a patient who, returning home at night, is convinced that when she turns her key in, the door to her apartment will blow up: terrorists have set a bomb to kill her, but she finds the apartment cold and empty. He adds:

> *The bomb fantasy frightened her, but it stopped her from feeling so alone. It's better to think someone is out to hurt you than that no one cares about you. Indifference is a catastrophe, and her paranoia was shielding her from it.*

Her story to herself (and others) is one of fear. But his analysis raises important questions about how our stories of fear of others or mistreatment by others might be experienced as a defence against 'connection'. Does such fear of the other also function as a way of 'shielding' us from indifference – a more frightening catastrophe?

In a diverse group of members such as those in the Toronto workshops, members talk about differences they experienced in terms of race, class, relation, religion, and sexuality. But the predominant difference in Toronto – as in New York – centred on racial difference. This focus is most notable in the SSG and the LSG. In what way do these stories and interactions 'shield' members from the more frightening possibility of complete indifference?

To add another layer to this possibility of indifference, after our first Toronto Workshop – one of the non-Canadian consultants noted how polite the members and staff were to each other and that there seemed to be a great sense of reticence pervading the interactions. This is not reluctance but more an inclination to be silent or non-communicative, reserved or possibly restrained in expression. We have begun to think of this as a form of stereotypical (though by no means applicable to all Canadians) 'reticence' not infrequently ascribed to 'Canadians'. When one of us (again a non-Canadian) was a consultant to the Large Study Group in the third Toronto Workshop, he found the dynamics difficult to understand, as though there was on top of this reticence a coded interaction going on which, as a non-Canadian, he could not enter into the mystery. By the third large study group, he was silenced and unable to speak to the dynamic. There are of course many nuanced differences between those new to Canada and those who have been in Canada for generations and certainly not everyone was 'polite'.

Emerging Themes

We turn to the key emotional themes which have emerged in the workshops so far and the unconscious mechanisms which the group as a whole utilises to defend against them:

- Hatred and rage
- Despair in the disconnectedness
- Shame

Hatred and Rage

We have observed that once the workshop is underway, people try to connect with each other, and to be engaged without being engulfed by an other or the group, to learn and grow and make a 'difference in the world' – especially in the community. Members tried in many ways to 'make contact' with each other 'as people' and had to contend with how difficult, and often impossible this is.

In the LSG, the degree of hatred was palpable as racialised women directed their rage to white women in the room as a means of working with their hatred of systems, structures, and individuals that have discriminated against them: rage at the figure of their white, older, very Canadian director. At one point in the LSG, the chairs around the director were moved such that the chairs created a funnel directly exposing the director to the membership. The intensity of the interaction on this occasion provoked consultations directed at the rage, but its intensity made it very difficult to consult to the fear of intimacy which the hatred may have been defending against.

Melanie Klein's (1946) work on defences in the paranoid-schizoid (P-S) and depressive (D) positions helped us making sense of some of the dynamics and processes we witnessed in the workshops around hatred. In particular, the fear of the bad objects annihilating from inside gave way to the characteristic defensive splitting and projection of bad objects. The affect was hatred towards the split and projected part-objects. The taking of the P-S position allowed the hatred to manifest and to be allocated at least in the white women in the membership.

Winnicott (1994) noted in his now well-known paper that the analyst consultant must have his or her own hatred 'well-sorted out and conscious'

(p. 350). Sorting this out well, is definitely a work in progress, because until and unless we are able to do so as consultants, we cannot effectively consult to or explore differences. Working with member's hatred raises counter-transference problems for consultants and if consultants have not worked through their own hatreds, and a tendency to 'hate back', then members are rarely able to work through their own problems with hatred.

Despair in the Disconnectedness

Although there was considerable difference to explore in the Workshop: sexuality, religion, age, gender, class, and profession, the key difference that was worked with time and time again in the LSG and SSG was that of race. At every LSG event, racialised women shared stories of their experience of painful discrimination – stories to which white women generally could not 'respond' – except to say, 'thank you for sharing your story'. Racialised men often flanked the racialised women and provided support to their efforts. The stories seemed to be focused – not so much on exploring the difference – but of impressing others about the painful consequences of that race-difference. Steiner in 1993 presented his theory of psychic retreats as states of mind that provide relief from unbearable anxieties at the cost of isolation and withdrawal. These powerful systems of defences help individuals to avoid anxiety by avoiding contact with other people and with reality. Being in the psychic retreat contributed to despair of disconnectedness, and this creates however an impossibility of linking and making connections and that in turn gives rise to the despair or un-connectedness.

For the white, woman director, there was enormous unconscious rage directed at her and other white members. We believe that the task of the staff, is to tolerate this aggressivity and to work with it while trying simultaneously to give meaning to what such rage might imply and defend against. This implies working through hatred and being able, as consultants, to know our own hatred, to receive it, and contain it.

Shame

Shame played an important function in blocking the capacity for white members to engage. In a fascinating text entitled *Shame and Its Sisters*, Sedgwick et al. (2006) refers to Tompkins basic set of affects placing shame at one end of the affect polarity shame-interest, suggesting that the pulsations of cathexis around shame, of all things, are what either enable or dis-enable so basic a function as the ability to be interested in the world. Like disgust, shame operates only after interest or enjoyment has been activated and inhibits one or the other or both.

In a similar way, shame according to Ikonen and Rechardt (2010) is a reaction to the absence of approving reciprocity. In its most basic form, shame is the stranger anxiety of an infant when trustingly reaches his or her arms towards an adult, and then notices that it is not his or her mother – he interrupts the approach, turns his head away, hides his or her face, and starts to cry.

Shame is often hidden, and in order to deal with it, it is important to know how to find it and make it conscious. ST seems to be able to help in the bringing to consciousness some of the shame associated with exploring differences. Nevertheless, shame is often difficult to recognise since it gets mistaken as guilt, which it resembles at least phenomenologically. However, the main difference is that guilt refers to an act of the person, either psychic or concrete, whereas shame refers to the whole person.

Shame generates anger, which is often directed against both the self and others. The images of revenge and violence brought forth by shame-rage, on their part, give rise to guilt (Lewis,1987). The anxieties typical of the psychic retreat, also called by Steiner (1993) as borderline position, are those of shame, humiliation, and embarrassment.

The immediate experience of leaving the psychic retreat is that of being exposed, observed, and seen and this can be potentially shameful. We believe that the experience of exploring differences is the equivalent of an experience of leaving the psychic retreat and where being seen in one's own differences has the potential to bring shame and humiliation. The urgent need, also described by Steiner (2011), for relief from these experiences of shame might force the members to move quickly into the P-S position by creating the bad objects through splitting and projection, and experiencing and giving an experience of hatred. What seems to be missing in our work is the challenge that any analyst has with his patients, which is to facilitate the shift to the depressive position where loss of the damaged and hated object can be mourned, and guilt can facilitate reparation.

This last aspect of the work is especially true when the membership belongs to the same organisation or community and has already developed a previous working relationship or will continue to work together outside the temporary experience of the workshop.

We want to learn much more about the shame of 'being different'; and why exploring this is important in terms of Self-Other transformations and why consultation is required. What matters more than the story is the storyteller who may experience a more conscious, integrated sense of self while speaking to someone who listens. Such integration is the opposite of shame, for shame is the dis-integration that happens when a self cannot find empathic recognition from an emotionally significant other.

Conclusion

It has been a powerful learning experience for us, and for many members to contemplate that shame, rage and outrage, rendered them helpless and yet could still remain in contact with others and the group. Learning from experience is an idea and an intention upon which the method is based. It means working, thinking, feeling in the moment, and recognising that this is extremely difficult to do. It requires members and staff to share their stories, to think as they feel, to step back from the feeling charge, and find language to contain the impulse to sit in the complexity and difficulty. We know from past experience, that this is the charge that enlivens many members, keeping them learning long after these events, but it can also be quite frightening and disconcerting.

Notes

1 Here social justice is understood as a political and philosophical concept which holds that all people should have equal access to wealth, health, well-being, justice, and opportunity. https://www.investopedia.com/terms/s/social-justice.asp
2 'Racialisation' is a social process of ascribing ethnic or racial identities to a relationship, social practice, person, or group that did not identify itself.

References

Brooks, P. (1994) *Psychoanalysis and Storytelling*. Blackwell.
Brown, A. D., & Humphreys, M. (2006) Organizational identity and place: A discursive exploration of hegemony and resistance. *Journal of Management Studies* 43: 231–257.
Coleman, A. D., & Geller, M. H. (1985) *Group relations reader 2*. A. K. Rice Institute.
Correa, M. E., Klein, E. B., Howe, S. R., and Stone, W. N. (1981) A bridge between training and practice: mental health professionals' learning in group relations conferences. *Social Psychiatry* 16: 137–142.
Ferro, A. (1999). *Psychoanalysis as Therapy and Storytelling*. (P. Slotkin, Trans.). Routledge.
Ferro, A. (2006). *Psychoanalysis as Therapy and Storytelling*, 2nd Ed. (P. Slotkin, Trans.). Routledge/Taylor & Francis Group.
Gabriel, Y. (2000). *Storytelling in Organizations: Facts, Fictions, Fantasies*. Oxford University Press.
Henley, J. (2013). Interview with Grosz. J – *The psychoanalyst's tale – why we need to tell stories to relieve our sorrows*. Available at https://www.theguardian.com/books/2013/jan/07/stephen-grosz-psychoanalyst
Ikonen, P., and Rechardt, E. (2010). *Thanatos, Shame and Other Essays: On the Psychology of Destructiveness*. Karnac Books.
Keith, N. (2010). Getting beyond anaemic love: from the pedagogy of cordial relations to pedagogy of difference. *Journal of Curriculum Studies* 42(4): 539–572.
Klein, M. (1946). Notes on some schizoid mechanisms. *International Journal of Psychoanalysis* 27: 99–110.
Lewis, H. B. (1987). Shame and the narcissistic personality. In D. L. Nathanson (Ed.), *The Many Faces of Shame* (pp. 93–132). Guilford Press.
Polkinghorne, D. E. (1988). *SUNY Series in Philosophy of the Social Sciences. Narrative Knowing and the Human Sciences*. State University of New York Press.
Sedgwick, E. K., Frank, A., and Alexander, I. E. (2006). *Shame and Its Sisters: A Silvan Tomkins Reader*. Duke University Press.

Steiner, J. (1993). *Psychic Retreats.* Taylor & Francis.

Steiner, J. (2011). *Seeing and Being Seen: Emerging from a Psychic Retreat.* Routledge.

White, K. P. (2002). Surviving hating and being hated: some personal thoughts about racism from a psychoanalytic perspective. *Contemporary Psychoanalysis* 38(3): 401–422.

Winnicott D. W. (1994). Hate in the counter-transference. *Journal of Psychotherapy Practice and Research* 3(4): 348–356.

Chapter 11

At Home at Work and Vice Versa

Exploring the Dynamics of Dual/Special Relationships in Group Relations Conferences and Organisational Life

Katherine M. Zwick and Seth B. Harkins

Introduction: Initial Hypotheses and Observations

This work was borne out of theories and observations in our shared 50 years of experience working in Group Relations Conferences (GRCs), organisations, and institutions. Our initial approach to the challenge of dual/multiple or special relationships[1] (D/Ms) in GRCs and organisations involved four hypotheses.

First, we hypothesised and observed that there has been an increasing trend across multiple disciplines in the United States over the post-modern era away from privileging objectivity, impartiality, and vertical hierarchy towards increasing and recognising as valid subjectivity, intersubjectivity, intersectionality, "special relationshipping," and matrix-based and/or collaborative leadership. We established this trend in our presentation at the A.K. Rice Institute's (AKRI) *Dialogues III* in 2016 (Crenshaw, 1989; Garza, 2016; Griffith, 2016; Haraway, 1991; Khaleelee & White, 2014; Zwick & Harkins, 2016).

Second, we hypothesised and observed that the Traditionalist Model of practicing and studying group relations (GR) and dynamics in the here-and-now does not offer a comprehensive way of observing, speaking to, and working with special relationships and their impact on authority and GR in here-and-now conferences. Therefore, it is failing to address authority and GR as they exist in modern life. We established this paucity of guidance in extensive literature reviews in 2016 and 2018, as well as in our empirical data for our Belgirate 2018 presentation, which we will further outline below (Zwick & Harkins, 2016).

Third, we hypothesised and observed that group dynamics are influenced by the presence of special relationships – both at GRCs as well as in at-home organisations and institutions – and that the difficulty working with them meaningfully indicates significant survival-level threats of several kinds posed by their presence. We offer theoretical hypotheses to understand better the influences and defenses enacted in the presence of special relationships for the field's consideration in part V of this chapter

DOI: 10.4324/9781003261483-15

and encourage further research to establish the presence of these and possibly other dynamics.

Fourth, we hypothesised and observed that GR as a discipline would benefit from developing an operational model, with new terms, a consideration of a code of ethics, and possibly a new basic assumption – "basic assumption: strangers" – for working with the impact of special relationships on here-and-now dynamics of small and large groups and institutions in a way that enhances our understanding of group and organisational dynamics.[2]

Research Design

Our research design was approved by the National Louis University Institutional Research Review Board and included three elements: an extensive GR literature review, a survey of GRC staff who have worked in United States GRCs, and interviews of US GRC Directors.

The Survey – Methodology, Results, Summary, and Conclusion

Methodology

We surveyed United States GRC staff via the online platform Survey Monkey through a 23-item Likert scale questionnaire. The questionnaire was designed to test the perceptions of US GRC staff about dual/multiple relationships (D/Ms) in US GRCs and organisational life.

We contacted potential GRC staff by emailing the AKRI list of 193 members. Of the 193 members emailed, 78 participated for a 40% participation rate.

Respondents were required to note what kind of staff role they had occupied at GRCs in order to participate in the questionnaire.

Respondents noted that their experience in a staff role in US GRCs started as long ago as 1973 and as recently as 2017. The largest number of respondents was from Chicago, Illinois, followed by Boston, Massachusetts, New York, the West Coast, and other regions (in that order). Of the respondents, GRC consultants represented the largest cohort, followed by administrators. Participation was fairly evenly distributed among directors, associate directors, and assistant directors for administration.

Results of the Survey

We have highlighted below a few specific survey items and their results for the purposes of this chapter.[3]

Perceived Prevalence of Dual/Multiple Relationships found in US GRCs As Reported by Questionnaire Respondents

Type of dual relationship	Percentage of respondents endorsed perceiving at GRCs
Previous Staff Member–Previous Staff Member Relationship	80.52%
Previous Staff Member–Previous Conference Member Relationship	77.92%
Previous Conference Member–Previous Conference Member	77.92%
Faculty–Student Relationship	76.62%
Colleague–Colleague at Same Institution Relationship	75.32%
Student–Student at Same Institution Relationship	61.04%
Boss–Subordinate Relationship	44.16%
Romantic Relationship Outside Conference	38.96%
Doctor/Therapist–Client Relationship	36.36%
Faculty–Teaching Assistant Relationship	29.87%
Consultant–Client Relationship	28.57%
Members of the Same Peer Support Group or Community (12-step, SMART Recovery, Church, Synagogue, etc.)	27.27%
Teaching Assistant–Student Relationship	23.38%
Members of the Same Community Organisation, Condo Organisation, or Similar (including PTA, other local organisations)	23.38%

In total, 95% of the 78 participants in our survey indicated experiencing "outside relationships" or dual relationships of some sort in GRCs in which they were in a staff role. These results indicate D/Ms are a significant factor and presence in GRCs in the US.

Staff Perceptions of How US GRC Directors Work with Dual/Multiple Relationships

The question we asked here was: "In your experience as a staff member at GRCs in which [D/Ms] were present, did the Director acknowledge the possible impact (beyond just the mere presence) of these [D/Ms] on the group dynamics arising in the conference?"

Options for responses	Percentage of respondents endorsed
Yes – always (all directors, every Conference) – always referred to this possibility using basic assumption … language but not with language regarding dual relationships per se	15.38%
Yes – always (all directors, every conference) – always referred to this possibility specifically using the language of dual/multiple or special relationships	21.79%

(Continued)

Options for responses	Percentage of respondents endorsed
No – never (no directors on any conference)	5.13%
Sometimes/some directors – referred to this possibility using basic assumption ... language but not with language regarding dual relationships per se	10.26%
Sometimes/some directors – referred to this possibility specifically using the language of dual/multiple or special relationships	21.79%
Sometimes/some directors – some directors on some conferences acknowledged the impact using only basic assumption language AND some directors on some other conferences acknowledged the impact using dual/multiple relationships (or similar) language	19.23%
I cannot recall	6.41%

As you can see from the endorsed responses, there was some acknowledgement and work with D/M relationships, but it is proportionally less than we would expect given the high prevalence of D/Ms perceived in GRCs. Additionally, the responses suggest that different directors work with or acknowledge D/Ms with significant variance.

Perceived Impact of D/M Relationships in US GRCs

A rounded 72% of respondents reported that the impact of dual and multiple relationships on GRCs and organisational life is unexamined in the GR literature regarding basic assumption group phenomena. 80% of respondents reported that the way D/Ms may be overlooked or unworked in conferences could be considered an "as if we are strangers" basic assumption dynamic.

Perceived Relevance of this Topic to Organisational Life Outside of GRCs

Ninety-seven percent (97%) of respondents indicated D/M relationships to be a significant dimension in the world of work and academic institutions. Ninety-one percent (91%) of respondents indicated such relationships are commonplace in the workplace and academic life.

Survey Summary and Conclusions

In general, the participants regarded D/M relationships to be a significant phenomenon in GRCs and in organisational life. The 40% participation rate indicates D/Ms and US GRCs is an important issue worthy of further examination.

D/Mrelationships in US GRCs involve a variety of permutations, each of which merits further inquiry in terms of impact. Less than 50% of respondents endorsed that Directors were *always* seen to have addressed the impact of D/M relationships on a GRC, even though 95% of respondents endorsed experiencing the presence of D/Ms in GRCs in which they served in staff roles.

A large percentage of respondents view this issue as unaddressed in the GR literature. There is a perception of considerable variance in the degree to which and the methods with which Directors and consultants acknowledge and work with the issue.

The results were positive for considering a possible "as if we are strangers" basic assumption.

The absence of research in this area suggests D/M relationships are a taken-for-granted phenomenon in US GRCs, indicating significant group-level defenses around working with and understanding the impact of D/M relationships on here-and-now dynamics.

The Interviews – Methodology, Results, Summary, and Conclusions

Methodology

12 US GRC Directors were interviewed. Interviews were confidential and anonymous. Each participant signed an Informed Consent. Interviews were conducted telephonically or via videoconference and were audio recorded for verbatim transcript analysis.

This inquiry was guided by this organising question:

> *What is the lived experience of GRC Directors of D/M relationships in GRCs?*

Four additional questions were posed:

> *How have D/Ms been exhibited in conferences you have directed or participated in?*
> *How have D/Ms influenced conference dynamics?*
> *How have you managed or addressed D/Ms in your role as Director?*
> *Is an ethics code necessary to guide professional practice in addressing D/Ms in group relations conferences?*

The interview protocol consisted of 18 pre-determined questions as well as additional spontaneous questions throughout, intended to explore answers in more depth where indicated. Interviews were between 29 and 129 minutes in length. We consider our experienced Director interviewees to be "high warranty voices" within the US GR community. The average number of years of experience of the Directors interviewed was 40 years of experience.

Of the 11 Directors who reported on their demographic information: 8 identified as Caucasian or White; 2 identified as African American, 1 identified as mixed, 6 identified as female and 5 identified as male. All reported their ages in the 60 and 70s. The Directors were living in various regions in the US, being fairly evenly distributed among the North East Coast, the Midwest, and the West Coast.

Results

100% of Directors interviewed reported:

- The presence of D/Ms at multiple conferences on which they were staff or directed
- Experiencing challenges working with dual, multiple, and special relationships in conferences
- Experiencing a lack of guidance or direction from existing GR literature to work with D/Ms
- Believing in the importance of addressing special relationships in the pre-conference work and throughout the conference

Two Directors interviewed reported a desire for continued opportunities to work on a staff with strangers and/or to attend conferences as a member who is a stranger to other members. 11 directors reported that D/Ms seem inevitable in conferences at this point in time, just as they seem inevitable in organisations.

One director reported that few or no D/Ms within conferences is more ideal than any (or more) D/Ms from the perspective of learning about the primitive group unconscious:

> *"I think the value [of group] relations is to have a stranger conference where it is absolutely here-and-now ... You get the more classical experience ... I think that it having multi-layers of [relatedness] to a staff member, for example, makes it harder to have the shock of whatever the most primitive levels are ... I'm not saying it's impossible. But it's much harder to do when all those other layers of relatedness are there."*

Some Quotations from Directors Interviewed on the Presence of D/Ms at Conferences

These quotations were chosen as representative of views reported within the interview data set:

> *"Dual relationships are ubiquitous."*
> *"You have [D/Ms] at almost every conference. How can you not have it?"*

"Part of [choosing someone you already know to work on GRC staff with you] comes from fear ... choosing someone that you don't know and can't trust... [You hire] folks you know and can rely on."

"Dual relationships are problematic any time you have a friend on staff."

"[The first conference where I was a member] the special relationships were student-teacher, and the conferences where I was on staff recruiting were people in supervision with me."

"I think [D/Ms] were there from the beginning. I mean, if women were chosen by their ... personal connections to the men ... That's how things were done in those days ... special relationships were there."

"[Staff selections were] based on insider relationships."

"I understand that in the early days of this work, half of the people at conferences were analysts sending their patients to conferences."

"Probably for as long as there's group relations conferences ... it's part of the basic structure of the conference, where you may have staff or you know staff or members, or staff and members who in sort of very clear-cut dual relationships that are kind of built into the conference structure ... Often ... [D/Ms are] a factor in staff choices."

"It's almost impossible to avoid all kinds of nested complicated relationships ... It's a fairly small community of people."

"Some Directors only want to hire people they feel entirely comfortable with."

Challenges Directors Face with D/Ms at Conferences Regarding *Students* on Staff or in the Membership

These quotations were chosen as representative of multiple views reported within the interviews.

"There were, at least within [a particular university-based conference] system, many staff that had gone through [its educational] programs of one sort or another, and in some ways were beholden to being on good terms, either in dissertations ... in many ways, in my mind, a very incestuous system."

"No [a teacher-student relationship in a conference] is not different [from a therapist-patient relationship in a conference] except in regard to one particular aspect of the student-teacher relationship, which is that none on my patients' livelihoods depend on their relationship with me."

"My understanding for students is that their professional development might very well be experienced as on the line. The analogy would be around sexual boundary violations between faculty and students."

"So what happens is the dysfunction of [the educational system] has to get imported into a conference, and, if you try to ... ignore it, any more

than you'd ignore the patient doctor relationship, I think you've got a potential problem."

"I think that coercion is there. I think also if you have power over someone's graduation or certification … that you're playing with something really hot."

Challenges Directors Face with D/Ms at Conferences Regarding *Patients* on Staff or in the Membership at GRCs

These quotations were chosen as representative of multiple views reported within the interviews.

"I think that's really hard on … the therapist to … stay in role, conference role, which is loaded for a staff member anyhow."

"It was somewhat surprising and upsetting to me that the staff were sort of regarding her more like a patient than, you know, a member."

"My instinct tells me … there's too much space for unconscious damage to occur."

"In some cases, it might be, it could be a very positive thing for both sides. So … that's a judgment call in terms of where the person is in therapy, what kind of therapeutic relationship it is."

"Things come in disguised packages."

"I have always been quite aware of the fact that one, there are [a particular staff member's] patients or prior patients [on staff or in the membership of a GRC] and two, I was taking them on. And … in a sense, was I getting at him by getting at them?"

"I think the therapy-patient relationship is complex and special."

"I think it's possible to put enough distance between a therapist consultant on staff and a patient, but it has to be carefully figured out how to hold several boundaries so that there's no damage done."

Challenges Directors Face with D/Ms at Conferences Regarding Business Partners or Other Types of Relationships on the Staff or in the Membership of GRCs

These quotations were chosen as representative of multiple views reported within the interviews.

"I think that [business colleagues at conferences] are not all the same, because … you want people in the same company to come together."

"So yes, when I know someone is married to somebody else on staff, that raises a flag for me … how well is the Director going to manage that? Because it has to be managed in one way or another."

"[Business relationships at a GRC] is a can of worms because ... I think the unfortunate part is that it ... ends up being very bifurcated. Good and bad."

"The fact that people come from the same company, and maybe that's one employer, that's like, that to me is not a problem. That's what you want to happen."

"My whole [business] staff went to at least one conference."

Director Methodology for Working with Dual/Multiple Relationships within Group Relations Conferences

Directors were asked to describe methods they used or observed being used for working with the presence and impact of D/Ms in GRCs.

We found that the methodology reported fell into six (6) categories, which we outline here.

Please note we put an asterisk next to reported methods that we understand to be a ritualistic practice. Rituals may serve as an organisational defense against greater understanding and against observing here-and-now dynamics (Hirschorn, 1988).

Reported Director Methods in Pre-Conference Work

1 The Director, in the staff work, names out loud the reasons they hired each staff person.*

    For example: *"And the Director, sometimes, if they really want to be open will say 'This is why I hired you' as a way to at least name some of the prior relationships."*

2 The Director, in staff pre-conference work, asks if any of staff members have special relationships with any of the members and removes Small Study Group (SSG) consultants from SSGs where there are salient ties between member(s) and consultant.*

    For example: *"I think the first thing you do is look at the selection of small groups and make sure that ... those relationships get marked so that staff members are as far as possible, not in intimate contact with ... anyone in the small group, where that is a strong relationship."*

3 The Directorate and admin team removes or minimises known member-member relationships from SSGs, often with input from consultant staff.*

    For example: *"I think at every single conference I ever was a staff member, it was [SSG assignments were] pre-selected ... which is making the assumption we can control for things."*

4 The Directorate and admin team place members of similar professions or institutions in the same Review & Application Groups (RAGs).*

> For example: *"If you're trying to cluster [within RAGs] people with a certain professional background and you have somebody on staff that's in the same background and sometimes that can govern the choice as opposed to not having a prior relationship."*

5 If a therapist or doctor is on staff with a patient, one Director describes their methodology as *"I alert the person on staff that they're likely to be scapegoated on staff if they don't share [that they are my patient.] I don't demand that they share it. I just alert them, in my experience, there's likely to be some unmanageability."*

> This Director does not openly share, in his role as Director, who is his patient on a conference staff or in the membership. The onus is on the patient to disclose. There is no indication of a further methodology beyond disclosure in this case.

6 Disallowing certain types of special relationships within staff or across the staff-member boundary.*

Therapist/Doctor–Patient Relationships

> For example: *"I would not want anyone who has had a patient-therapist relationship ... I would not want both of them on staff ... I really think that's too much."*
> *"I've basically not had anybody ... I don't like the idea of having one of my [patients] in a conference I'm in."*
> *"I think it's too risky."*

Additional Quotations from Directors on Methodology for Working with the Presence and Impact of Dual/Multiple Relationships within GRCs

> *"[D/Ms are] absolutely unavoidable. I think the only thing you can do is pre-work. You know ... how do we manage not to let this get in the way of member learning, first of all."*
> *"I always ask [of staff members], 'Do you have a patient or student or someone like this in the conference?'"*
> *"I have generally worked very hard to bring all of that [D/Ms] to light."*
> *"All staff have the obligation to acknowledge those relationships where they exist."*

"You have to keep the role [you are in at the conference] very, very absolute."

"You're gonna either lose it [an effective holding environment for the conference] by not being able to manage it. Or you're gonna lose it by acting as if you're managing it, when you know damn well, you're not."

"[There's a] critical need to have very clear and tight boundaries because that's part of what we're trying to teach."

Director Thoughts on Instituting a Code of Ethics Regarding Working with D/Ms in Group Relations Conferences

We asked the Directors interviewed if they had a desire for a code of ethics within the AKRI in order to help navigate working with D/Ms at GRCs.

A desire for a code of ethics was mixed among the Directors. Some rejected this as imposing regulations that could not be effectively implemented. Some liked the idea but wondered how an ethics code could be implemented. Some thought an ethics code was a good idea.

All the Directors indicated training in the area of special relationships in conferences was one way to address the challenge of working with D/Ms in GRCs.

Emblematic Quotations from Directors in Support of a code of ethics

"I think it would be great, and I think it would be really difficult to implement."

"I like the idea of a Code of Ethics."

"Unless an organisation has a healthy relationship to its values, it's fucked up."

"I think a Code of Ethics would be nice. I can't imagine how it would get implemented … especially because everyone does have such complicated relationships. You know, I'm not sure how that would even look."

Emblematic Quotations from Directors Noting Difficulties with a Code of Ethics

"The idea that we clearly need some hard and fast guidelines doesn't work in my sense because you're trying to reduce something … that is very complicated."

"You have to look at each situation differently, because there's no simple rules and regulations [for] attachments."

"I am much more into informed consent of … the process and to what extent we prepare people beforehand and to what degree do we work with them after hand in order to integrate the work. But that seems to me an equal, ethical challenge."

In answer to the question: would an informed consent for conference participation mitigate the concern for patients in the membership or on staff with therapists on staff? *"No, I don't think so ... I don't think you can ... manage the irrational by making a rational choice."*

Interviews Summary and Conclusions

According to the 11 Directors we interviewed, D/Ms have been present in GRCs for a very long time – some say from the very beginning of GRCs within the US. These experienced Directors acknowledged that D/Ms are a reality of contemporary organisational life. They also recognised the challenges posed by D/Ms, particularly the impact when unaddressed or insufficiently addressed; hidden (intentionally or not) relationships, in particular, are generally thought to dilute, erode, or inhibit staff and member learning.

There was some variance in Director self-appraisal of their respective adeptness at addressing the presence and impact of D/Ms in conferences they have directed. Most Directors interviewed agreed that skillful addressing of D/Ms and their impact in conferences is sometimes a significant challenge. Director methods for dealing with D/Ms include expecting openness and honesty about them from staff, leading in un-concealing them, and exercising informed judgment in assigning members and consultants to SSGs in particular, where the number of special relationships is more often than not attempted to be reduced.

Director methods for addressing D/Ms in GRCs were reported as predominantly ritualistic in nature.

There were mixed opinions regarding a code of ethics but agreement that training is needed for GRC Directors in managing D/Ms in conferences.

Experienced Directors agreed that there is a lack of GR literature to guide practitioners in addressing D/Ms in GRCs and organisational life.

Why Do We Have So Much Difficulty Working with D/Ms in a Significant and Meaningful Way?

In this part, we put forth some of our theories as to why we collectively as US GR practitioners have so much difficulty working with D/Ms in a significant and meaningful way in GRCs.

1   Practitioners in the US have little guidance from existing GR literature about how to work with the presence and impact of D/M relationships in GRCs or organisational life.
2   The GR literature asks us, primarily, to leave special relationships "outside" of GRCs and to approach here-and-now conferences "as if" those outside relationships are either not present or are not significantly

impactful in terms of understanding the here-and-now system-as-a-whole. We are asked to enter here-and-now conferences and take up a consultancy stance "without memory or desire" (Bion, 1961).[4]

3   We hypothesised – and our interviews with Directors validated – that staff bodies at US GRCs approach the topic of special relationships *ritualistically*. The ritualistic naming of special relationships – without further work – may serve as an organisational defense against greater understanding (Hirschorn, 1988). Greater understanding – beyond ritualistic mechanisms or attempting to control for special relationships – of the impact of D/Ms in the here-and-now may bring about primitive fears of exile due to a perception that one may be engaged in (emotional, structural) incest or nepotic enactments, and/or relationships that subvert the hierarchical norms we (pretend to?) agree to. Thus, the ritual protects us from going deeper, feeling these feelings, and contending with the impact of these dynamics on the group-as-a-whole. We also hypothesise that there are defenses against *adaptive* use of special relationships by engaging in their ritualistic naming without further study.

4   Related to number 3 above, we further hypothesise, as we have mentioned earlier, that there may be an "as if we are strangers" basic assumption undergirding much of group dynamics in contemporary US GRCs as well as in organisations at large wherein special relationships exist. While we do not have the space or task here to offer our full thoughts on this possible basic assumption, we want to refer to it in connection with our research and hope to put forth an article for the international community outlining the qualities of and evidence suggestive of this possible basic assumption ("BA: strangers").[5]

Why Might We Defend against Acknowledging or Working with Maladaptive Elements Related to D/Ms?

Special relationships can introduce into here-and-now systems, or reveal, threats to individual, subgroup, and group-as-a-whole survival in various ways. Some of these threats are related to potentially *maladaptive* elements of D/Ms.

Inbreeding and Failure to Thrive

An abundance of outside affiliation being imported into a here-and-now system threatens to create an inbreeding or repetition of imported ideas and relationships within the here-and-now system. This reminds us of the image of an ouroboros (closed circuit, eating itself) rather than a nautilus (open system).

Too much affiliation – not enough diversity in a system – could thwart evolution, the growth of ideas, or the ability to see a system clearly. There are not enough outsiders or newcomers to the system. The over-affiliated system – with highly salient ties imported into the here-and-now – could eventually fail to thrive. This is similar to how we understand inbreeding working genetically in species.

An outside affiliation being imported into a system may in some ways threaten to close a system. These dynamics may be even harder to detect or skillfully work with if we, culturally in GR work, act as if they do not exist or do not have an impact on the here-and-now system (this section informed in part by Aram, Baxter & Nutkevitch, 2012).

Incompetency and Exile

D/M relationships imported from the outside may be particularly prone to seduction and corruption – across boundaries of authority, role, and task. Particularly, but not only, when special relationships involve an authority-subordinate relationship. These dynamics may become more corrosive or harmful in the group consciousness if we act as if they don't exist or do not have an impact on the here-and-now system (Laing, 1969; Pepper, 2014).

We may have difficulty admitting to our vulnerability to corruption or being corrupted due to fear, shame, and guilt – similar to the feelings generated by the incest taboo – and a desire to be seen as competent and by so being (competent), avoid exile or annihilation from the group or system (Freud, 1919, 1930; Mauss, 1990; Sophocles, 2006).

Special relationships can call into question the competence of staff members who have special relationships with other staff or with conference members. Fears of being perceived as incestuous, nepotic, or conversely benefitting from incest or nepotism, threaten perceptions of personal competence and may subvert the agreed-upon hierarchical norms: rules, overt and covert, concerning training, order, merit, objectivity, and "fairness" or our "right to work." Similar fears and feelings related to special relationships may inform group member dynamics as well.

A group-level incest taboo – and the enormous shame even the hint of incest may provoke at the group level – may make it challenging, if not impossible, to look clearly at the vulnerability we all have to losing our integrity, to violating a boundary, or to becoming seduced out of a role (for example), in the presence of imported D/M relationships.

These dynamics may become even more intense or impactful on the group unconscious when we act "as if" they don't exist or do not have an impact on the here-and-now system. (Pepper, 2014) Perhaps the unconscious line of thought is, then, "Better to pretend this does not exist and is not influencing us – because were this to come to consciousness and into view of the group, would the Emperor be found to have no clothes? Would our supposition of order, fairness, and objectivity flowing from the top down be revealed to be if not a sham in its entirety, then at least significantly more complex?" (Pepper, 2014; White, 1986, 1997).

Why Might We Defend against Working with or Acknowledging *Adaptive* Elements Related to D/Ms?

The Threat of Subjectivity

Outside affiliation may introduce significantly more *subjectivity* into a system that traditional GR theory wishes to observe *objectively*.

Intersectionality studies, network theory, and post-modern political theories assist us in understanding that special relationships and even salience within relationships may positively and adaptively subvert hierarchical order for the benefit of a system or task, and that salient ties can be an integral aspect of functional, collaborative, and cooperative systems (Alford, 1994; Butler, 1990; Chrislip, 2002; Collins, 2000; Crenshaw, 1989; Garza, 2016; Haraway, 1991; Karl & Baker, 2001; Khaleelee & White, 2014; Lorde, 1984; Simmons, 2015; Zwick & Harkins, 2016).

A key component of adaptive special relationshipping[6] is transparency about salience, process, decision-making, and power-sharing. It does not abandon as silent, irrelevant, or unimportant the complex ties people may have with each other within a system or from outside a system, but rather investigates them and attempts to utilise them in the service of a task or tasks (Garza, 2016; Griffith, 2016; Zur, 2017).

Adaptive and functional special relationshipping may offer us the model of the Matrix – a complex web of relationships and affiliations – as an innovative way to understand and achieve authority, power, leadership, followership, and membership. The Matrix is compared and contrasted to the Totem (Freud, 1919). A more in-depth description of our conceptualisation of the Matrix model is in the Glossary below.

The orderliness and control presented in the Totem model to manage the flow and structure of authority is directly subverted by the Matrix, which recognises as valid, adaptive, and productive complex, intersubjective, and overlapping relationships being imported into a here-and-now system or task (informed by Haraway, 1991).

With adaptive special relationshipping, movement into and out of positions of authority is not necessarily orderly or predictable nor as controlled as within a Totem model.

Toppling an (Imagined?) Totem

The Matrix model for understanding and relating to authority structures as necessarily subjective and intersectional would challenge a more patriarchal, Euro-centric tradition of authority structuring, which goes to the very heart of GR theory itself, founded upon a more objective, Eurocentric, colonial, and patriarchal model descending from The Scientific Method and Modernism (Khaleelee & White, 2014; Zwick & Harkins, 2016).

The threat adaptive special relationshipping could pose to a pervasive method of asserting patriarchal, Euro-centric dominance, then, is quite potent. Perhaps the unconscious line of thought is, "Better to denigrate as 'there-and-then' or 'irrelevant outside information' the importation and importance of special and salient relationships into the here-and-now system, because transparent, open and collaborative D/M dynamics could threaten the desired flow of orderly top-down authority structuring. The Totem may be toppled."

One question we might ask to challenge this possible unconscious motivation to suppress or keep as "outside" material the presence and impact of D/Ms is: how strong is the Totem if it can be toppled simply by looking at, including, validating and working with what is already present? We can pretend the Totem stands alone in a vacuum in space; but that does not make it so.

Overall Summary and Conclusions

Survey and interview data indicate D/Ms as a phenomenon present in contemporary life that needs to be addressed in GRCs. According to our literature review, surveys, and interviews, there is a paucity of GR literature regarding D/Ms. There is an equal paucity of research in this area.

Organisational life is more interdependent, smaller, and hidden than prior to the Digital Age, perhaps smaller *again,* making D/Ms a significant issue for GRCs to address more effectively.

Survey and interview data suggest D/Ms need to be more effectively addressed in GRCs. A ritualistic addressing of this phenomenon may explain one reason D/Ms are taken-for-granted in GRC culture in the US.

There are mixed perceptions about the need for a code of ethics in order to work more adeptly with D/Ms at GRCs, but there is a solid belief that D/Ms should be addressed in the training of GRC Directors and Consultants.

We conclude there is likely an "as if we are strangers" phenomenon in GRCs and in organisational life. This points to a possible "as if we are strangers" basic assumption ("basic assumption: strangers") writ large in organisational life. This basic assumption can undergird or be separate from other basic assumptions and known group dynamics; for example, a pairing or subgroup within a group or organisation may have a *relational valence* to engage in dynamic work or anti-work on behalf of the group-as-a-whole due to an outside or pre-existing or special relationship. The outside, pre-existing, or special relationship may be covert or overt in its influence on the group dynamic and may be known or not known to the group-as-a-whole in the here-and-now.

The "inbreeding" of ideas via imported special relationships, corrupted special relationships, and nepotism is a significant issue that appears to already exist within GRCs and organisational life. Addressing D/Ms more effectively in US GRCs may serve to increase GR' relevance to organisational life as well as create more realistic and transparent learning for GRCs staff and members.

Likewise, learning from adaptive special relationshipping and understanding the real, functional, and helpful ways that special relationships can be utilised, openly and overtly, in the service of an organisational task may add significant learning about collaboration, power-sharing, and matrix-based leadership to the GR field.

The standard practice in the Traditionalist Model of reducing or eradicating known special relationships or ritualistically naming them without further work to understand their impact on the here-and-now may belie the intensity of the threat that is posed by special relationships to the hierarchical, orderly understanding of authority relationships GR has sought to study.

But acting *as if* we are strangers does not, we think, rid our conferences or organisations of the *impact* of special relationships on organisational dynamics. In fact, and rather, we seem to fail to have the mechanisms or methodology to see them, understand them, address them, reduce corrupted special relationships and enhance adaptive special relationships in the service of the task where we find them.

While we say they should not be here, are not here, or should have no bearing on here-and-now dynamics, special relationships may in fact be the undercurrent of much or all of what is happening – or is not happening – in contemporary GRCs and in organisational life.

Proposals for Future Research and Group Relations Conference Tasks

We propose systematic field observations, surveys, and interviews of GRC staff from other countries to compare and contrast with our results would help us gain a greater understanding of how this issue is being dealt with more broadly and may serve to create better dialogue and cross-cultural learning regarding managing dual relationships within GRCs internationally. We also propose surveys and interviews be conducted about the presence and impact of dual relationships in organisations outside of GRCs to assist us as a field in gaining greater clarity about the prevalence of D/Ms as well as the dynamic issues they present in organisational life.

We propose ongoing review of literature in other disciplines, such as psychology, anthropology, business management theory, organisational leadership theory, intersectionality studies, and political theory for evidence of an "as if we are strangers" basic assumption in group functioning.

We propose GR small study workshops and conferences wherein a specific task of the event is to understand the impact of special relationships on the here-and-now.

Appendix: Glossary of Terms and Notes

Dual, Multiple, Special Relationships ("D/M Relationships" or "D/Ms" here): a relationship wherein there are two or more individuals that have at least one additional relationship that exists outside the current relationship. Another way to think of this is "multiple roles in relation to each other" either in the same context (institution, organisation, or event) or across multiple contexts.

Special Relationshipping: the activity of forming a special relationship for the advancement of an agenda, such as those related to career or organisational task. Synonymous with "networking," but applied beyond career-advancement activities and groups (informed by Forret & Dougherty, 2004).

Nepotic: of or related to nepotism; a relationship or role that is dependent upon favouritism.

Structural Siblings, Parents, Children: in the model of the mind and/or in the structure of an organisation, group, or conference, we can be said to have sibships with those lateral to us, can be structural parents to those subordinate to us, and can be structural children to those who have authority over us. (informed by Lévi-Strauss, 1963).

Structural/Emotional Incest ("Incestuous Special Relationship" "ISR"): occurs when there is behaviour that violates the explicit or implicit rules of generally agreed upon engagement in a structural family relationship (in an organisation or biological family). Structural incest may involve seduction of authority or subordinate, but not always. Seduction, whether explicit or implicit, is a common enactment of incest. ISRs are a "means to an end." The "end" is typically about gaining or maintaining power and authority or (felt or real) security or safety from annihilation or exile. Enactments of structural incest are *maladaptive special relationshipping.* A common trait of ISRs is that they are often secretive or enacted thoughtlessly or unconsciously or without transparent process, though the keeping of a secret is not always conscious nor is the incestuous enactment always conscious. We hypothesise that enactments of structural incest seem more likely in competitive, top-down authority structures wherein power is not easily shared and where the means to reach a role of power or authority is experienced as elusive, impossible, or too lofty to attain by traditional means in the culture of the institution or group (informed by Freud 1919, 1930; Lévi-Strauss, 1963; Pepper, 2014).

Adaptive Special Relationshipping ("ASR"): can be thought of as utilising, in an open and transparent way, networks of relationships for the purposes of advancing an institutional task. ASRs are similar to networking and have the important element of being openly discussed and worked with consciously within the system. In this model, leadership and authority may be shared, may change fluidly depending on a given task, and may be considered "flatter" than the authority relationships in a Totem or hierarchical model. "Grassroots" movements with "no leader" may depend on ASRs; note that there is usually a "leader" in grassroots movements, but there may be no figurehead per se as leadership is negotiated and reassigned depending on the task. ASRs may occur in institutions wherein the culture is one of collaboration and power-sharing, wherein perceived access to power and authority is experienced as close, possible, and non-defensively engaged with (informed by Crenshaw, 1989; Garza, 2016; Haraway, 1991).

Relational Valence: the valency, or proclivity, that an outside relationship, between two or more people, may have to experience or enact a dynamic or behaviour inside the current group. The group could be a family, institution, horde, mass, small group, social group, conference, etc. (Bion, 1961).

Matrix vs. Totem: a Matrix, as applied to an institution or group, can be thought of as a fluid, dynamic web of relationships and roles, wherein people may have existing D/Ms outside of the current role-relationship. The Matrix acknowledges ways in which power-sharing and special relationships inform leadership and authority and is particularly interested in Adaptive Special Relationships. This is structurally quite different from the Totem authority structure, which views authority and leadership solely hierarchically and seeks to maintain objective and often rigid/prescribed means by which to "move up" in authority and leadership (informed by Burke 1998; Collins, 2000; Haraway, 1991; Ritzker, 2013).

Field: both noun and verb form. In noun form, a field – or web, matrix, map, landscape – of authority relations, rather than merely or simply a Totem. In a field of authority structures, there is a recognition of complex intersecting authority relationships, which may be informed by imported relationships into a system. We have also referred to this as a "matrix map" of relationships wherein members of a system seek to illuminate complex authority structures existing within relationships in a system. For example: in a GRC, perhaps a consultant is on staff with a student, and they both are students of the conference Director; at the same time, there is a member in the conference who is the consultant's practicum supervisor; at the same time there is a member who goes to synagogue with the Director. In verb form – *fielding* authority structures would mean to invite a system to notice how and where top-down hierarchy is not present in its simplest form or is being influenced by other authority structures or outside authority relationships.

Traditionalist Approaches to Special Relationships in US Conference Life[7]

1 Reduce the number and type of special relationships known to be potentially present in the administrative construction of SSGs.
2 Reduce the number and type of special relationships known to be potentially present in the administration of assigning consultants to SSGs.

3 Feelings, thoughts, and fantasies about a person with whom we have an outside relationship – if these are predominantly associating to the outside relationships, this is a "there-and-then" dynamic and not explicitly relevant to here-and-now work or dynamics.

4 Request of staff as well as members to let go of "memory and desire" about outside conventions, including prior knowledge of and associations to individuals in the here-and-now system.

5 Hypothesise the bringing in of material about an outside relationship as a group defense against here-and-now work (BA fight/flight, pairing, dependency, me-ness, etc., as applied).

6 Hypothesise that member behaviour that "pulls" on a staff person to engage with the membership in a "friendlier" way as a seduction of the staff person originating in the membership (not originating in the staff body).

7 Hypothesise that seductive behaviour of this type falls within the current basic assumptions known to us (basic assumptions dependency, fight/flight, pairing, oneness, and me-ness).

8 Make transparent/overt known special relationships within the staff body, when possible; this action is sometimes treated as a "purging" of special relationships, as if stating their presence is an act of letting go of them for the duration of the conference.

9 There is a preference to reduce the number and type of special relationships in the staff body.

10 Significant (highly salient or influential) special relationships are considered a potential impediment to the work in the here-and-now in conferences.

Notes

1 The reader is referred to the glossary and notes in the appendix for definitions of terms, including dual and multiple relationships, Traditionalist Model, and other concepts.

2 Ms. Zwick first began presenting about "basic assumption: strangers" in 2015. We offer future research and GRC tasks in part VI.

3 In the future, we may seek to publish the full results of the survey in service of the work that GR practitioners are engaging in internationally.

4 Please refer to our notes below to read more about the Traditionalist Model we are referring to.

5 Please also see Zwick (2015) and Zwick and Harkins (2016).

6 See glossary regarding the concept of special relationshipping.

7 Based on the authors' combined 30 years of experience attending as members and working as staff on multiple Group Relations Conferences and Events as well as an extensive group relations literature review 2015–2018. Informed particularly by Bion (1961); Aram, Baxter and Nutkevitch (2012); Brumner, Nutkevitch and Sher (2006); Hayden and Molenkamp (2002); Rice (1965); Colman and Bexton (1975); Colman and Geller (1985); Cytrynbaum and Noumair (2004); and DeLoach (1988).

References

Alford, C. F. (1994). *Group psychology and political theory*. Yale University Press.

Aram, E., Baxter, R., & Nutkevitch, A. (2012). *Group relations conferences: Tradition, creativity, and succession in the global group relations network*. Routledge.

Bion, W. R. (1961). *Experiences in groups*. Routledge.

Brumner, L. D., Nutkevitch, A., & Sher, M. (2006). *Group relations conferences: Reviewing and exploring theory, design, role-taking, and application*. Routledge.

Burke, N. (Ed). (1998). *Gender and envy*. Routledge.

Butler, J. (1990). *Gender trouble: Feminism and the subversion of identity*. Routledge.

Chrislip, D. (2002). *The collaborative leadership fieldbook: A guide for citizens and civic leaders*. (n.l.) Josey Bass.

Collins, P. H. (2000). *Black feminist thought: Knowledge, consciousness, and the politics of empowerment*. Routledge.

Colman, A. D., & Bexton, W. H. (Eds). (1975). *Group relations reader 1*. A.K. Rice Institute.

Colman, A. D., & Geller, M. H. (Eds). (1985). *Group relations reader 2*. A.K. Rice Institute.

Crenshaw, K. W. (1989, January 1). Demarginalizing the intersection of race and sex: A black feminist critique of antidiscrimination doctrine, feminist theory and antiracist politics. *The University of Chicago Legal Forum*, 140: 139–167.

Cytrynbaum, S., & Noumair, D. A. (Eds). (2004). *Group dynamics, organizational irrationality, and social complexity: Group relations reader 3*. A.K. Rice Institute.

DeLoach, S. S. (1988) *Study group consultancy: Elements of the task*. Author.

Forret, M. L., & Dougherty, T. W. (2004). Networking behaviors and career outcomes: Differences in men and women? *Journal of Organizational Behavior*, 25:3 419–437.

Freud, S. (1919). *Totem and taboo*. Routledge Classics (2001).

Freud, S. (1930). *Civilization and its discontents*. Hogarth Press and the Institute of Psycho-analysis.

Garza, A. (2016, February 12). *Black Lives Matter*. Speech presented at University of California Santa Cruz – Martin Luther King, Jr. Convocation in Civic Auditorium, Santa Cruz, CA.

Griffith, E. (2016, March 24). Why the Black Lives Matter founders are among the world's greatest leaders. *Fortune*.

Haraway, D. (1991). *Simian, cyborgs, and the reinvention of nature*. Routledge.

Hayden, C., & Molenkamp, R. (2002). *Tavistock Primer II*. A.K. Rice Institute for the Study of Social Systems.

Hirschorn, L. (1988). *The workplace within: Psychodynamics of organizational life*. Boston, MA: Massachusetts Institute of Technology Press.

Karl, K. A., & Baker, W. (2001). Achieving success through social capital: Tapping the hidden resources in your personal and business networks. *Academy of Management Executive*, 15:3 146–147.

Khaleelee, O., & White, K. (2014) Speaking out: Global development and innovation in group relations. *Organisational & Social Dynamics*. 14:2 399–425.

Laing, R. D. (1969). *The politics of the family and other essays*. London: Tavistock Publications Limited.

Lévi-Strauss, C. (1963). *Structural anthropology*. Translation by Claire Jacobson and Brooke Grundfest Schoepf. Basic Books.

Lorde, A. (1984). *Sister outsider: Essays and speeches.* Ten Speed Press.

Mauss, M. (1990). *The gift: The form and reason of exchange in archaic societies.* Translated by W. D. Halls. Routledge.

Pepper, R. (2014) *Emotional incest in group psychotherapy: a conspiracy of silence.* Rowman & Littlefield.

Rice, A. K. (1965). *Learning for leadership: Interpersonal and intergroup relations.* Tavistock Publications.

Ritzker, G. (2013). *Contemporary sociological theory and its classical roots: The basics.* McGraw Hill.

Simmons, M. (2015, January 15). The no. 1 predictor of career success according to network science. *Forbes.*

Sophocles. (2006). *Oedipus Rex.* Cambridge University Press.

White, W. L. (1986, 1997). *The incestuous workplace: Stress and distress in the organizational family.* Lighthouse Training Institute; Hazelden.

Zur, O. (Ed). (2017). *Multiple relationships in psychotherapy and counseling: Unavoidable, common, and mandatory dual relationships in therapy.* Routledge.

Zwick, K. (2015, December 5). *"As If" we are strangers: Exploring this basic assumption.* Lecture at the Grex 3rd Annual Membership Meeting. Home of Andrea Fraser.

Zwick, K., & Harkins, S. (2016, September 17). *With memory and desire? Inquiring into the unexplored dynamics of dual/special relationships in conference and organizational life in the 21st century.* A.K. Rice Institute for the Study of Social Systems' Dialogues III Consortium. The Cenacle. Chicago, IL.

Chapter 12

LFA as a Learning Community

Experiencing Living and Learning in the Conference Space and Territory

Luca Mingarelli, Giada Boldetti, Simona Masnata, and Gilad Ovadia[1]

Background – The Story of LFA – Past and Present

Learning From Action (LFA) is an application of Group Relation Conferences (GRCs) (Armstrong, 2005; Brunner et al, 2006). We like to call it a "Working Conference" because of the dialogue between action and reflection. It is an opportunity to explore and connect different cultures and models of Therapeutic Communities (TCs) and GRCs. It was created by Hinshelwood and Pedriali in 2000 as a learning format for TC (mainly for mental disease patients) and Mental Health (MH) Service workers so that they could experience similar living conditions to patients treated in TCs (Hinshelwood and Skogstad, 2000; Mingarelli, 2009; Jones, 2010; Gale et al, 2012).

About ten years ago, after the death of his friend Pedriali, Mingarelli asked Il Nodo Group[2] to give continuity to this kind of workshop in order to manage and co-lead it in collaboration with Hinshelwood. Il Nodo Group authorised Mingarelli and Hinshelwood to manage LFA autonomously.

At the beginning, in 2010, there was an Italy-UK staff: Hinshelwood was the Director and Mingarelli was the Associate Director. Now Hinshelwood has taken on the role of Scientific Supervisor of LFA. From 2011 to 2016, Mingarelli was the Director, then Boldetti became the first woman Director, with Mingarelli as Associate and or Codirector. In LFA 2019, Mingarelli was the Director, and Ovadia, from Israel, was the Associate Director. This was the first time with a non-Italian or UK Associate Director. This made it really an international team, with Italian, UK, Israeli and Hungarian members. In 2017 and 2019, two editions were also held in Japan.

The OPUS paper by Hinshelwood, Pedriali, and Brunner (2010) explains the fundamental intentions of LFA at its birth:

> These Workshops are the product of several sources of stimulation, the Therapeutic Community development in the UK and in Italy, the development of community care in Italy, and the Group Relations tradition of experiential learning in terms of methodology. The Workshop is founded on the assumption that actions can carry messages. Indeed,

DOI: 10.4324/9781003261483-16

words can also be actions upon each other, which, thus, carry implicit messages as well as the overt ones. For instance, swearing is for an impact, rather than for its precise symbolic content and there is a kind of 'action language' which puts pressure on the care-giver to enact with the person, rather than to understand the communication in a verbal dialogue. To 'read' such messages requires subjective and intuitive functions, just as much as cognitive and symbolic ones.

So, patients in TCs are generally unable to access a symbolic touch and people who work in TCs have to develop the ability to understand other kinds of languages to get in contact with them. For this reason, when the LFA was started it was strictly offered to TC and MH Service workers. Exploring the TC culture and the aim of helping MHS workers using GRC methods were the primary intentions (Barone et al, 2010).

During the ensuing years, some innovations have slightly changed the original project and we opened participation to other professionals from profit-making sectors. It generates the opportunity for bridging between the world of mental illness and the rest of the world.

Primary Task and Daily Life

The primary task of this Working Conference is to offer an opportunity to explore how unconscious and non-verbal communication and group dynamics shape decision-making processes and influence accountability and various other aspects of "working together" in this temporary learning community.

In order to connect with the primary task, it is essential to understand that in LFA the work is real. Participants carry out daily activities in a community dimension that approaches the TC, and at the same time, they explore communication, unconscious dynamics, decision-making processes, and accountability.

The staff facilitates and supports the participants in carrying out the activities, monitors the climate and the dynamics of the system and subsystems, and manages the meetings and groups in order to provide the participants with the best conditions to connect with the unconscious dimension and learn from experience.

The challenge of the primary task of LFA is to offer an exploration that simultaneously takes place in the different parts of the structure of the individual and the group. The effort of the staff is to allow learning in a situation of very high stress.

The Idea of Using Daily Life Activities

LFA is inspired by the model of the TC, where operators and patients share daily life, and patients are encouraged to perform tasks such as cooking and taking care of the home, as well as actively participating in decision-making processes (Ferruta et al, 2012). These issues are all present in LFA and constitute the core of the activities; they are the actions that generate the thought, the relationship and the assumption of responsibility, the field in which the dynamics develop, and where the unconscious works in the system.

Quoting Hinshelwood (2010): "Community should offer its members the opportunity of actively working together while taking into account the emotional situations developing in the daily life which reminds them of their experience" ... "To some extent we can say that the workshop is a TC itself, conceived to help TC workers to explore the processes developing around the daily doing".

The challenge is how to use the tools of everyday life to allow participants to explore, bring attention to processes, unconscious dynamics, and relationships while they are shopping or cooking, washing dishes, or organising leisure time so as to be able to learn from it.

GRC and TC Combination

In the construction of LFA we paid attention to how TC and GRC cultures can work together in this conference.

Location is usually in a hostel for this reason, the cost of LFA is lower than traditional GRCs, which are usually held in a 4-star hotel.

Location and their roommate are the first impacts for participants when they arrive. With no single bedrooms and 2–4 members per room, it's not possible to choose a roommate, as this is the condition of patients entering a TC. This is the first occasion LFA members have to empathise with the patients they care for. This impact is very important to understand some feeling their patients experience when they enter a TC, a situation that it's easy to take for granted (Main, 1946). We point out this step of entering a community in the Director's speech that starts the Opening Plenary (OP) when we talk about the establishment of a temporary learning community.

It's important to look at the schedule (Figure 12.1) to understand the LFA structure.

LFA takes less than 2½ days. The original format lasted an extra day. We reduced the format by one day to facilitate recruitment and participation.

The Community Meetings

The daily schedule has a basic structure similar to a GRC, with Opening and Closing Plenaries, Review and Application groups, and large study groups, adapted in this event as community meetings (in TC language).

Community meetings every morning and evening provide a "sandwich" structure that contains the day's activities.

The decision-making plenary (DMP) is an innovative event that has the task of exploring decision-making and accountability in setting up the groups that will perform the basic activities (self-managed by the

FRIDAY, 19 OCTOBER / VENERDI'	SATURDAY, 20 OCTOBER / SABATO	SUNDAY, 21 OCTOBER / DOMENICA
11,45-12,45 Registrazione dei partecipanti e spuntino / Registration and snack	08,00-09,00 Colazione / Breakfast	07,00-08,00 Colazione / Breakfast
13,00-14,00 Riunione Plenaria di apertura/ Opening plenary	09,00-10,00 Riunione di comunità del mattino 1 / Morning community meeting 1	08,00-09,00 Riunione di comunità del mattino 2 / Morning community meeting 2
14,00-14,30 Pausa / Break	10,00-10,15 Pausa / Break	09,00-09,10 Pausa / Break
14,30-16,00 Riunione decisionale plenaria/ Decision-making plenary	10,15-10,45 Gruppi decisionali 2 / Decision-making groups 2	09,10-09,40 Gruppi decisionali 4 / Decision-making groups 4
16,00-16,15 Pausa / Break	10,45-12,30 Attività 2 / Activities 2	09,45-11,30 Gruppi di Applicazione / Application Groups
16,15-17,15 Gruppi decisionali 1 / Decision-making groups 1	12,30-14,00 Pranzo / Lunch	11,35-12,30 Attività 4 / Activities 4
17,15-18,45 Attività 1 / Activities 1	14,00-14,30 Tempo libero comunitario 2 / Community free time 2	12,30-13,30 Pranzo / Light lunch
18,45-19,00 Pausa / Break	14,30-14,45 Pausa / Break	13,30-14,00 Lavaggio piatti & pulizie conclusive / Washing up & cleaning
19,00-20,00 Riunione di comunità della sera 1 / Evening community meeting 1	14,45-15,15 Gruppi decisionali 3 / Decision-making groups 3	14,00-15,00 Riunione plenaria conclusiva / Closing plenary
20,00-20,15 Pausa / Break	15,15-15,30 Pausa / Break	15,00-15,15 Commiato / Leave-taking
20,15-21,30 Cena / Dinner	15,30-16,45 Gruppi di revisione / Review groups	
21,35-22,15 Tempo libero comunitario 1 / Community free time 1	16,45-17,00 Pausa / Break	
	17,00-18,30 Attività 3 / Activities 3	
	18,30-18,45 Pausa / Break	
	18,45-19,45 Riunione di comunità della sera 2 / Evening community meeting 2	
	19,45-20,00 Pausa / Break	
	20,00-21,30 Cena / Dinner	
	21,30-22,15 Tempo libero comunitario 3 / Community free time 3	

Figure 12.1 2018 LFA Schedule

participants). The DMP immediately follows the OP and puts participants powerfully in contact with the theme of LFA: decision-making and account-ability: think-decide-act.

This event, in a similar way to the OP of the GRC Organisational Event, is aimed at generating the three activity subgroups through a process of self-organisation, in which the groups in charge of the three essential areas of daily living – cooking, cleaning, and leisure – come together.

The Director of Activities (DOA) leads this event, giving the group a sim-ple directive but linked with the authentic needs of the community organi-sation for the following days. The event is very stressful, as it has to balance the need to consider the best way to divide into groups as well as the need for action, due to real-time pressure, as the time of the event runs quickly, and the community is going to eat just a few hours later.

Over the years, we have observed various ways of dividing and organis-ing. The two main issues are:

1 ability during activity (stay in the same activity where you're capable all the time or rotate in the other activities as well).
2 the number and the quality of human relations (interact with the major-ity of people without a fixed group or develop relations mainly in the same group in order to improve the growth of the group).

It's very interesting how, in the last two LFAs, participants decided to change groups every time, so no group remains the same during the con-ference. This choice generated an uncomfortable situation and a feeling of guilt for this during the conference. But it's very close to the reality of real relationships in internet social networks, where one can observe the formation of virtual groups *with soft edges.*

Decision-making groups (small/medium groups, generally 11–14 members with a consultant) have the task to plan activities exploring the group decision-making, and they make the experience of taking roles and the inter-connections among groups including the issue of negotiating the division of the daily budget.

Activity groups are double tasked events aimed at reflecting and learning about the different modalities of, and possible struggles with, working together and relating to the small groups, whilst at the same time working on the task of performing daily activities for the survival of the Community. Consultants are part of the Activity groups and actively participate in the activity.

During the course of LFA it often becomes evident that participants tend to perceive the activities as "good" moments, whilst reflection times are seen as "difficult" moments, thus opening up the dilemma between thinking and acting.

In the OPUS paper, Hinshelwood, Pedriali, and Brunner (2010) describe how "action can become a defence against reflection" and refer to how "participants often engage in activities in order to satisfy a narcissistic need, rather than in order to learn something new". This shows how taking action does not necessarily correspond to learning from activities and actions.

Mario Perini (2017), in his paper on language of achievement, says: "Mind and reality, emotions (aggression, love) and transformative actions are at the interface between thinking and acting in work organisations, no matter whether in factories or therapeutic communities or in the core of system management and governance. I would even say that the doing/thinking dilemma is a founding element of mature organisational cultures".

Action has, as Freud said, two possible aims – one is to *use* reality to release tensions (and discharge energy), or the other aim is to *change* reality in some way via thinking as an experimental activity. LFA underlines the first as well as the second.

Trying to Compare How the Two Cultures Are Represented in LFA, We Made This Very Simplified Scheme

From the GRC:

- Management of the conference made by GRC staff composed of a directorate and consultants
- Opening and closing plenary
- Attention to the construction of structure as a container and the timetable

- Management of the three T's: Time; Task; Territory
- Review and Application Groups.

From the TC:

- Culture of inquiry (Main 1983)
- Presence of practical activities including the use of money
- Presence of the majority of the staff in all community meetings
- The function of the consultant during the activities is slightly different than in a GRC because, beyond the usual role, consultants collaborate closely with community members. This is an important example for TC operators: to work actively with participants without losing their role
- Concept of a democratic community. Even if it's not a simple thing, it's very important to develop a democratic process in TCs that welcomes people with poorly structured Egos because this process helps Ego growth

We think that an important reflection for people who work in TCs (with persons who have severe disease) is: how much decision-making power users are stimulated to exercise and how much they are helped to be aware that they are exercising it. So, the experience in a TC must be an opportunity for active participation and mastering a role in community life.

The meeting or the clash between these two cultures animates many debates within the staff during the conference and after it in the individual reports and in sometimes thick correspondence by email (Long, 2000).

Giovanni Foresti (consultant in several LFA editions) after LFA 2015 shared this reflection with the staff:

> GRCs are often said to be a temporary learning organisation. Their task is a rather abstract conceptual paradox: studying group dynamics even while they are developing is a contradiction in terms, for things are tested in a given moment and then studied at a later stage. This occurs in a dialectic between abstract and concrete that is a continuous and turbulent flow, of which the subject must gain consciousness in his own time, in his own way and on his own. A paradox that the style of management staff can make more concrete/plausible or frankly absurd/Beckettian.
>
> The experience in the LFA, instead, is immediately tangible: more real in the political/historical sense of the word. It is an experience which is 'real' and strong: we need to get organised so that we can eat, keep clean and rest. It is impossible not to grasp the urgency and concreteness of the task and responsibilities that are logically and clearly derived from it.
>
> The key word is therefore *real*: a temporary organisation that is, indeed, provisional but not abstract/fictitious ... The theoretical theme

is the role of acting: the infamous acting that indeed is always the risk inherent in action. Frequently during the LFA staff wonder (as in TCs) how much to determine and give a direction or how much to let the membership and the individuals explore how and what to do/think.

After LFA 2016 there was a lively exchange of views by e-mail about how to manage mistakes. In TC culture it is fundamental to work on mistakes and failures in a group modality.

During the closing plenary of LFA 2016, Mingarelli said that the name he could associate to that LFA edition could be Learning From Mistakes – instead of LFA – because of the number of mistakes made by the staff.

Foresti in his report wrote:

> The item(s) that continue(s) popping up in the (alas narrow) surface of my mind is the mistakes/learning link: GRC culture versus TC culture or paternal culture versus maternal culture. The problem is an unresolvable paradox, as we know. If you stress the vertical axis, strengthening the staff image, you diminish the confusion but enhance the paranoia. Besides, you run the risk of promoting dependence. If you weaken it, all the conflicts are left at the horizontal level where they tend to become molecular and diffused/widespread.

Diamond comments on Foresti's notes:

> I think there was a link this year between the vertical ('autocratic' authority/horizontal (democratic authority) axis issue that also relates to the mistakes/learning link.

Mingarelli wrote:

> LFA unique identity comes from an integration/hybridisation/copula between the culture of TCs, with the horizontal axis and democratic/ maternal mode, and GRC, with a more vertical axis and the exploration of authority-paternal mode; LFA lives in this generative tension and open question: which one of the two modes is more useful during the LFA for providing the learning of the individuals and of the whole community.

Ovadia's comment after LFA 2016 was:

> We use the structure and setting of GRC, but LFA is another creature. If the GRC is focused more on leadership, authority and groups as phenomena by itself, and in organisations, LFA is about individuals in the organisation and the fragility of human experience …

LFA can give to human services professions the opportunity to meet themselves with simple tasks of daily life but in uncomfortable dependence. This combination of daily life adjustment behavior and dependency creates an amount of deprivation that gives the opportunity to each one of the members or staff to meet himself/herself in a deprived situation and to learn from that.

So, it provides a space to the individual learning about himself or herself connected to the Winnicott concept of 'the capacity to be alone'.

LFA can help the workers to learn about countertransference in relatedness to situations with deprived population of patients or customers.

The role of Consultants in the Decision-Making and the Activities

In each of the working groups on decision-making and activities, every group has a consultant to accompany it. The task of the consultants in any given workshop is similar to that of the consultants in an organisational event in a GRC.

The consultants can demonstrate different dimensions to the group – from addressing the group level and its attitude to the primary task to questions probing group authority and leadership through to the nature of decision-making and execution (Stapley, 2006). The group's need to act to carry out the daily tasks brings along with it many fantasies about the quality of the product and its performance, as if these were the only goals of the workshop, so much that contemplation, reflection, and learning from experience can be pushed into the corner. These manifestations may result, for example, from the development of group narcissism, competitiveness, and defences against failure, as well as performance anxiety in the face of time limitations. These pressures chiefly exist in food-related activities, where the consultant may offer an explanation that will block the pressure on the group to make a snap decision to act quickly without performing proper thinking and processing actions. However, in activities relating to cleaning, the consultant can point to various negative reactions and emotions triggered in association to cleanliness, including evasion, avoidance, or belittling the task.

Similar to the role of staff in TCs, the consultant is close to the participants and constitutes part of the group, quite unlike the world of GR. Thus, the consultant may take part in preparing the food, arranging tables, and the like, which affords him an inside view while he himself is in action. This position also facilitates personal dialogue with the participants, which is sometimes similar to an organisational event.

This form of the consultant's participant presence may also arouse adverse reactions from the group that appear in the disregard and denial of the consultant's function in the group work process. The question as to how the consultant's identity is maintained demands his considering how to position himself during the activity and how to act at any given moment.

In this way, the consultant can convene the group for observation, which can also take place during a short break in the kitchen as the consultant invites the participants to reflect on their learning experiences.

In the group dealing with cleaning or in organising leisure activities, the consultant can make himself available and wait for the group in the meeting room or offer learning tracks within the time units for the activities or during preparations or at their close.

Precisely this concreteness in performing the tasks carries the potential for many misunderstandings, disassociations, and disorientation. Such, too, is the case in excess focus on execution. The consultant accompanies the participants in a similar manner to the staff in a TC. Through transfer imagery, his presence reminds the participants of the working reality from which they hail.

Staff Structure

The staff and its deployment is chosen by the director as in the traditional GRCs style; the differences from the traditional GRC tradition are the following:

- the staff is smaller (max 7 staff members for about 40 participants); this also facilitates having a lower fee than the traditional GRC, which gives the opportunity also to educators, nurses, etc. to register;
- the staff is almost the same in different editions, which gives continuity to the action research and to be able to contain the anxiety and possible fragmentation of the membership – this is more similar to the tradition and need of a TC, where the more stable and solid the staff is, the more effective is the work.

Staff Meetings (SM)

The schedule is almost the same in different LFAs. In the time before the LFA the directorate has some web meetings to discuss and decide on the design and schedule and to plan the recruitment strategy.

The Administrative team is composed of two members; this has been decided seeing that in LFA the management of the boundaries between inside and outside (i.e. shopping, money, leisure management of the house, etc.) is very complex.

Six editions ago, Mingarelli, as Director, decided to create a new role: the DOA. Usually, this role has been taken by the associate director or co-director; this choice is coherent with the fact that the activities are the core of LFA; the DOA leads meetings with the consultants to support them in their difficult role of facilitating the task of activities.

Another new innovative role is the treasurer: with the decision to introduce the real "money" in the LFA one of the two Administrators has to become the treasurer during the activities; there is a budget every day and the different groups have to negotiate between themselves and with the treasurer the amount of money needed.

Hinshelwood[3] views the treasurer as "an important innovation, and he exemplifies the TC. He *enacts* a communication. He puts a certain member in a role with unspoken characteristics – responsibility, honesty, etc. Mostly that is unspoken and is implicit. In a TC (or MHS) this is radical – if you give a patient a role of treasurer, he has a role of responsibility and reliability quite against the role of patient. He 'says' to the patient, 'you are quite capable of being a normal person, however many symptoms you have.' And that is different from the message always given to patients which is, 'you are quite incapable of being normal, and we will concentrate only on symptoms and not on your capacity for responsibility.'"

The interaction with money is another point of observation of what happens in the LFA dynamics. Over the years the treasurer has assumed a supporting role for the understanding of the activities, as his observations about the behaviour of the participants negotiating the money needed for the different activities are integrated into the consultants' visions (Kets De Vries, 2011).

International Network

LFA has developed its own way to create an international network of institutions that can be involved with in different roles; Every year there are at least six partners and two or three sponsors in addition to Il Nodo Group, which is the main organisation that hosts, organises, holds, and manages LFA. This enlargement of the network field is another difference from traditional GRCs that generally have a maximum of two sponsors. The idea is to generate a sort of cooperative enlarged system or group of organisations in a sort of consortium or community of communities that are interested in this action research for several reasons and support the realisation of LFA. Some sponsors include CSGSS (USA), OFEK (Israel), and Mito & Realtà (Italy). Some of the partners have included Fondazione Rosa dei Venti Onlus (Italy), Mulberry Bush Organisation (UK), Thalassa House TC (Hungary), OPUS (UK), TCTC (UK), International Network Democratic Therapeutic Communities (INDTC), and Association Group Psychotherapy (Japan).

The agreement is individual for each organisation and every year has to be renegotiated and renewed; sometimes it is more commercial and for others it is more scientific. Usually we offer discounts and visibility of the organisation's logo on the flyer. We share the director's report and in exchange we ask support in the recruitment and in the design and the submission of participants' reports.

Remarks on the Use of the Concept of "ACTION"

"Daily activities, especially those linked with concrete needs, if considered from this point of view, become vital functions both because they represent real needs and because they stimulate the development of a thinking activity" (R. Hinshelwood, unpublished paper).

Freud concludes his article *Totem and Taboo* with the statement, "In the beginning was the action" (Freud, 1989). The action is keenly related to the drive for the satisfaction of needs and is quite simply a part of the human experience. The words as products of emotion and thinking arrive later in human development, as well as in child development.

In choosing to utilise the concept of action, the emphasis has been placed upon the continuity of Bion's beliefs in general, as well as that which applies to groups, as noted in his book *Experiences in Groups* (Bion, 1961) which describes the Northfield Experiment's contribution to the conceptional basis for community treatment. Further, Bion uses the concept of action as part of the vertex (Bion, 1970). The emphasis in selecting the concept of action over the concept of doing is based on the sequences of emotion-thinking-action, action-thinking-emotion, not necessarily on the productivity of the result, although the result itself is important (Bion, 1962; Ferro, 2006). An investigation of the concrete action which relates to reality versus mere talk about concepts is important within the context of meeting individuals suffering from cognitive disturbances, delayed comprehension, depression, language deficiencies, emotional overload, and similar disorders found within the TCs. Such disorders disrupt the emotion-thinking-action sequence structure and have a direct impact on decision-making and execution.

Yet many things within the workshop could be deliberated within Winnicott's (Winnicott, 1971) system of concepts of "playing and reality" and of "being and doing," which are also related to observing the actions involved in daily life. However, remaining within the dimension of action enables us to maintain the focus on learning from the experience, observing a more basic, primary tier mental functions, as required by staff working in TCs and similar frameworks (Perini, 2017). The participants can observe the work of the team at the decision-making stage and afterwards in execution, noting when actions constitute a substitution for words. Actions can be goal-oriented and precise and can be a productive result of a planning process.

Working in groups necessitates the creation of modes of cooperation, concurrent action, and consideration of attention and sensitivity to the place/territory in which "the other" is found. The action within the group must achieve a concrete goal in a given time, demanding coordination, dialogue, and mutual understanding, which is frequently difficult to achieve due to the varying levels of the participants' fluency in the English language in which the conference is conducted. Experiencing these gaps which are augmented when problems must be resolved when negative feelings of frustration, stress, and disappointment arise as the unwanted results of actions considered to require the use of containment functions. These group encounters are reminiscent of similar encounters which participants confronted as staff members in the TC, thus enabling distinctive learning (Baum, 1990).

Notes

1 Many thanks to Giovanni Foresti, John Diamonds, and Robert Hinshelwood for the valuable contribution made in the drafting of the chapter.
2 Il Nodo Group is a scientific cultural not-for-profit Association that has developed training and consultancy activities in cooperation with The Tavistock Institute. It is the main sponsor of the residential ALI (Authority Leadership and Innovation) GRC, the Italian formula of the Tavistock method, which has been taking place every year since 1998. Il Nodo Group is also managing GRCs innovative events, such as ECW (Energy Creative Cooperation and Wellbeing joint Organizations) and LFA.
3 Hinshelwood's personal communication to Mingarelli in 2016.

References

Armstrong, D. G. (2005), *Organization in the mind: psychoanalysis, group relations and organizational consultancy*, Karnac.
Barone, R., Bruschetta, S., Giunta, S. (2010), *Gruppoanalisi e comunità terapeutica*, Franco Angeli.
Baum, H.S. (1990), *Organizational membership: personal development in the workplace*, State University of New York Press.
Bion, W. R. (1961), *Experiences in groups*, Tavistock Publications.
Bion, W. R. (1962), *Learning from experience*, Heinemann.
Bion, W. R. (1970), *Attention and interpretation*, Tavistock Publications.
Brunner, L. D., Nutkevitch, A., Sher, M. (eds) (2006), *Group Relations Conferences: reviewing and exploring theory, design, role-taking and applications*, Karnac.
Ferro, A. (2006), "Clinical Implications of Bion's Thoughts", in *International Journal of Psychoanalysis*, 87:4, 989–1003.
Ferruta, A., Foresti, G., Vigorelli M. (2012), *Le comunità terapeutiche*, R. Cortina.
Freud, S. (1989), *Totem and taboo*, W. W. Norton.
Gale, J., Realpe, A., Pedriali, E. (2012), *Comunità terapeutiche per psicosi*, Alpes.
Hinshelwood, R., Pedriali, E., Brunner, L. D. (2010), "Action as a Vehicle for Learning: The Learning from Doing Workshop", in *Organisational & Social Dynamics*, 10:1, 22–39.
Hinshelwood, R., Skogstad, W. (2000), *Observing organisations: anxiety, defence and culture in health care*, Routledge.
Jones, R. M. (2010), *The body of the organization and its health*, Karnac.
Kets De Vries, M. F. R. (2011), *The hedgehog effect. The secrets of building high performance teams*, Wiley, Hoboken.

Long, S. (2000), *The international team: a discussion of the socio-emotional dynamics of the team* (paper presented at the International Society for the Psychoanalytic Study of Organizations Symposium, London).

Main, T. (1946), "The Hospital as a Therapeutic Institution", in *Bulletin of the Menninger Clinic*, 10 66–70.

Main, T. F. (1983), "The concept of a therapeutic community – variations and vicissitudes", in M. Pines (ed.) *The Evolution of Group Analysis.* (p 217): Routledge & Kegan Paul.

Mingarelli, L. (2009), *Difficult adolescents: an autobiography of a TC*, Ananke.

Perini, M. (2017), "Action and thought in the work group", in M. Ringer (ed.) "Thinking in groups and teams: Surfacing new thoughts", in *Gruppo: Omogeneità e Differenze*, pp 123–136.

Stapley, L. (2006), *Individuals, groups and organizations beneath the surface*, Karnac.

Winnicott, D. W. (1971), *Playing and reality*, Routledge.

Section 4

Post-Meeting Reflections

Introduction

In this section, just two participants (both from Israel) offered to write a chapter and think, with the benefit of hindsight, about their subjective experiences of the meeting and their associations. They bring important undercurrents into relief, both political correctness (overt as well as covert manifestations) and the "container" function of group relations.

In *The father is a little bit crazy and the mother doesn't serve enough nourishing food: Political Correctness in Group Relations,* Yermi Harel writes about political correctness (PC) and political incorrectness (PIC) and the space between them and invites us to continue to open up dialogues about racism, politics, language use in the group relations world and the importance of keeping this space alive going forward. Using various frameworks, he examines two "happenings" during the meeting and suggests that the GR community is well placed to explore the "internal racist organisation" as a place to hold difference and other.

Sivanie Shiran in *A Home for the Soul: Reflections on Belgirate VI,* wonders whether the group relations community came to some kind of crossroads in the last meeting. She talks about an acknowledgement of the importance of searching not only for a space for psychic growth and also a physical space and a space for numinousness – harnessing the power of the spirit to transcend painful experience. She uses Analytical Psychology and two particular associations to illuminate ideas around these three themes. She ends with a fascinating question.

DOI: 10.4324/9781003261483-17

"The Father Is a Little Bit Crazy and the Mother Doesn't Serve Enough Nourishing Food"

Political Correctness in Group Relations

Yermi Harel

"The Place Where We Live"

The opening plenary of the Belgirate VI conference discussed many of the political and social issues that have caused disquiet all over the world, including Donald Trump in the US, Jair Bolsonaro in Brazil, Matteo Salvini in Italy, and the capitalistic government in Chile. Many of these leaders stand out for their political incorrectness (PIC) behaviour. The tension between political correctness (PC) norms and PIC leadership has been apparent from the beginning of their tenures and created a feeling as if the responsible adult had left the building.

Another factor that added to the sense of frustration in the conference was the setting. The hotel, "the place where we live", changed owners and became less friendly and unfamiliar. The famous Italian food which had been served in the past was very disappointing this year. Some of the participants shared an ironic metaphor about the hotel and the conference, saying "the father is a little bit crazy and the mother doesn't serve enough nourishing food". Isn't this metaphor, to some extent chauvinistic, reducing value and politically incorrect, not suitable in 2020? In the spirit of feminist understanding and the "MeToo" movement, haven't some of the classical traditional psychoanalytic concepts, such as penis envy, good enough mother, name of the father, good and bad breast, become politically incorrect?

In the following pages, I will discuss two episodes which occurred during the Exploratory Event of the Belgirate VI (2018), to highlight the relevance of political correctness to contemporary Group Relations world.

Case 1

During the second session of the Exploratory Event, I joined one existing group named Black/Brown, which consisted mostly of African Americans. The group was focused on internal dynamics concerning their being Black/Brown, their unique vulnerabilities, discrimination against members, and conflict between members of the group and the late Bruce Irvine. The

DOI: 10.4324/9781003261483-18

members did not welcome me or other newcomers who joined for the second session, and even viewed our presence as an interruption. While they continued with their affairs, I thought to myself how the hostility and inhospitality of the Black/Brown group made me feel scared and a sense of self-silencing as I censored myself from expressing the fear. Perhaps, I thought, this is how Afro-Americans sometimes feel in the white world. This was power struggle. It was as if the group and their leaders were saying: "We, the Black/Brown, have the power and the opportunity to decide what issues we will discuss, and we do not care what you feel, even if it is terror".

Case 2

In the closing plenary of the Exploratory Event, one of the members, the chairperson of OFEK, commented that the behaviour of the Black/Brown group was egocentric and childish. This remark – "childish" – was perceived as a massive insult, as if crossing a line. A type of mistranslation, perhaps a confusion of tongues, occurred between the speaker and the vulnerable listeners. Although both heard the same word, it meant something different to each one. To say childish to Afro-Americans means something different than to say it to other groups. Perhaps childish is corresponding with "boy" and this is diminishing and insulting. In Group Relations, we work on the relations, relatedness, and the massive projection that everyone carries, on both an individual level and a group level. PC in the context of GR says there is boundary that you should not cross. But the mistranslation can also be viewed as a power struggle. The reflection "you behaved childishly" is demeaning. So, the group and their leaders respond by saying: "Hey, this is not acceptable, it is below the belt. Stop the game and punish the speaker". This is what we deal with in Group Relations: projections, relatedness, and relationships.

Political correctness is a term used to refer to language that strives to give the minimum amount of offense, especially when describing groups identified by external markers such as race, gender, culture, or sexual orientation. It aims to reduce the alienation and marginalisation of socially and economically disadvantaged groups, which include poor people, women, racial and ethnic minorities, LGBTQ+, and the disabled. The term is sometimes used derisively to ridicule the notion that altering language usage can change the public's perceptions and beliefs, as well as influence outcomes. In public discourse and the media, it is generally used as a pejorative, implying that these policies are excessive or unwarranted.

The term PC first appeared in Marxist-Leninist vocabulary following the Russian Revolution of 1917. At that time, it was used to describe adherence to the policies and principles of the Communist Party of the Soviet Union (that is, the party line). During the late 1970s and early 1980s, the term began to be used wittily by liberal politicians to refer to the extremism of some left-wing issues, particularly regarding what was perceived as an emphasis on rhetoric over content. In the early 1990s, the term was used by conservatives to question and oppose what they perceived as the rise of liberal left-wing curricula and teaching methods on university and college campuses in the US.

Those who are most strongly opposed to political correctness view it as censorship and a curtailment of freedom of speech that places limits on debates in the public arena. They contend that such language boundaries inevitably lead to self-censorship and restrictions on behaviour. They further believe that political correctness perceives offensive language where none exists. Others believe that "political correctness" or "politically correct" has been used as an epithet to stop legitimate attempts to curb hate speech and minimise exclusionary speech practices. Ultimately, the ongoing discussion surrounding political correctness seems to centre on language, naming, and whose definitions are accepted.

In its more extreme forms, political correctness holds that such acts do not just give offence but are acts of violence that threaten the psychological safety of minority groups.

Slavoj Žižek (2015), the Slovenian philosopher, claims that political correctness is not a term for politeness, nor a conspiracy against the American way of life, but a way of using language that hides the problems of society without doing anything to solve them.

Political correctness stems from the understanding that racism and inequality exist, and that instead of fixing those problems, prettier language will do the trick – as if by using inoffensive words and avoiding crass jokes, we can paint over the filth of reality. Politically correct expressions, to Žižek, become patronising because they highlight inequalities. As the philosopher notes: "one needs to be very precise not to fight racism in a way which ultimately reproduces, if not racism itself, at least the conditions of racism." The subtext of every carefully chosen, politically correct expression, is that there are still people in a position so privileged that they need to refer to "others" in a way that is not offensive.

Politically Correct and Jokes

Avoiding politically correct language is also about calling things by their name. Sigmund Freud (1905), in his *Jokes and Their Relation to the Unconscious*, describes the societal nature of humour. He claims that "our enjoyment of the joke" hinges on it revealing something that is repressed in more serious talk. Freud argues that the success of the joke depends upon a psychic economy, whereby the joke allows one to overcome inhibitions.

In February 2019, Ishizuka and Stephens (2019) published an article which showed how the legendary children's books by Dr. Seuss were racist. They claimed that 98% of the characters in those books were white, while the other 2% were cast as inferior. For example, Asian characters are frequently shown in stereotypical clothing such as "rice paddy hats", with bright yellow skin and slanted eyes. But, as Dr. Seuss notes, "I like nonsense, it wakes up the brain cells. Fantasy is a necessary ingredient in living, it's a way of looking at life through the wrong end of a telescope, and that enables you to laugh at life's realities". In a way, it saddened me that the PC slaughtering knife reached Dr. Seuss and his unique humour. Can we no longer see differences for what they are – nothing else than differences? And can we no longer simply name them, perhaps even with a joke, even if occasionally some offense is given? The delicate border between racist humour and good humour is sometimes ambiguous and unclear, but this does not mean that all humour should be banned and censored.

In my opinion, jokes and politically incorrectness share some similarities. Freud wrote that jokes have three characters: the joke-teller, the listener, and the butt. In PIC, there are at least three characters, with more and more appearances being made by a fourth: the speaker, the listener, the butt (some minority group), and sometimes the censor, the patriarch, and the castrating father. Both jokes and PIC language share the same basic motivation, which is the desire to touch the repressed material of the conscious and the unconscious. John Cleese, a Monty Python character, said: "Political correctness will lead us into a humorless world, reminiscent of Orwell's *1984*".

Internal Racism

Fahkry Davids (2011) is a British psychoanalyst who describes himself as coming from Asian origin, a brown-skinned man who grew up in South Africa, and someone who has experienced apartheid, along with racism in the UK. He opens his book *Internal Racism: A Psychoanalytic Approach to Race and Difference* by showing the complexity and the relation of microaggressions against minorities:

> To be black in a white world is an agony. This is because the white world is racist – if you are black, you are seldom allowed to be an ordinary, regular human being. Instead, at every turn, you are confronted by hidden stereotypes that can spring to life in a flash, push violently into you, destabilize you and make you think, feel and act in ways that are wholly determined from the outside, as if you yourself had no say in the matter. This can turn even the most innocuous of situations utterly fraught.

In his book, Davids elaborates on the concept of the "defensive organisation" based largely on Steiner's (1987, 1993) work on the "pathological organisation". This "defensive organisation" is the result of a failure of object dependency, which causes the infant/child to create "a highly organised and efficient phantasy system, felt to be primarily responsible for his or her care." That system, a narcissistic construction, is essentially defensive against true object relating. This, however, is a "pathological organisation", whereas what Davids presents is an internal racist organisation as a "normal defensive organisation". He posits that "a relationship between self and racial other exists universally in the inner world". The "racial other", to Davids, is a universal internal object, along with self, mother, father, and superego. Furthermore, the relationship between self and racial other is located within a "defensive organisation". Thus, he argues, "the internal racist organisation is a pathological organisation that occurs in the normal mind".

This leads to an interesting proposition. Because racism resides in the normal part of the patient's mind, it regularly escapes analysis, which is focused primarily on the pathological. Racism, therefore, is at least potentially ubiquitous and is a compelling face of the expected relationship of self and other. If one accepts such a wide view of racism and sees it as a general attitude towards variously designated, ethnically identified others, the contemporary world is dramatically indicative of this thesis in many alarming and frightening ways. In GR, as opposed to psychoanalysis, we can have the opportunity to be in touch with "the internal racist organisation" and do some explorations on this structure and the relation between self and racist other.

Politically Correct and Language

Language shapes our reality and tells us how to think about and respond to that reality. Language also reveals and promotes our biases. According to these hypotheses, using sexist language promotes sexism and using racial language promotes racism. For Jacques Lacan, language is responsible for inflicting lack in the subject, because "language cannot say the whole truth", which becomes a form of symbolic castration. We are not castrated by our fathers, but by language, which castrates our fathers too. If we speak and belong to linguistic communities (that is, if we are human), we will always be marked by lack. Lack is our payment in return for a place in society. Due to the impossibility of words to fully convey unmediated reality, the symbolic order we are subjected to is a producer of lack.

Lacan claimed that "the unconscious is structured like a language". With this dishonestly simple aphorism, Lacan initiates his return to Freud and to the project of psychoanalysis as taken from the perspective of linguistics, structural anthropology, set mathematics, and topology. In its content and structure, this is a simple statement of analogy, comprised of a subject, a verb, and an object clause, that sketches lines of equivalence between the unconscious and language through the notion of structure. For Lacan, "the unconscious is the discourse of the Other", something that comes from outside and forces himself on you, and is like political correctness, which also originates from outside and forces his codes on you. Political correctness can be viewed as a belligerent, aggressive, and domineering act that wants to set the rules, but, according to Lacan's theory of language, it can instead be an act of subversion, an act that aspires to change reality by changing language and by changing the unconscious.

Kristeva (1980), in her book *Desire in Language: A Semiotic Approach to Literature*, attempts to expose the limits of Lacan's theory of language by revealing the semiotic dimension of language that it excludes. She argues that the semiotic potential of language is subversive and describes the semiotic as a poetic-maternal linguistic practice that disrupts the symbolic, understood as culturally intelligible rule-governed speech. In the course of arguing that the semiotic contests the universality of the Symbolic, Kristeva makes several theoretical moves which end up consolidating the power of the Symbolic and paternal authority generally. She defends maternal instinct as a pre-discursive biological necessity, thereby naturalising a specific cultural configuration of maternity. Although she claims that the maternal aspects of language are repressed in symbolic speech and provide a critical possibility of displacing the hegemony of the paternal/symbolic, her very descriptions of the maternal appear to accept rather than contest the inevitable hegemony of the symbolic.

Murder Father, Dead Father

In *Totem and Taboo*, Freud (1912) puts forward a foundation myth of the origins of culture. He describes the primal parricide committed by the original horde who killed and devoured their father, who had possessed all the women and ruled through terror. This murder was followed by remorse and guilt (as the sons both hated and loved their father). Rosine Jozef Perelberg (2015) makes a distinction between murdered father and dead father. In murdered father configurations, the individual is not able to conceive of the role of the father in the primal scene. In dead father configurations, the paternal function is more clearly established. Psychoanalysis starts with the death of the father. As a modern discourse, it situates modernity in the murder of the father (the primal patricide), which we can understand as the murder of the ideal of an omniscient and omnipresent higher entity. What follows this murder is the take-over of the sons, who establish a new order, based on democratic principles, guaranteeing the non-monopoly of paternal dominance. In this exchange, father's death is expected to result in the liberty of the sons from his rule, but psychoanalysis warns us about this rather hasty conclusion. The death of the father does not free subjects from his overwhelming authority, rather, it opens new issues and problems. It is the goal of psychoanalytic inquiry to explore the nature of these new potentials. Gilles Deleuze (1965) claims that "the only difference between before and after the death of God, is instead of being burdened from the outside, man takes the weight and places them on his own back".

One difference after the death of the father (or God) is the creation of law, through which the father imposes his social order on the child. Maria Aristodemou (2010, 2011) hints at this phenomenon through the title of two of her papers: "Where God Was, Law Will Be" and "Home is Where the Law Is." Aristodemou emphasises the law's role as representing the "name of the father" and acting as a lighthouse for society. Today, further questions arise. Do we live in a time when the law no longer functions to provide social and psychic stability?

Schwartz (2002) claims that political correctness represents the attempt to eliminate the father, often referred to as the patriarch, who is seen as having deprived us of our connection to mother and all her goodness. In fact, what has really deprived us of our connection to mother's goodness is not the father, but reality itself. Political correctness therefore represents an attempt to destroy reality. Attempting to destroy the father as the representation of reality represents a different way of constructing meaning than we have in the traditional Oedipal arrangement. While the traditional arrangement made organisation possible, anti-paternal psychology undertakes the destruction of all organisation. When organisations give themselves to political correctness, they therefore reorganise themselves towards self-destruction, a process Schwartz (2010) labels organisational nihilism.

The Pendulum of Politically Correct and Politically Incorrect

Simon Western (2016) finds that both politically correct and incorrect share similar ways of gaining satisfaction through aggression, idealising their identities, and a desire for a new authoritarian social settlement. Ideologically, they both hold an underlying belief system that identifies present day as a fallen world, where morality and authority are no longer strong and clear. The politically incorrect tribe believe we have fallen from a better past and look to nostalgia for their inspiration and guidance. Concurrently, the politically correct tribe believe that today's morality has fallen or failed, and blames hyper-capitalism and its effects – consumerism, greed, powerful elites, and a rampant media – all which undermine their "liberal-progressive" agenda. Both desire a new authoritarianism to support the specific kind of new morality they wish to impose on others. PIC does this overtly, PC – covertly.

The dialectic space between PC and PIC is important and should be maintained. We have many internal censors. Žižek sees political correctness as a form of modern totalitarianism. "There is something so fake about political correctness", says Žižek, something that, according to him, prevents a true overcoming of prejudice and racism. We do not need another domineering father from outside. In the other way in GR arena, there is a constant worry of casualty which comes with caution about whether one may, inadvertently and with no control for the vulnerabilities of other, cause offense or humiliate and degrade.

We understand now that PC culture hides racism under the rug and does not actually minimise or prevent its effect. Everything that is hidden has the potential to explode in the future. This line of thinking can shed light on the rise of Trump, the politically incorrect president, directly after Obama, the politically correct president.

There is similarity between the Winnicott's "false self" and politically correctness. There is a self-discipline that can be experienced as politeness. It is a code, an ethics, of how you should behave and how you should dress, and in the case of PC, how you should speak. What is right and what is wrong. You cannot live if you do not have a developed false self and apparently you cannot survive without PC. Between the "modern totalitarianism" as Žižek understands PC, and pure PIC speak, there is the path of compromise that is especially important for the GR community. We don't want to insult or humiliate anyone, but we should remember that the work of group relations is dealing with projections, relatedness, and relation. In a Winnicott spirit, "the place where we live" should contain truth and false, humour and seriousness, roughness and softness. It is the freedom to move and live literally and symbolically.

Epilogue

After the conference, some of the participants went to see Strauss' *Elektra* at La Scala (not a formal territory of the conference), which is based on ancient Greek mythology and focuses on Elektra's furious lust for revenge. The opera grants a window to the unconscious and provides an opportunity to feel her agony and listen to the reliving of her father's murder. We witness a strange battle between remembrance and forgetting, as Elektra's actions are driven wholly by the effort to forget the present, in order to restore the past. All is in vain, of course, because it is impossible to reverse time. Everything is too late. This belatedness becomes Elektra's destiny. The result was a very modern, expressionistic retelling of the ancient Greek myth, which presents raw, brutal, violent, and bloodthirsty horror. What a happy end to the conference, named "The place where we live".

References

Aristodemou, M. (2010) Home is where the law is: A humbug reading of the Wizard of Oz, in Taking Oz Seriously: A Symposium on Law and Literature, *Southern Californian Interdisciplinary Law Journal* 20: 9–19.

Aristodemou, M. (2011) Where God was, law will be? Kant Avec Houellebecq. *Australian Feminist Law Journal* 34:1 3–21.

Davids, F. (2011) *Internal Racism: A Psychoanalytic Approach to Race and Difference*. Red Globe Press.

Deleuze, G. (1965) *Pure Immanence, Essays on a Life*. Zone Books (2001) p71. The chapter on Nietzsche is a translation of an essay originally published in 1965.

Freud, S. (1905) *The Joke and Its Relation to the Unconscious*. Penguin Classics (2003).

Freud, S. (1912) *Totem and Taboo*. Routledge Classics (2001).

Ishizuka, K. and Stephens, R. (2019) The cat is out of the bag: Orientalism, anti-Blackness, and White supremacy in Dr. Seuss's children's books, *Research on Diversity in Youth Literature* 1:2 Article 4.

Kristeva. J. (1980) *Desire in Language: A Semiotic Approach to Literature and Art*. Columbia University Press.

Lacan, J. (1966) *Ecrits*. Translated 1977 by Sheridan, A. Tavistock Publications.

Lacan, J. (1960–61) *Le Séminaire. Livre VIII. Le transfert*. Ed. Jacques-Alain Miller. Editions de Seuil. (1991). p139.

Perelberg, R. J. (2015) *Murder Father, Dead Father: Revisiting the Oedipus Complex*. Routledge.

Schwartz, H. S. (2002) Political correctness and organizational nihilism. *Human Relations* 55:11 1275–1294.

Schwartz, H. S. (2010) *Society against Itself: Political Correctness and Organizational Self-Destruction*. Routledge.

Steiner, J. (1987) The interplay between pathological organizations and the paranoid schizoid and the depressive positions, *International Journal of Psychoanalysis* 68: 69–80.

Steiner, J. (1993) *Psychic Retreats: Pathological Organizations in Psychotic, Neurotic and Borderline Patients 19*. Routledge.

Western, S. (2016) Political correctness and political in-correctness: A psychoanalytical study of the new authoritarians. *Organisational and Social Dynamics* 16:1 68–84.

Žižek, S. (2015) *Big Think* video. https://www.youtube.com/watch?v=IISMr5OMceg&t=13s

Chapter 14

A Home for the Soul

Reflections on Belgirate VI

Sivanie Shiran

In this chapter, I'd like to explore the stated theme of Belgirate VI – namely, *The place where we live – A space for group relations* – and my lived experience of the theme in the conference. Specifically, I want to "walk around" the related images, real and imagined, of the container and the contained, just long enough, perhaps, to see if some new understanding of the dialectic between them may be born of it. I hope to do that by tapping into my subjective experience of the conference venue and membership, various associations they aroused in me, and by attempting to elucidate some of these themes with the aid of insights borrowed from the field of Analytical Psychology.

The Setting

When I arrived at the train station in Belgirate, I had a palpable sense of excitement and anticipation. It was my first time attending the conference and I came with the hope that something might just happen here, that some new learning might emerge. I looked around at the people stepping forth from the train at this tiny station and wondered which of them would be my fellow sojourners. When I discovered two other women on the platform, one much older, the other much younger than I, felt a sense of poetic justice settle in. It felt "right" somehow, as though we were aligned with the greater cosmos. So much so that when a random citizen at the station voluntarily offered to drive us to the conference location, none of us seemed to hesitate. It wasn't so much a naiveté that I experienced, but rather a deeper feeling that somehow this is what "the author" intended; I was merely collaborating with the larger narrative waiting to play out.

When I arrived at the long-anticipated conference venue however, I was surprised to find a rather shabby hotel. Despite its grand location on the shore of Lago Maggiore, the hotel where participants were to reside during the conference appeared bare and run down. The rooms were very basic, more reminiscent of a student dormitory, and the water in the bathtub took a while before its colour was appropriate for bathing. The food too, in spite

DOI: 10.4324/9781003261483-19

of the culinary reputation of northern Italy, was also very basic and functional, with only minimal attempts at appeal. "It used to be a family establishment, very homey …" a random participant in line at the dinner buffet shared with me, "… shame, it seems to have fallen into real neglect".

C.G. Jung, borrowing from the Greek word for sacred space, coined the term "temenos" to refer to the vessel in which transformational processes take place. Drawing on alchemy as an analogy for the analytic process, he insisted that the temenos must offer secure and continuous containment for the transformational process to occur.

In his autobiography, "Memories, Dreams, Reflections", Jung (1963) further contemplated the meaning of this archetype. Reflecting on a dream that he had while constructing his own house in Bollingen, Jung came to appreciate the home as both a gestational container for our individuation process as well as a concretised reflection of our current psychic state.

The temenos known as "Belgirate" no longer seemed to be holding up. The peeling paint, old furniture, uninviting food were all evidence that some of the energy, once cathected, was no longer invested in the container. While there was a felt sense of community in the membership, there was a lack of vitality in the space that struck me at odds with the task at hand. Something was crumbling, but it was not yet clear what that might be.

In Search of Spirit

The first hint appeared in the opening plenary, where we heard two keynote lectures. For the purpose of this article, I will refer to them only in broad brush strokes. The first lecture was given by Shmuel Ehrlich from Israel and harkened us back to the parents of group relations and psychoanalysis. It was as if we first needed to locate ourselves amongst the ancestors if we were to stand a chance of understanding our place in the world at all. It felt like an attempt to centre and ground us, lest we (the membership) all fly off, spiralling into our ego-centric subjectivities, as often happens in GR conferences.

John Hill (1996), in his article, "At Home in the World" noted that "home", beyond a mere physical shelter, may be understood as a stable inner psychological dimension to which one can return so as to integrate new experiences. Indeed, locating ourselves on a stable point in time-space continuum as we embarked on the work of Belgirate VI seemed an important pre-requisite for integrating any new developments that might yet emerge.

The second keynote lecture, given by Rosemary Viswanath, transported us further Eastward.[1] Journeying to India, the plenary was asked to consider a new prism through which to understand the work of group relations. What caught my attention during her lecture was not so much the content, but rather the way she comported herself while speaking. Her whole being seemed to emanate a certain attitude – at once secure in her inner authority and equally humble before the greater powers of the universe.

This attitude seemed to invite the membership towards a new alignment. If Ehrlich's lecture grounded us in relation to our roots, Viswanath's lecture seemed to reach upwards towards the open sky. Its impact was to usher into the plenary, if only briefly, a moment of grace. I suggest that this shift, while unspoken, seemed to silently bespeak a communal realignment along, what Erich Neumann (1954), a prominent student of C. G. Jung, termed the "ego-Self axis". Neumann claimed that this alignment constitutes an important shift in attitude on the part of the ego (i.e. our centre of consciousness) towards what Jung termed "the Self". Unlike the Kohutian definition of self, the Jungian "Self" refers to both the essence and totality of the psyche, incorporating both conscious and unconscious elements. Jung claimed that the God image present across cultures is in fact evidence of this powerful archetype driven by the self-ordering principle. Thus, according to Neumann, when the ego and Self are aligned, there is a healthy dialogue between the two and the ego remains open to birthing new contents from the unconscious into consciousness. In those moments in the plenary, it was as though we were preparing for a new psychic birth of sorts.

And indeed, the subsequent keynote lecture given by Zachary Green, delivered. At the podium, Green seemed to summon great courage as he presented a new model that incorporates spiritual dimensions into the more traditional group relations model. His behaviour implied that much was at stake and the undercurrent of emotion was palpable. As he crossed an invisible cultural taboo in the GR community, he seemed to brace himself for the judgement he suspected would be rendered that day. It felt as though some new quality, some new aspect of our collective psyche, was finally being let out of the proverbial closet and into the sunlight.

It struck me that this new emphasis on spirituality was not unrelated to the decaying temenos of the hotel. Perhaps our old psychic habitat had reached its limit and a new one was now needed in its place. Like a lobster that readies to grow, its old shell first needing to be shed.

Mircea Eliade (1957) reminds us that

> ... Habitations are not lightly changed, for it is not easy to abandon one's world. The house is not an object, a 'machine to live by', it is the universe that man constructs for himself by imitating the paradigmatic creation of the Gods, the cosmogony. Since the habitation constitutes an imago mundi, it is symbolically situated at the center of the world.

Interestingly, Mircea Eliade's description of "home" – the place where we live – is remarkably close to Jung's definition of the Self – the archetype of a supra-ordinate, organising principle of psychic wholeness, which sits at the centre of one's being. According to Eliade, the home, as an imago mundi, links between the three worlds (the underworld, the profane, and the sacred heavens), thus not only making order of the world but at the same time acting as a container and unifier of diverse archetypal polarities. As with the Self, the home serves both as the centre, the very essence of the universe, and its totality all at once. Mircea Eliade explained that temenos has a numinous quality to it, because it incorporates teleological dimensions, paradoxically offering it a sense of placelessness and timelessness.

Listening quietly in the plenary, it felt to me as though the group relations community was in search of a new home, a new psychic habitation.

Spirit in the Diaspora

The keynote lectures in the plenary were followed by a plethora of parallel sessions that presented various adaptations of the traditional GR model in diverse settings. The covert subtext in many of those presentations appeared to be an attempt to gain the branding, and implied legitimacy, of the "group relations" label. What could truly be deemed part of the group relations tradition and what was already too far past the mark, seemed to be the question on (or rather "under") the table. The model was being stretched in so many different ways that it begged the question – does this still warrant the name "group relations" at all or is it really something else? The often, unspoken, undertone in the audience was a parallel one of judgement – is this really "group relations" anymore? It was as though only by exploring the work in new *settings*, new *forms*, could we hope to catch a glimpse of its defining features. As the physical container of Belgirate withered, talk of the *spirit* of group relations seemed to increase. The unexpressed question seemed to be "what is the *essence* of the *spirit* of group relations?"

Conference Membership

This dialectic between the "*place* where we live" and the "*spirit*" that resides in it reverberated as a felt experience in the conference membership as well.

During the exploratory event, a central conflict erupted between two membership constituencies with histories of being uprooted (the Jews and African Americans and African-Europeans). Past traumas were re-opened as both laid claims to experiences of racism in the here and now. For example, the newly appointed Director of the Group Relations Programme at the Tavistock Institute questioned whether OFEK (the Israeli group relations organisation) protested paying "dues" to the UK due to the shift in leadership from a Jewish woman to a Black man; while the director of OFEK apparently experienced the reference to money as having an anti-Semitic undertone and later accused members of the "people of colour" group as acting childishly, provoking a parallel response in that constituency.

In the face of this confrontation between institutional and racial subgroups, my experience was that all thinking was under threat of shutting down. But where thinking ends, imagination begins and I found myself gripped internally by two very strong associations which emerged spontaneously. The first association was to the Alvin Ailey dance troupe in America, and specifically to their signature masterpiece entitled "Revelations". The second association was to the musical drama, "Fiddler on the Roof". I will explore each of these associations in turn.

Alvin Ailey, *Revelations*

The Alvin Ailey American Dance Theater (AAADT) was the first African American dance company to exist in the United States. Striving to make a social and political statement, the founder, Alvin Ailey, established an exceptional troupe and in 1960 went on to choreograph their signature work known as *Revelations*. It has been performed before countless international audiences for over fifty years.

Choreographed when Ailey was only twenty-nine years old, Revelations is an intimate reflection on the powerful heritage of African American culture, inspired by his childhood memories of attending services at Mount Olive Baptist Church in Texas. Through a suite of dances, it illustrates the faith and tenacity of the African American people while journeying from slavery to freedom (DeFrantz 1996). Using spirituals, song-sermons, gospel songs, and holy blues, Ailey paid homage to his heritage which he described as "sometimes sorrowful, sometimes jubilant, but always hopeful" (Ailey 1986). The dance moves intertwine impossible strength and ethereal grace, expressing deep grief and holiest joy, and offering tribute to the resolve and determination of a people.

The work is divided into three sections "Pilgrim of Sorrow", "Take Me to the Water", and "Move, Members, Move". According to Ailey, "Pilgrim of Sorrow" expresses African-Americans' collective pain, as well as their collective prayers to escape slavery (Ailey 1986). "Much of the movement in this section possesses the downward energy characteristic of African dance, and the costumes are all brown, signifying both a coming out of the earth and a going into the earth" (Ailey, 1986; DeFrantz 1996).

The second section, "Take me to the Water" brings to life a baptism. All of the dancers in this section are dressed completely in white, symbolising the cleanliness, purity, and ancestors (Blanco 2008) involved in the spiritual rebirth.

The third and final section, "Move, Members, Move" illustrates a Sunday morning at church. The music in this section is upbeat and the grand finale, "Rocka My Soul in the Bosom of Abraham", brings together the entire smiling cast to improvise and celebrate the joy of life. This is intended as a praising of God and conveys the intense joy that striving towards spiritual wholeness brings.

Revelations is a highly charged piece of work. Despite edits throughout the years, Revelations has kept emotion at its core, eliciting affective connections from its audience as well as its dancers. Matthew Rushing, who was a 12-year member of AAADT, for example, was quoted as saying that he "loves his role in 'Wade in the Water' ... because it allows him to tap his own spirituality" (Croft 2006).

Fiddler on the Roof

My second and almost simultaneous association during the exploratory event at Belgirate VI was to the musical comedy, "Fiddler on the Roof" directed and choreographed by Jerome Robbins. The show played on Broadway between 1964 and 1972 (longer than any previous Broadway show) and has remained immensely popular ever since, with countless revivals and productions around the world, including a movie version.

The show, based on a story by Sholom Aleichem, depicts the quintessential diasporic life of an Ashkenazi[2] Jewish community in a small shtetl[3] in Eastern Europe at the turn of the 20th century. In fact, the producers originally worried that its ethnic particularity would appeal to only a narrow audience. But due to its focus on universal themes such as family, love, dignity, and tradition, the show succeeded in reaching broad popularity.

It tells the story of an impoverished Jewish milkman, Reb Tevye, who struggles to maintain a traditional life amidst the tides of change and against the backdrop of growing anti-Semitism which eventually forces the entire community from its home, from its beloved village *Anatevka*.

The central metaphor of the show, inspired by a painting by Marc Chagall, is a fiddler playing on a rooftop. His music is meant to symbolise the beauty and soul of Jewish tradition. But the fiddler's position on the rooftop is also intended to remind us of the culture's precariousness as the Jews are forced to wander and adapt to distant lands and their culture is under constant threat of extinction.

Interestingly, just before the community's forced departure in the show, the wife of the main character is seen sweeping their emptied home. When questioned about it by her husband, she explains proudly, "I won't leave a dirty house". My interpretation of this scene is that she refused to leave behind the dust – i.e. the *spirit* – of the place.[4]

Walking Around the Images

Taking a teleological approach to the interpretation of symbols, C. G. Jung suggested that we amplify their meanings, i.e. walk around them, long enough to approach their underlying significance and catch a glimpse of where they may be leading us. Indeed, my spontaneous association to these two productions during the exploratory event at Belgirate aroused in me a strong feeling of being guided somewhere.

Both associations lead us directly to the core experience of being uprooted as a people. In our state of liminality, betwixt and between psychic structures, the membership constituencies with histories of being uprooted as a result of their racial identities acted like a lightning rod, giving expression to the anxiety aroused by the possibility of homelessness.

Both works speak to the collective *soul* of a people and underscore the importance of a spiritual life that acknowledges the numinous in our midst. Moreover, the two works emphasise the importance of containing and embodying that spirit. They remind us of the precariousness of the spirit's *vessel*. In Revelations, the reference is to earth, country, and body, while in Fiddler on the Roof, the reference is to our physical and communal homes.

Both of these associations speak directly to the resilience of the human soul and its ability to endure, even in the face of being uprooted from its container. When confronted with the experience of losing "the place where we live" – i.e. our homes, our bodies – spirit is able to transcend painful experience and persevere by remaining connected to the larger Self.

As we sat together to reflect on the exploratory event, it seemed to me that these images, spontaneously emerging in my unconscious, were pointing us in an important direction. As the hotel – *the place where we lived* – fell into neglect, the group relations community seemed to draw closer to *spirit*. It seemed to be asking itself without a viable vessel to contain the work, can group relations preserve its *essence*, its soul?

On reflection, I wonder whether the group relations community may be searching to strike a balance between the container and the contained; between form and spirit; between body and soul. On the one hand, there is a need for a physical centre that can serve as a place for ritual pilgrimage, offering a temenos for psychic growth. Certainly, the Tavistock Institute has often been regarded as the historic centre of group relations. But in recent years, we have witnessed a growing number of initiatives that propose to serve as containers (Yossi Triest and Avi Nutkevitch in Israel, for example, initiated the establishment of a *"Center"* for the study of the Psychoanalytic-Systemic Approach and Zachary Green and Rene Molenkamp chose to name their organisation "Group Relations International"). On the other hand, these initiatives have aroused a degree of suspicion in the broader community and seem to tap into a fear (justified or not) that establishing a centre in any one location will essentially doom the *sacredness* of our work to profane power ploys. Yet if we refuse to authorise any "body" how shall we ever hope to find a home for the soul?

Notes

1 Interestingly, Jungian interpretations of fairy tales and myths have often regarded movement towards the East as a journey towards individuation (*Von Franz, 1977*).

2 Ashkenazi denotes Jews of European origin.
3 Shtetl is a Yiddish word meaning "small village".
4 This interpretation draws on work done by the Jungian Analyst, Henry Abramovitch, who wrote about temenos as it relates to the Analyst's move from one office space to another and, specifically, to an interpretation he offers in that article to a symbolic ritual encountered by one of his clients while in the process of moving home.

References

Abramovitch, H. (1997). Temenos Lost: Reflections on Moving. *Journal of Analytic Psychology*, 42:4 569–584.

Ailey, A. (1986). *Revelations* video. Viewed: February 15, 2008 and April 18, 2008. http://web.mit.edu/21m.670/www/unit-2.htm

Bachelard, G. (1964). *The Poetics of Space*. Orton Press.

Blanco, M. (2008). MIT Course #21M.670. Lecture, 21 February.

Croft, C. (2006). Alvin Ailey's beloved masterpiece is still a revelation. Special to *The American-Statesman*. Thursday, 9 February. www.austin360.com/arts/content/arts/stories/xl/2006/02/9arts.html

DeFrantz, T. (1996). Alvin Ailey. In Salzman, J. et al (Eds), *Encyclopedia of African-American Culture and History*, Vol 1, MacMillan Press.

Eliade, M. (1957). Consecration of a Place: Repetition of the Cosmos in *The Sacred and the Profane*. Harper & Row.

Hill, J. (1996). At Home in the World: Sounds and Symmetries of Belonging. *Journal of Analytical Psychology*, 56:4 575–598.

Jung, C. G. *Collected Works of C.G. Jung, Volume 7: Two Essays in Analytical Psychology*. Princeton University Press.

Jung, C. G. (1944). *Collected Works of C.G. Jung, Volume 12: Psychology and Alchemy*. Princeton University Press, Routledge.

Jung, C. G. (1963). *Memories, Dreams and Reflections*. Collins, Routledge & Kegan Paul.

Lambert, P. (2010). *To Broadway, To Life!: The Musical Theater of Bock and Harnick*. Oxford University Press.

Neumann, E. (1954). *The Origins and History of Consciousness*. Routledge & Kegan Paul.

Neumann, E. (1957). *Man and Time: Papers from the Eranos Yearbooks, XXVI*. Princeton University Press.

Index

Note: Locators in *italics* represent figures and **bold** indicate tables in the text.

Ingram Content Group UK Ltd.
Milton Keynes UK
UKHW022000280323
419333UK00007B/68

9 780367 370725